Donated by Pat Woods,
October 2022

TALKING OF RUGBY

TALKING
OF RUGBY

AN AUTOBIOGRAPHY

Bill McLaren

Stanley Paul
London Sydney Auckland Johannesburg

TO MY WIFE, BETTE

Stanley Paul & Co. Ltd

An imprint of Random House UK Limited

20 Vauxhall Bridge Road, London SW1V 2SA

Random Century Australia (Pty) Ltd
20 Alfred Street, Milsons Point, Sydney, NSW 2061, Australia

Random Century New Zealand Ltd
18 Poland Road, Glenfield, Auckland, New Zealand

Random Century South Africa (Pty) Ltd
PO Box 337, Bergvlei 2012, South Africa

First published 1991
Reprinted 1991

Paperback edition 1992

Typeset in 11/13 Garamond by
SX Composing Ltd, Rayleigh, Essex
Printed in England by Clays Ltd, St Ives plc

A catalogue record for this book is available from the British Library

ISBN 0 09 177296 6

Contents

Photographic acknowledgements

The author and publishers would like to thank the following photographers and agencies for the use of their copyright photographs in this book: Colorsport, AllSport, *Hawick News, Glasgow Herald*, Derek Lunn, Robert Perry, *South China Morning Post*, Keith McMillan, Simpson.

TALKING OF RUGBY

1

That Fateful Day

My life was turned upside down one fateful day in October 1948. I learned I had contracted tuberculosis of the lungs. I would have to go into a tuberculosis sanatorium and be confined to bed for some four years. I might *eventually* be cured of a disease that was regarded as desperately serious and, worst of all, I would not play rugby again. The roof fell in on my world. A few days before I went into hospital I found my father in tears at the prospect before me.

I had been playing for Hawick since I had returned in February 1947 from war service in Italy. On the September holiday Monday 1948 I was playing against Glasgow Academicals and, late in the game, when I tackled Russell Bruce, the Scottish international, I found it hard to get to my feet again. I didn't know what was wrong but I had just completed a very demanding course in physical education and had been feeling a bit 'wabbit.' Shortly after, however, I was on my way home down a steep hill called The Miller's Knowes, running down because I always ran home as a means of keeping fit. I had to stop because I was overcome by a paroxysm of coughing. My doctor arranged for me to have an X-ray. The next thing was a meeting with the tuberculosis physician for our area. I got the news that the X-ray had shown serious damage to my left lung and that I would have to see a TB specialist. When he heard that I'd been playing rugby football the previous Saturday he threw his eyes to the heavens incredulously, saying I could easily have had a massive haemorrhage on the field. He told me that I would be in hospital for four years, and probably confined to bed for all that time.

I had just graduated as a teacher of physical education up in Woolman-hill College in Aberdeen and had begun teaching. As well as playing rugby for Hawick, I'd managed to get into a game between a Scottish fifteen and the Army in 1947, which was a form of trial match, and I had played in an official Scottish trial as well. Not only that, I'd been appointed vice-captain of the Hawick Rugby team, under Wattie Scott, for the season 1948-49. To have to leave all that behind for four years in hospital was a shattering prospect. I'll never forget the journey into Bangour Hospital on which I was accompanied by my girl friend Bette, and by my father and my sister Kit. I was only 24.

2
Heroes And Ambitions

From my very earliest days I had wanted to play rugby football for Hawick and for Scotland. It was a desire that was bred in the bone if you like, because although my father had come from a football background in the Loch Lomond area, he had been completely converted to rugby football, when he came to Hawick. His full cousin, in fact, was Donald Colman of Aberdeen, who was capped at football for Scotland and was the Aberdeen trainer for many years when Paddy Travers was the Manager. Once in the thirties, my father took me to see Aberdeen play a Scottish cup tie in Edinburgh and we had lunch with the Aberdeen team. I was seated next to Willie Cooper. Memories from childhood are often the strongest and it always has been something of a surprise to me that in all the years since, without reference, I have been able to name that Aberdeen team: Johnstone, Cooper, McGill, Fraser, Falloon, Thomson, Beynon, MacKenzie, Armstrong, Mills and Strauss. I remember Eddie Falloon as a very small player with a big heart, Matt Armstrong as the main goal-scoring centre-forward, and Willie Mills as what would now be described as the 'playmaker.'

So, as you can imagine, Aberdeen always has been my favourite football team, but there never was any danger of football replacing rugby in my sporting affections. How could it be otherwise for a boy born and bred in Hawick in the Scottish Borders where rugby has been interwoven into the historic tapestry of the district since the 1870s, with each local rugby club providing a focal point of interest for virtually every inhabitant, young and old, male or female? Moreover, my father, as I have said, was an ardent convert and he had always stimulated my interest in Rugby Union, right from the time I could walk almost. Every Christmas

5

time I always got a new rugby ball and as soon as it was light I was off, whether it was snow or sleet or whatever, down to the local pitch to play.

I was brought up on stories of the great Scottish players of the twenties, many of whom I never saw play but knew all about: John Bannerman, Herbert Waddell, Jimmy Nelson and Doug Davies and all the other fine players who had given Scotland such a great era. And, of course, down at Mansfield Park, our home ground, where I used to go with my father to see matches at a very early age, the great Hawick heroes included Willie Welsh, Jock Beattie and Jerry Foster, so I had an all-consuming desire to wear the green jersey of Hawick. When I was a boy it was regarded as one of the great privileges to be allowed to carry the kit of one of the Hawick team down to the ground for him, apart altogether from the penny or twopence you might be given for doing so! It usually also meant that you got into the match free of charge. Like every local schoolboy I wanted to represent the town and emulate my heroes. That was the number one ambition, closely followed by that great desire one day to play for Scotland.

I remember being taken by my father to see a Scotland v England game in the 1930s at Murrayfield when I must only have been about 8 or 9 years old. I can remember the thrill of being at Murrayfield and I can still see a big powerful Scottish full-back who used to play for Cambridge University. D.I. Brown was his name. He looked like a heavyweight boxer to me, with his broken nose and rugged features. I was also lucky enough, when I was just twelve, to be at Twickenham in 1936 when England played Scotland. I was sitting in the North stand that time with my father and a couple of his factory friends, and Jock Beattie, my great local hero, was captain of Scotland. It was actually to be his last international match. Also playing in that game was Robert Barrie who worked for Braemar Knitwear Limited where my father was factory manager. I remember being introduced to Rob Barrie on the High Street once and was just speechless at the thrill of talking to this great Hawick stalwart. When he got his first cap against England on that day in 1936, of course I was doubly thrilled to be up there in the North stand. Unfortunately, Rob Barrie tackled Hal Sever, the Sale winger, a big powerful man, and knocked him down but, in doing so, he broke a collar bone and had to go off the field. Of course, in those days there were no such things as replacements and Scotland played on with 14 players and lost by 9 points to 6; and so my heart was broken because not only did Scotland lose but Rob Barrie was injured.

When my father took me to Twickenham again in 1938, on one of those Cook's Tours where you paid about £6.00 and got down there by train and back again with a trip round London in one of those old buses thrown in, Scotland won the Championship in the great Wilson Shaw match in which Shaw scored two tries and Scotland won by 21 points to 16. That was some experience for a lad of 14 years of age. It really was something to treasure. I've still got the dog-eared programme of that match, and some of the English names come readily to mind – full-back G.W. Parker of Blackheath who kept England in the game till the last with penalty goals, centre Peter Cranmer of Moseley, a big, strong scrum-half in Coventry's J.L. Giles, the Wheatley brothers of Coventry and that great Waterloo hooker, Bert Toft, who permitted Scotland only six scrummage strikes in the entire match. So, it was a great day but Wilson Shaw and Tommy Dorward were the two that captured my attention because I'd heard a story that Tommy Dorward from Galashiels had travelled away through to Glasgow, which in those days was a very long journey indeed, three and a half hours I would think, just to practise his half-back combination with Wilson Shaw; and how well it worked on the day because Shaw scored the two crucial tries that brought Scotland a magnificent victory. That is some memory. Of course, there was no such thing in those days as squad sessions. Players used to meet on the day of the match, so Dorward and Shaw's practice was a very unusual commitment on the part of two players to hone their partnership. In a way it was the forerunner of the modern squad sessions although in those days it wasn't taken nearly as seriously as squad sessions are taken now. Actually Scotland's halves for the French match of 1948 asked permission to arrive on the Thursday so that they could practise together. This was refused by the SRU who told all the players that a practice would be arranged for the Friday 'for those who choose to turn up'!

I used to play matches between great international sides with myself playing all thirty players. We lived in Salisbury Avenue in Hawick, a kind of quiet, semi-private roadway and I used to go out with a ball that I'd created, a whole lot of paper all tied up with string in the shape of a rugby ball, the reason being that if I mis-kicked that in the Avenue it wouldn't break a window. So with my paper ball I used to go out and enact the international matches. I'd kick off for Scotland and I'd catch it for England and I'd pass it along the back line playing each man in turn. I would feign tackles, put the ball into my one-man scrummage, heel it with my foot, punt and chase. I just loved creating Scottish tries!

I remember once being out in the Avenue on a Sunday enacting one of my rugby matches, Scotland v England, and I was thumping this paper ball all over the place. Unfortunately the wife of one of our neighbours complained to my father that I was disturbing the sabbath, which in Scotland at that time was reasonably sacrosanct. My father insisted, despite my protestations, that I must stop right away and I had to go inside. I remember taking a very dim view of that and being very resentful because, apart from anything else, Scotland were leading England by 36 points to nil at the time!

There was another occasion when I was playing a game in our back green when we used to live down at Weensland Road. The green measured about 12 yards by 12 yards and beyond it was part of my father's vegetable garden. I used to play matches on that little paddock and you could convert a try (nobody kicked penalty goals in those days, it was all running and handling!) by kicking the goal over our garden shed in which there were bicycles and my father's garden tools. One day I landed a beautiful goal, a cracker, which was unfortunately followed by the crack of a pane of glass. I'll never forget the 'choking' I received from my mother who had been doing the dishes by the window in the back kitchen just as my paper ball hit it and cracked the pane. My punishment was to have to take an extra spoonful of cod liver oil which, together with castor oil, was reckoned in those days to be the cure for all ills, and a sure-fire way to keep young children glowing with health. So my two sisters, Jess and Kit, and I had to take our regular doses. No cod liver oil capsules in those days. Just a muckle spoonful of the ghastly stuff! How I detested it. I'd rather have had a good skelp on the lug! But such trials were negligible compared to the joys of my 'international' matches with that paper and string ball. I was lucky too in that just about 150 yards from our house there was a big area of grass which was left that way for youngsters to play on. It was kind of circular. We used to call it just 'the pitch' and as boys we used to play all kinds of things down there – mainly rugby football, but we also played hockey with our fathers' walking stocks and a tennis ball. I remember getting a rocket because I used my father's best walking stick for playing hockey down there, and the head came off! I didn't really want to let on about it but I didn't manage to keep it a secret for very long. My father had plenty to say about that. We played all kinds of games there but mainly rugby football and I remember the outstanding player amongst us was a fellow called Rob

Robson; 'Tough' Robson they called him, a great big lad from down in the Weensland area. Everybody wanted to be in 'Tough's' side!

When I was a laddie of about eleven or twelve years old, I used to go up the stairs into a spare room we had and I would do commentaries, impersonating the great rugby commentators of the day. The two I remember from my earliest days were H.B.T. ('Teddy') Wakelam and Howard Marshall. They were the established BBC radio commentators; Howard Marshall as much on cricket as on rugby football, and Teddy Wakelam, of course, a great rugby man. I used to draw up, in a huge ledger, fictional teams comprising the great players of that period. I'd have games like Scotland v the World and Britain v the Rest and I would write in very clear hand-writing the reports of the matches with a huge page devoted to describing all the action and then a big gap with: Half time – Scotland 32 – The World 0. I then used to do my commentary impersonations for those great matches.

My father used to tell, too, of the occasions during the summer months when he would come round the corner of the Avenue from work to find me sitting on the garden wall doing the commentary on a kind of little 'Olympic Games.' I used to organise sprint races and longer races. I marked out the track in the Avenue with bricks and with chalk markings and my friends would be running the races and I would be doing the commentaries. So from that early part of childhood I clearly enjoyed communicating sport even to an unseen audience although, at that time, it never occurred to me that one day I would be doing just that for the BBC. One other thing I remember about those early commentaries – I also used to put in the 'square one . . . square three' bit myself! Readers who are old enough will remember the fellow who used to sit beside the commentator and give the number of the 'square' in which the action was taking place. In the *Radio Times* of the day there was a diagram of the pitch divided into the sections numbered from 1 to 8 so that listeners could follow which area of the ground the play was in when the chap gave the number of the square. Nowadays radio commentators themselves automatically tell their audience exactly where the play is and the television viewers can see for themselves with an occasional little hint from the commentator.

I was very lucky as a youngster, still at primary school, in that my father took me to our local rugby ground, Mansfield Park, to see Hawick play so that I was well acquainted with the players of that time, not only my own Hawick heroes but other Border stalwarts such as Jock Allan of

Melrose, Jack Waters of Selkirk, 'Doddy' Wood of Gala, Bob Grieve of
Kelso and, of course, I'd heard about Jimmy Graham of Kelso. Andrew
Bowie, a good friend, who won about fifty seven-a-side medals in a
Hawick jersey and later was on the committee of the Scottish Rugby
Union, used to travel with me to games occasionally and once he told me
about playing against Jimmy Graham, the great Kelso flank forward of
the twenties and thirties. The first of Kelso's five capped loose-forwards,
(flankers, as they're called nowadays) Graham was a devastating player, a
big, raw-boned farmer who, as they say, 'didn't take many prisoners.'
Bowie had got clean away, was sure he was going to score, but he heard
Jimmy Graham coming behind him: 'I knew from the pounding of the
footsteps who it was,' he said. 'So I just made up my mind that, just as I
felt he was going to tackle, I'd give a little jink and scoot away for the try.
Well, I heard him coming and I gave a lovely little jink right enough, but
he simply cut me in half!'

Another one of those stories that made those great international
players kind of revered figures to me concerned Doug Davies, the
famous Hawick forward who was capped twenty times for Scotland way
back in the twenties, and played in Scotland's first Grand Slam side in
1925. Doug was known very much as a kind of iron man. He was a
Border farmer with arms like rocket launchers, a very powerful fellow
indeed, and once at Murrayfield for Scotland he lowered his head about
ten yards from the line, charged and went straight into the goal post. The
whole goal post shook but it didn't make any difference to Doug, who
went over and scored the try and then trotted back down the field again,
none the worse for wear!

As a boy I saw the legendary G.P.S. 'Phil' Macpherson, who captained
that Scotland Grand Slam side of 1925 and who played for Edinburgh
Academicals, one of the outstanding Scottish club sides in the 1920s and
1930s. I was just a schoolboy at the time but I can remember seeing him
play against Hawick at Mansfield Park. He got the ball with about thirty
yards to go and half of Hawick between him and the line. He left them
all standing. He was such a phantom figure with lovely change of pace
and beautiful balance. He seemed to float past people just as Barry John
was later to do. I can still see Macpherson scoring at the end where the
old Hawick changing pavilion used to be and where there now is the
social centre.

Another of the great Scots I remember seeing was W.M. Simmers of
Glasgow Academicals, an outstanding Scottish back of that era, who

played for Glasgow Academicals. One of his sons, Brian, played for Scotland as stand-off half, and another, Graeme, was a stylish architect on the rugby field, wonderfully skilled and a superb tactician, who came very close to winning a cap. 'Max' Simmers was at the end of his career when I saw him play. He had been a wing and centre, and very quick in his day, but he had lost a little bit of his pace and was at full-back against Hawick for Glasgow Academicals. He still gave an immaculate display and, whilst Border people tend to be highly parochial, I remember him getting a great reception from the crowd on that day. They recognised him as a genuine class player.

One of my local favourites was Willie Welsh. My father's generation regarded Willie as one of the finest all-round footballers ever to play for Hawick. He was best known as a loose-forward and he had speed and exceptionally safe hands. He was skilled enough to have played as a back and, indeed, he did so on a famous occasion, the Jed-Forest final of 1932, that I heard about as a boy when a Hawick seven, containing five forwards, were 0-15 down at the change-over to a powerful Dunfermline seven containing internationalists Harry Lind and Alf Wilson. Some of the Hawick support were leaving the ground and they missed an incredible Hawick rally in which Willie Welsh played a major role, helping Hawick to an 18-15 victory.

Welsh scored a debut try in his first international against the 1927-28 Waratahs from New South Wales, gained 21 caps in all and toured Australia and New Zealand with the 1930 Lions, playing in the third Test against the All Blacks. Whenever I was in Wales for an international commentary, the famous Ivor Jones, of Neath, Wales and Lions and later president of the Welsh Rugby Union, always enquired about Willie Welsh, who had been a colleague on that 1930 tour and whom Jones described to me as 'one of the truly great forwards.' George Dobson, the stocky, little Melrose scrum-half, used to tell of a game against Hawick in which he decided to be very crafty by not trying to break at all for much of the game, thus lulling Hawick's defenders into a false sense of security. 'I just bided my time,' said George, 'and then a big gap appeared and I was sure I would score so I had a right go. Whereupon Willie Welsh hit me like a ton of bricks with a thumping tackle, and I remember him whispering in my ear: "Now then, ma laddie, dinna try that again!"' Once, 'Border Callant,' who wrote regularly about rugby in the now defunct *Bulletin* newspaper, gave it as his view that *There are glimpses of Willie Welsh in parts of McLaren's play.* These glimpses might have been just fleeting ones but I was so proud of that reference that I still have the cutting in an old scrapbook. Welsh turned to the Rugby League game mainly because of the employment recession in the thirties, but afterwards returned to Hawick and I remember once when he attended a Hawick training session aimed at the sevens. As a former outstanding sevens player who had experienced the professional game too, clearly he had a wealth of lore to pass on to those of us just starting to earn our spurs. I was thrilled at the thought of Willie Welsh giving the benefit of his experience but it lasted only a few minutes. The president of the Hawick Club, Willie Burnet, who had played against England in 1912 and had been an international referee, had to remind Willie that, as a professional, he was banned from taking part in club affairs. That was the end of Willie Welsh's coaching of the Hawick seven. Of course, Willie Burnet was technically right. The Hawick Club would have been in hot water with the Scottish Rugby Union because the law was clear and strictly implemented. You could be banned for just talking to a Rugby League representative in those days. Clearly, however, the Welsh case was an embarrassing situation which deprived us of some words of wisdom from a man we all held in the highest respect.

Welsh was a contemporary of Jock Beattie, another of my boyhood idols. A local joiner, Beattie was an immensely strong man who played for Scotland 23 times as middle-row lock and who captained Scotland against England at Twickenham in 1936. Something of a character, Beattie had distinctive bow legs and once a wag in the crowd shouted, 'Hey, Jock shut your legs! There's a coach and horses coming!' On another occasion a Hawick player, well-known for feigning injury, went down yet again; but since Hawick were 3-6 down to their ancient rivals, Gala, with time running out, Jock called out as he ran past the stricken victim, 'Come on, mun, oo henna time for that th' day!'

Off the field, Jock was hardly ever without his favourite pipe, stuck jauntily in the corner of his mouth, and he always had a stub of a pencil stuck behind his right ear. He could charm a dinner audience with his quick-fire repartee, often poking off-the-cuff fun at whoever caught his eye. He made a memorable quote as warning to the Hawick team in their changing room when he was club president. They were due to play a vital game against Langholm who were renowned for their non-stop action and fierce tackling. 'Now, mind, boys,' said Jock, 'they hellers frae Langholm will be efter ee th' day and dinna forget, sometimes wi' Langholm there's thoosands o' the buggers oot there!'

One afternoon in 1977 I was on my way down to Mansfield Park when I noticed the kenspeckle bulk of Jock, sitting on a roadside bench alone and watching the river Teviot meander by. So I stopped the car and went over to join him. He knew that he was dying but the old humour and quick wit still were evident as he fascinated me with his reminiscences. I felt so sad at the thought of this rugby giant being stricken by incurable disease. A few weeks later he had gone. If there is such a thing as immortality, surely it is simply in the memory you leave behind. In which case, Willie Welsh and Jock Beattie are immortal.

3

From School Rugby to the Senior Game

My recollection of rugby at Hawick High School is one of enthusiastic and helpful teachers, but we gained a grasp of the basic skills simply by playing games. That, compared with now, is chalk against cheese. Even in the years immediately after the second world war the changes were fundamental. When, as a teacher of physical education in my home town of Hawick, I had some 60-70 boys, aged from ten to twelve, for rugby coaching, there was one ball between two boys; we started with a warm-up session, then a lengthy spell of individual and unit skills, practising in small groups so that every boy was constantly involved, and only then did we have a coached game as the grand finale. When I was a boy, our teachers encouraged us in the best way they knew but I do not recall any organised skills practices or unit work. At most, thirty of us would have just two rugby balls so that two teams just played a game with occasional breaks whilst Mr Geddie, Mr Ironside or Mr Frame stressed a point or two. Mr Ironside was a woodwork teacher who played scrum-half for the local junior club, Hawick YMCA, and he could scorch you like a blowlamp if you made the same mistake twice. But he was a tremendous enthusiast and I liked him because he would sometimes tell my father that I wasn't a bad player! Jack Frame was my Harden house master and I thought the world of him. He was a science teacher but, in my eyes, his great claim to fame was that he played centre for the Hawick 'Greens'; he was a big, blonde player with a bit of style. Once I had split my knee in a fall and on the morning of an inter-house match, he asked what the trouble was. When I took off the bandage he had one look and advised me not to play. I was hoping against hope that he would let me play and I had a lump in my throat the size of a golf ball for the rest of the day. Perhaps because of all the practice I had enjoyed, either by myself or with pals, down on that much loved pitch in Oliver Park, I was chosen to play for the Hawick High School first fifteen when only in my third year. My hero then was a big senior boy called Douglas Lumsden, son of a local minister, who was in my eyes a veritable giant.

One day we played against Selkirk High School who were neighbouring rivals of ours. We had heard that they had a big, coloured lad called Soga and that he was their danger man. (I'm pretty sure that he also was an outstanding cricketer who eventually played for Scotland.) Imagine my horror on discovering that he was directly opposed to me at centre, and that, from a distance, he looked like a well-fed Frank Bruno. I won't ever forget looking up the pitch the moment before kick-off and seeing that muckle, dark fellow. My knees weren't actually knocking but I would have given anything to be transferred to the forwards! However, I don't think big Soga scored until late in the game and that was regarded as a minor triumph for those of us quaking to our bootsoles at the prospect of having to keep the handcuffs on him.

Another formidable opponent was Billy Borthwick of Galashiels Academy. They were our strongest rivals and Billy was built like a garage but he could run as well so that when he got up a full head of steam, it was like trying to stop a runaway meat-wagon. We heard stories about Billy playing for the Academy in the morning and junior Gala Star in the afternoon. In any event some of us knew that Billy would give us a hat-full of trouble – and he generally did.

I cannot be sure whether it is still there to this day but, for at least thirty years, a photograph of the Hawick High School first fifteen of 1938 hung alongside other team photos on a prominent stairway wall in the school. It was a picture that caused me some embarrassment because there I sit in the front row, just a laddie amongst older colleagues, with a smile on my face, unaware of the fact that I was wearing a rugby stocking on one leg and a short sock on the other! As they say in Scotland, I certainly was 'given my character' for that faux-pas which stood out like a sore thumb – or like a short sock!

I revelled in all sport at Hawick High School. Having already been a member of the Trinity Primary School relay and tug-of-war teams, I loved the rugby, cricket and athletics at secondary school. At rugby I frequently would stay behind with friends Bobby McGee and Ian Bett to continue practising long after the other boys and teachers had gone. At first my mother worried when I came home late on the Wednesdays but soon accepted that additional rugby kick-about in the Volunteer Park.

In one tug-of-war contest we were opposed to Wilton School who had a big, heavy lad, Billy Knox, as their anchor. Our team always found it difficult to beat Wilton because of Billy's weight. This time, however, his rope slipped up to round his neck and we got them going. Even with Billy's face getting redder and redder, we kept on pulling till victory was achieved. That was not regarded as very sporting but as Billy was little the worse for wear perhaps the end justified . . . !

A sporting highlight at the High School was when my younger sister Kit and I were senior athletics champions in 1939. My older sister, Jess, who was more of an artistic type, always reckoned that her best ever event was the three-legged race with her pal Jenny Riddle!

Academically I never reached even my limited potential. Once I got only 16 per cent for arithmetic and my father was so 'black affronted,' not to say damned annoyed, that he refused to sign my report card! I recall my mathematics teacher, William Redpath, who we used to refer to with some affection as 'Gandhi' because he bore some resemblance to the Mahatma, saying to me: 'You know William, it is a complete waste of pen, ink and paper you trying to pass higher mathematics!' He used to call me William Pythagoras McLaren because that theory always caused me some trouble! But in the three weeks preceding the examinations I really did get down to the slog and you can imagine his surprise when I did gain my higher maths, admittedly somewhat narrowly, with a mark of 52 per cent to be precise! What is more I got my Higher Leaving Certificate which in those days was the top passport to fame and fortune! The shock of that achievement reverberated through the entire staff-room! I believe that even Miss E. Vera B. Fisher was impressed by the fact that I had squeezed through in lower French. My own satisfaction at having gained the reward of, admittedly, a belated slog moulded my attitude thereafter so that I always tried to respond to any challenge with my best effort.

A word about Miss Fisher. For some time, this stocky, stern soul and I had something of a running battle of wills. She was my French teacher and a very good one at that, but one who obviously found some difficulty in fostering in me, a deep interest in, and knowledge of, the French language. From the kick-off, Miss Fisher and I never were guaranteed to be on model friendly terms. This was accentuated in my case by the fact that we always had a French lesson on the Wednesday afternoon. By unfortunate choice that was followed by our rugby, two whole periods of it. Needless to say, my whole school week centred on the Wednesday rugby sessions. I just couldn't get out of Miss Fisher's class quickly enough. The trouble was she made sure that I didn't. To my prejudiced mind, Miss Fisher seemed to keep us in after the bell so that we didn't get to rugby as quickly as we wanted to. My resentment grew with each passing Wednesday but it didn't make any difference. Even so, there have been times when I have looked on Miss Fisher in a kindly light. Thanks to her, I was able to ask the French coach, Jacques Fouroux, in his own language, or what passed for it, if he had had a good journey, slept well and eaten well and whether there were any late changes in his squad! This was achieved, admittedly, in 53 per cent lower French grade, but Monsieur Fouroux seemed to appreciate the effort and I found him helpful and co-operative.

As a general rule, promising young rugby players in Hawick have a step-ladder to the stars that starts with friendly competition among Hawick's six primary schools, the next rung being the various grades at Hawick High School, which leads to two semi-junior clubs, PSA and Wanderers, then to four junior clubs, Trades, Linden, YM and Harlequins, prior to elevation to the senior Hawick 'Greens' side. My own generation, however, were denied that promotional journey because of the start of the second world war, during which a Hawick Rugby League was formed. The eight teams who competed were a mixture of factory, school and boys' organisations – Trades, Boys' Brigade, Innes Henderson (later Braemar Knitwear Ltd), Pesco (Peter Scott and Co Ltd), Air Training Corps, Lyle and Scott, Pringle and Hawick High School. Still just seventeen, I was a member of the organising committee; the secretary was H.B. 'Barrie' Laidlaw, who later became an international referee. I played for the High School side and later for a combined Pesco-High School fifteen and we had some very enjoyable games in which local rivalry was intense. One game I shall always remember was against Pringle (now Pringle of Scotland Ltd), for I was marked by Tom Simpson who wasn't as big or as heavy as me. Marked is the word for, whereas I was expected to be the big shot in midfield, in fact I was reduced to being a very little shot as Tom hit me with a series of shuddering, copybook tackles. I seemed to spend much of the match on the floor. That provided a salutary lesson never to under-estimate an opponent and always to have some alternative strategy at hand just in case things do not go quite according to plan! Tom was one of several fine players who took part in that competition, among them being David

Valentine, capped for Scotland (as indeed was his brother Alex) and later a huge success in Rugby League, and Tom Wright, who played for Scotland against Australia in 1947 before he, too, went to Rugby League. Jack Hegarty played for the ATC and later was capped six times as a back-five forward and Jim Chalmers, gifted with startling side-step and quick take-away, later had a spell in Rugby League too. It was in September 1941 that a memorable event took place, a Border junior sevens tournament at Philiphaugh in Selkirk, in which 15 teams took part including 5 companies of the Royal Welch Fusiliers who were stationed in the district. It was decided to send a Hawick PSA seven which I was asked to captain. The age limit, we were told, was to be seventeen but on arrival we discovered that some players were over twenty and that the real limit was nearer twenty-two. So we were pretty chuffed when we won by beating Selkirk 8-0 in the final after disposing of a Kelso seven in the semi-final that included Sandy Charters and Archie Lockie, who later were in the Kelso side which won the Scottish unofficial championship in 1947-48. Our seven that day were just laddies – Tom Wright (16 years old), Bill McLaren (17), Jim Turnbull (17), Jock Wright (Tom's younger brother, 15), Jack Millar (18), John Campbell (16) and Willie Fraser (19).

At this time, too, I was playing pre-call-up wartime Rugby for Hawick and you can imagine the thrill of playing in a green jersey alongside the inimitable Jock Beattie, by then a veteran player, and Rob Barrie, both of whom had featured in the Scottish team against England in 1936 when I was taken on my first visit to Twickenham. One game in particular comes to mind because Hawick lost to the King's Own Scottish Borderers fifteen by 3-11 and the star was one Tommy Gray. He then was a second lieutenant and he gave us a rough time because he was so quick and slippery and had the most adhesive hands. He left me gasping in a flash of light once, prior to scoring a clinching try. Little did I know then, in October 1941, that some nine years later, on 18 March 1950, I would be sitting in the Murrayfield stand alongside my fiancée, Bette, having been given permission for a day out of East Fortune Sanatorium, watching that enthralling finale to the Scotland v England game in which the same Tommy Gray, with a special built-up boot to accommodate a foot half blown-off during the war, stroked an eminently missable conversion of Donald Sloan's try straight between the uprights for an eleventh hour Scottish win by 13-11.

Although many of the experienced Hawick players already were in the forces and the Hawick sides of 1940 and 1941 were nothing like as strong as they would have been in peace-time, one hardly can describe the thrill of wearing the green jersey. It was an ambition realised, an ambition fostered by those stories told to me about the Scottish greats of the success era of the twenties, by my own admiration of the famous Hawick players of my youth, and also by my mother's warm admiration for her cousin, Walter Sutherland, 'Wattie Suddie' to his host of supporters, who had played 13 times for Scotland as a wing and was a double international, having also sprinted for Scotland, and who lost his life when a stray shell landed in the very last days of the great war. That famous doyen of Scottish Rugby writers, Andrew 'Jock' Wemyss, once told me that Wattie Sutherland was the greatest wing he had ever seen. I was very proud to hear that and when I told my mother about it, it really made her day.

For a lad of just seventeen, it was some experience to train and play with the 'Greens' players of that early war spell. There were some characters among them. Tommy Fraser was no imposing physical specimen although he had a joiner's strength, but as a wing forward he was turbo-powered, a non-stop dynamo of a player who seemed always to be at the elbow of the man with the ball. Jimmy Lumsden had all the gifts and stature of a Welsh stand-off, a lively, cheeky chappie, sharp and cute. John Hogg could neither hear nor speak, but his instinct of where to be and what to do was quite uncanny as was his seemingly instant reaction to the referee's whistle. He was one of the fastest hookers I can remember and it would have been a close contest had he and Colin Deans, each in his prime, been matched over 100 metres. As the youngster among them I frequently was the butt of their fun: a pail of freezing cold water thrown at me when in the team bath, a gag at which one of the finest uncapped wings, Wattie Scott, a brawny farmer, was a past master; and once, after a training spell when I emerged into the darkness to cycle home and couldn't find my bicycle. I eventually discovered it, floating in the air, tied to the crossbar with a length of rope. I never did find out who was responsible but I suspected that one James B. Lumsden was the ring leader! They were great times although as a boy of fifteen I had heard Mr Neville Chamberlain, on that fateful Sunday morning, telling us we were at war and now, almost three years later, my call-up was approaching. There had been time, however, for a series of Hawick games against Army sides stationed at Stobs Camp, a huge military area just four miles out of Hawick. We beat one Army outfit 54-0, the AA Unit 33-0 and a Royal Marines side 19-0. In the Inverleith sevens in

Edinburgh in 1940 we had reached the final with a side comprising Bert Turnbull (a stocky flying machine), Jimmy Rae (who had been my teacher of physical education at Hawick High School just a few months previously), myself at stand-off, and Jimmy Lumsden at scrum-half behind a forward trio of Tommy Fraser, John Hogg and Willie Fraser. In the final we met Edinburgh University whose back division included a huge fellow called E.C.K. 'Euan' Douglas. That name is engraved on my memory. We were already behind when he went for a break but I had him in my sights and I sailed in in copybook style. I expected to send him crashing to earth but instead he gave me a steam-hammer hand-off that almost took my head off my shoulders. I hit the deck. He scored. There are moments when you feel a right fool. That was one such for me and it did not ease the pain nor mitigate my sense of failure when I heard after the match that Euan was a champion international hammer thrower. Hawick players were expected to make tackles count! That and other obligations were brought home to me by older men with an intense love of their club and of the game and who expected the standards created by great players in the past to be maintained and, where possible, improved. One had the feeling of a host of Hawick players long since gone, looking down stern-eyed from their Rugby Valhalla just to ensure that the pride and passion they had experienced in wearing the green would be felt also by all those who came after.

We used to train on Tuesday and Thursday evenings and play matches on the Saturdays, the rest of the week being given over to whatever other pursuits one wanted to follow. Of course in those wartime days those other pursuits included fire-watching (taking turns at keeping guard during the nights in case of air raids), other air raid precaution work such as packing gas masks, and checking fire fighting equipment, and Home Guard duty. Where would the modern player find time for such vital duties with rugby involving so many extraneous commitments? The demands placed on modern players are an indictment of the whole set-up and in a sense a betrayal of what the game was meant to be in the eyes of those great men who set it on sure foundations long ago. Rugby Union was supposed to be a recreation providing a break from the daily grind. It had its place in the scheme of things and certainly in Hawick we took it, and preparation for it, very seriously indeed. But it was never meant to be virtually a seven days a week job, which is what it almost has become. Top players, and those aspiring to such status, spend part of every day on one or other aspect of rugby. There are even midweek and

Sunday squad sessions at almost every level. Rugby Union is the luckiest game in the world for wives and employers. Wives are the salt of the earth when one considers the demands made by the game on their husbands' spare time. And even allowing for the benefit to employers of having a kenspeckle class player on their staff the amount of leave of absence granted to such players is staggering. Small wonder that the Scottish Rugby Union sought to repay at least some of this employer co-operation by including the occupation and the name of the firm he works for in the biography of each player in the official match programmes on international days.

We played a lot of cricket and golf as well during those pre-call-up months. More of golf later because it has been such a massive part of my sporting life. In cricket we played in a form of league competition in our beautiful Wilton Lodge Park where later I was to spend some thirty years of my life coaching rugby and other games to three generations of Hawick boys and girls. I was a bit of a bash with a bat, never content to stay for any length of time but intent on gathering a few quick runs with a bit of swish and swash and inevitably falling to a wild swipe at a straight ball. I used to take some pride in having played for Hawick at rugby, cricket and golf although one painful cricket memory remains. Hawick and Wilton were playing Carlisle at home in Buccleuch Park. Carlisle included the Lancashire and England Test bowler, Len Wilkinson. There had been some publicity about that in our local papers. On the day Wilkinson proved devastating. I think we were 28 for seven or something like that when my turn to bat came. I walked down the steps of the pavilion and as I passed my father, who was sitting in the front row of members' seats, he said jocularly: 'I don't suppose you'll be very long, Bill, will you?' I took guard but don't remember even seeing the ball; I just heard the click of the stumps being hit and saw the umpire's finger raised. And there was that long walk back to the pavilion and a wink from my father. And to think that Wilkinson was supposed to be a slow bowler. I reckoned that ball passed me at about a hundred miles an hour!

Being in the local Home Guard was some experience which we all took very seriously. Talk about Captain Mainwaring and his squad of TV fame! We had a few like them. We used to meet for drill and instruction during the week and Sundays were given over to route marches and to battle manoeuvres. They were a scream because there were times when no one seemed to know what anyone else was doing. But in typical

British fashion we seemed to muddle through and it was very enjoyable because it was so important.

When I was called up in July 1942 and reported to 13 Platoon, 'B' Company, no. 8 Primary Training Corps at Beverley, near Hull, all kitted out in my Home Guard uniform as instructed, the welcoming sergeant, who looked like a replica of Attila the Hun, took one look at me and gazed skywards in obvious pain. I had my Home Guard gaiters on the wrong way round!

I remember the feeling of intense sadness as the train took me up the hill past Stobs and Riccarton on my way to Army service. It was a voyage into the unknown and at eighteen in those days you were an innocent abroad and initially felt very much alone. It didn't help when we were told that we would be confined to barracks throughout our six weeks of initial training at Beverley – apparently because the Army did not want to subject their new green innocents to the dangers of Hull, in particular those ladies of the night who plied their ancient trade as do all such in ports of call for the seafarer. As if any of us would have known what to do with a lady of the night even if we had come across one!

4
The War and
Missed Opportunities

The rigid disciplines of Army life posed no problem for me throughout the four and a half years of my service. I had been accustomed to firm discipline from early schooldays when my headmaster at Trinity Primary School had been Mr Robert Burns. He had lost both legs in the first world war and had to negotiate his way about the school with the aid of two walking sticks which he would thump down on a desktop with a crack like a pistol shot when displeased. No one in his right mind risked falling foul of Mr Burns. Our PE lesson would consist of Mr Burns hurling a tennis ball at pupils sitting at their desks and woe betide anyone who didn't make a clean catch. Yet I have fond memories of the way in which he encouraged in us a deep love for our native town and its traditions.

In 1934, when I was eleven, the great honour was bestowed on me of making the welcome speech to Cornet Will Brydon, as principal of our annual town festival, the Common-Riding, on his visit to our school. This had to be done before a big audience of teachers, pupils, parents and a band of the Cornet's followers. After several visits to Mr Burns's office to let him hear my welcome speech I became word perfect, for he took great care to ensure that his pupils were thoroughly well prepared for whatever they were to attempt. Even to this day I can remember most of that address with its 'we yield not in our love of our native town' and the closing recitation in which I wished the Cornet on 'behalf of my fellow pupils' a safe journey throughout his Cornetship. What pleased me even more was that, following that school ceremony, Bobby Appleby, a close friend of my father; who was to have a principle role as Cornet's Acting Father, sidled up to me and said: 'Well done, Billy' whilst pressing half-

23

a-crown into my palm. You could do a lot with half-a-crown in those days ... and I did just that!

Then at Hawick High School one came under the influence of the Rector, Mr. A.M. Watters, a short, stocky man who once administered to my palm six of the belt because I had broken a rule by playing with a ball before the PE teacher had arrived in the gymnasium. Our PE teacher was a woman, Jessie Harper, a strong disciplinarian with a voice like troops marching over a gravel bed but a wonderful character and a super motivator. She was as fit as a flea, skinny as a rake and she called a spade a spade. I never did break that rule about the ball again. Nor do I remember feeling any bitterness about getting six of the best for that offence. What I do remember is that it taught me a lesson. All of which might be worth consideration by those who nowadays tumble over backwards to ensure that those who break the law, juvenile or adult, are not punished in a way that would make them think twice about committing the same offence or crime again.

What with those experiences, and the discipline of Hawick Rugby Club, whose genial president in those early war years, Mr Oliver Robson, made it clear to every player just what standards were expected both on and off the field, Army life became very acceptable and enjoyable. One of the first questions I was asked was which regiment my father had served in. When I replied, 'Royal Artillery' that was it. I was going into the Royal Artillery. I was posted to a training regiment at Harrogate where I was made to feel at home by visits to the home of 'Jock' Blackadder who had been a Hawick Rugby stalwart and was a friend of my father. What a personality he was, and full of fun, and of course we spoke a lot about Rugby and of his contemporaries.

Then to my surprise, and to everyone else's, the Army decided to send me to a WOSB (War Office Selection Board) to assess my fitness for a possible commission. Perhaps they already had decided that everyone would be a lot safer if I directed the guns instead of actually firing them, because anyone who turned up for initial training with his gaiters the wrong way round was liable to stick the shell in back-to-front – apart altogether from what he might do with the cordite. We had four days of intensive examination and I always had the feeling that my rugby football experience had a lot to do with my being accepted for OCTU, (Officer Cadet Training Unit). One of the tests to which we were subjected was a form of twenty-a-side moving melee in a restricted space, in which the ball had to be carried over the opposing line. The examining officers were all dotted around the edges of the battle area and they must have been impressed because I got the highest marks. Of course it was right up my alley. Anyone who has played for Hawick against Gala, even in wartime, has to be made to measure for that sort of free-for-all. Whilst other lads were inclined to stand off and await developments I revelled in the hurly-burly and enjoyed every minute. Thank God for Mansfield Park and Hawick Rugby Club!

Officer training was done at Alton Towers in Staffordshire after OCTU at Wrotham in Kent. It was whilst I was in Kent that I played for Army sides in Maidstone and Tonbridge, and I recall the thrill of playing in direct opposition to Tommy Kemp of Richmond who had played three times for England in 1937 and 1939 and who was also to play for them against Australia and Wales after the war in 1948. What passed for a team-talk to our side was a warning that T.A. Kemp was an England international and would require close watching. They could say that again. He had great hands and he was the quickest off his mark that I had played against. What impressed me most, however, was that clubs in the south of England were social centres. I recall being quite surprised when, after tea, everybody then enjoyed a dance and a chat until it was time for us to get back to the business of preparing ourselves for overseas duty.

I was posted to 79 Squad, 121 OCTU, Honourable Artillery Company, Royal Artillery at Alton Towers in Staffordshire from February to May 1943. One tragic event stays in the memory. We were billeted on the top floor of the magnificent main building and we were shattered and grieved when one of our room-mates was found dead after having apparently fallen out of a window. It was at Alton that one came across Captain A.A. Bray, a tall, gangly, lantern-jawed officer/instructor who seemed a bit eccentric at times but who was universally popular with the squad members and not only because he had been awarded the MC. We then finished our officer training at Catterick Camp between May and June 1943. All I remember about that period is that, following a training exercise out on the moors, it was discovered that part of a range-finder was missing. Hungry and 'bushed,' all of us were packed into vehicles and driven out into the wild there to 'boogle about' in the darkness until the damned thing was found. We never did find out who had lost it. Perhaps that was just as well.

One of our officer training tests was to be taken to Wales and a place called Pennmannmawr, there to be subjected to what was termed a 'battle course.' One of the gags was to take us up into the mountains, bed us down for the night in wee tents, then about three o'clock in the morning, waken us with thunder flashes and other bangers, whereupon we had to find our own way back to our base camp. It would have been hard enough in daylight in strange country. In darkness it was positively lethal. There were guys staggering into the base throughout the day and one came in with a broken leg having fallen into a slate quarry. As if that wasn't enough, every arrival had one other obligation before being given anything to eat. We had to take a dip in the Welsh briny for a stipulated length of time. I have been in some cold water in my time; family outings to Scremerston near Berwick, for example, where a dive into the North Sea gave one the new and unwelcome experience of a frozen head. But Pennmannmawr took the biscuit because it still was wintertime and felt like Siberia.

Another Army wheeze was to set us the task of getting from one point to another without being shot. To do so we had to crawl, in full kit, the length of a wall that was about two-feet high. The sergeant, who clearly was related to Genghis Khan, warned us that the bullets would be real ones so we had better keep our heads down. To the crack of gunfire we wriggled and crawled our way to safety whereupon one of our mates claimed that the sergeant had been kidding, that they wouldn't dare risk firing live bullets. 'Is that so? And what are those marks on your haversack that you carried on your back?' said a colleague. There were two neat bullet holes through the top of his pack. I have seen fellows visibly blanche but this one really did go a whiter shade of pale.

On another occasion we had to throw smoke shells before charging 'the enemy.' We had been warned to count the shells going off to make sure that all had fired before we did the valley of death bit. The count was wrong because one of our lads stood on an unexploded cannister and was enveloped in what looked like white flames. He was badly burned and a makeshift stretcher had to be built before he could be carried that long distance over very rough territory to hospital. We never saw him again. The ways of the British Army seemed strange and startling in those far-off days. Yet they transformed a bunch of raw innocents into proud and reasonably confident young officers, fitter than they had ever been and with a clear impression of the responsibilities they would have to bear, and of what henceforth would be expected of them. When I went home on embarkation leave I felt like a million dollars, as well as a wee bit self-conscious, with my officer's uniform on and with its one pip. It was in Weensland Road that I received my first salute. As the

private approached I wondered if he would salute a mere second lieutenant and if he did not, what should I do? But he did and I remember feeling just a bit embarrassed at such an historic event happening in my own
home town.

In July 1943 I embarked at Liverpool on a troopship bound for North
Africa and two incidents stand out from a brief stay in the desert. Most
of us were struck down with dysentry and I had a crying need for relief
during a desert training exercise. In some haste I shot round the side of a
huge sandhill and was in the process of ridding myself of the entire contents of my intestines when I heard a loud cry of 'Oeufs, oeufs!' As I set
a new standing high jump record for the Middle East, a greasy, bearded
face appeared, that of an Arab selling eggs. There are situations in life
when you feel that you are at some disadvantage, especially as at that
moment the very thought of an egg was nauseating. I didn't actually take
out my Webley 38. I couldn't. It was lying alongside my breeks – just
out of arms length! But the bearded one got the message. I was blissfully
alone again.

We made the long train journey from Algiers to Bizerta. I think it took
us about two and a half days. Every time the train stopped the officers
and the other ranks brewed up at the side of the track. The tea was great
but all we had for food was bully beef. We used to put three or four tins
of the stuff into a big pot with a pile of margarine and heat it over the
fire, whilst mixing it into a kind of mince. At first it was scrumptuous
but by the third or fourth stop you were getting fed up with it, and
eventually I went right off it altogether. I haven't eaten stewed bully ever
since! In a similar way I was put off spam as well. We were on one of
those flat-faced LST troop carriers heading from Bizerta to Italy. I was
kind of kidding myself on that I was something of a seafarer because I
had lasted the troopship journey from the UK to North Africa without
once being sick, whilst those all around were depositing the contents of
their stomachs into various parts of the ocean. On this trip to Italy, too, I
was in good shape – that is until I went down for breakfast one morning
and found several American officers already tucking in. One of them was
actually spreading marmalade on a slice of spam! That did it. I joined the
under-the-weather brigade at a rate of knots on deck and made my contribution to sea refuse whilst doing quite a lot of deep breathing.

For the next two years, throughout the Italian campaign, one settled
down to being a member of 20/21 Battery, 5 Medium Regiment, Royal
Artillery. I joined them just after they had survived the Salerno landings

and was immediately made aware of the camaraderie among all ranks and their intense pride at being in a very good and dependable outfit. It eventually became a proud boast of 5 Medium that, for the last great push of the campaign, General Freyberg of the 2nd New Zealand Division asked specially for 5 Medium to be part of his support artillery. Once when he came to meet our officers and to explain the attack plan he asked me where I came from, and as soon as I said 'Hawick' he responded with; 'Ah, they play Rugby there, don't they?' I wondered if this knowledge had been based on the fact that my local hero, Willie Welsh, had toured New Zealand with the Lions in 1930 and played in a Test against the All Blacks. Almost the first thing that John Young, our 'D' Troop commander, pointed out to me, away down the Gaeta Plain, was the site of a huge railway gun with which the enemy used to fire massive shells a huge distance, as much for psychological value as for actually hitting targets. It was a matter of some satisfaction some time later when we passed in the vicinity and saw this mighty weapon as a captured prize.

I was the only Scot among a shower of English officers, but they were super chaps – Captain Tom May, Captain John Young, Lieutenants Nick Nicholas and Harry Burrows in our troop; and five sergeants I would have trusted my life to – Alfy Tarr, Fred Jordan, Jack Soppitt, 'Boots' Cranford and Bob Hilditch. Then there was Battery Sergeant-Major 'Mo' Fell. He really ran the show and young officers, wet still behind the ears like myself, leaned very heavily on his experience and instincts. He had a delightful way of letting a young officer know in most subtle terms that he was a bit of a yo-yo but I thought the world of him, and the folk back in the UK perhaps didn't appreciate fully just what the world owed to those sergeants and sergeant-majors, the salt of the earth, who could scorch other ranks like a blow-lamp but who knew their job and were quite fearless in doing it.

I really did revel in life with 5 Medium. It was a good feeling just to be part of what the young mind saw as a genuine and fair fight against evil, and I soon discovered that 5 Medium had quite a reputation for accuracy and efficiency. They could do some damage too. Having been accustomed to training on 25-pounder guns I was mightily impressed when I compared the size of the hole they made to that created by a 5.5 shell. In a medium regiment we were inclined to refer rather disparagingly to the 25-pounders as 'pea-shooters' but the 25's still did a very significant job, although there was one occasion when I had reason to hope they might be a bit more effective. We were making our way up a steep hillside, just after our infantry had cleared it of the enemy, to create an observation post on top of this mini-mountain called Monte Lignano. Suddenly we were being shelled . . . by 25-pounders! One could only surmise that they had miscalculated their angle of sight or range because their shells were not clearing the mountain top. Surprise instantly changed to panic and I remember my wireless operator and I actually clawing at the earth with our hands to try and create a wee hole into which we could flatten ourselves.

Certain incidents remain fresh in the mind. Cassino was engraved on our hearts. We seemed to be there for ages and from the observation post from which we directed our gunfire we could look across the valley to that imposing monastery which gave the enemy an unrivalled view of the entire countryside. It was a lonely job to be Observation Post Officer. You always felt very vulnerable and the only company usually was your signaller. At Cassino the post was a broken-down farm cottage on top of a hill. You had to crawl the last 200 yards to it on your stomach so as not to let the enemy see any movement – as if he didn't know perfectly well that that was the obvious place for an OP. Fortunately, he found that as difficult to hit as we did the monastery itself although, if I remember rightly, for a time we went out of our way not to damage the monastery but to deal with enemy positions on the lower slopes. Once I had to report on the success or otherwise of our aircraft in dropping supplies to a beleaguered infantry group who were cut off on one of the hills on the lower slopes. Food would carry one colour, ammunition another. It all brought home to us just how accurate and efficient our airmen were and how brave and resolute our infantry were as they battled in the most unhelpful terrain for every single inch of advance.

There were times when we thought we would be stuck at Cassino for the rest of the war. The enemy position seemed impregnable and it dominated the vital Route 6 to the north. One taste of success was very welcome. The enemy had a six-barrelled mortar, called a Nebelwerfer, which they used to wheel out from a cave down on Route 6, fire off six shells, and wheel it back into the safety of the cave. Nebelwerfers frightened the living daylights out of you because they made a screeching, whining noise as they flew to their target, just like Stuka dive bombers, and they had a considerable psychological value apart, altogether, from accuracy which could explode six shells within roughly the same area. We tried desperately to knock it out. At night from the OP you could see the flame as it fired but we always seemed to be too late to catch it because they could move it like a wheelbarrow very quickly into its safe haven. So we hit on the idea of having our guns loaded and trained on the target area with a gunner holding on to the lanyard ready to fire on the order. Eventually it worked. When we at last advanced up Route 6 it was lying upside down and wrecked. We gave ourselves a wee pat on the back for that.

Our 5.5 guns made quite a racket when they went off, so you can imagine the effect of 1500 guns all firing at the same time. Which was what occurred at a place called Acquafondata, from which a barrage was to be laid down to support an infantry attack. The guns all were sited in a huge valley. The barrage was to begin at 9 p.m. When it did it was like Guy Fawkes night only much noisier. It was deafening, and devastating as an example of the fearsome firepower at the Allies' command. We were all glad that we were at our end of it and not theirs. At one time the guns became so hot that the gunners were able to fry eggs on the barrels. One rare personality among the gunners was a lad called Mumford. He came from Doncaster and was as Yorkshire as Herbert Sutcliffe, Len Hutton and Hedley Verity. He never was liable to win a beauty contest and he called everything a 'smeerie' but nothing got him down and he was the life and soul of the party. I've often wondered what became of Gunner Mumford. Wherever he is I'll wager he is still making people laugh. I'm sure he was one of the gunners who expressed their feelings when the regiment made the grave mistake, already recounted, of assigning me to the task of leading us through Ravenna. Royal Engineers had laid down white tape guidelines after having cleared the track of mines. What rather caught me by surprise was that the white tape seemed to lead round the town and not through it. The end result was that I led our regiment round Ravenna three times and I remember my embarrassment.

That was the last time I led the regiment anywhere, although I recall being on motorcycle duty as a kind of glorified despatch rider shooting ahead of the battery to indicate which way to go whenever there was a junction. I managed that all right without disaster but we had been on the move, and in and out of action, with such non-stop regularity and with so little sleep that once I found myself in a ditch with the motorbike several yards away. I had fallen asleep on the bike, happily without serious injury either to me or to the machine.

Our regimental commander was Colonel 'Crusher' Hayes, a huge, bull of a man, one of the old school who tended to enter where angels feared to tread. I thought the world of him because he was a man of principle and integrity although he gave me a fearful rocket on one occasion when, during one rest period, our Battery soccer team had played a local side. That was at a place called Potenza; their team were a very skilful lot, but we got a 1-1 draw which pleased us but not the Colonel. In his view we had been guilty of over-robust tactics that ruined the good relations that had been created between us and the locals. As I was the only officer in our team and, in his opinion, had been the worst offender, I got the full blast. Of course, as the only rugby man in the team as well and by far the heaviest at some 14½ stones, I think I did go over the score in attempting to intimidate tricky little Italians. But 'Crusher' felt that the good name of the regiment had been besmirched and said so in no uncertain terms. I have a photograph still of that eleven. By golly, we were a tough-looking lot, like a bunch of dance-hall bouncers. But we could play too and my recollection is that the lads couldn't understand what all the fuss was about!

On another rest occasion I received a firm dressing-down from our second-in-command, Major Pearce, for playing records too often and too loud in the mess. My taste in music always has been towards New Orleans jazz and blues with a touch of Nana Mouskouri, Shirley Bassey, Dean Martin, Tom Jones and Elvis Presley thrown in. The only two records in that mess that appealed to me, however, were one of Tannhauser's Pilgrims' Chorus and Doctor Henry Levine and his Barefoot Dixieland Philharmonic playing 'Muskrat Ramble.' In truth I did play them quite a lot. There wasn't a lot else to do. Clearly they did not appeal to Major Pearce. So I was marched in to his office and warned of the consequences if I did not cut down the racket. I never was over fond of Major Pearce after that.

They were enjoyable times nonetheless. There were great feelings of pride at being part of the effort and at being with such a first-class regiment. I was hugely impressed by the fact that none of those southern English officers who were my colleagues ever seemed to flap. Tom May and John Young always seemed to be quite confident about what should be done and how to do it. John Allen, whom I last met years ago down in Mumbles, near Swansea, on the eve of a Wales international, seldom seemed to be fully awake, but he was a man of strong character and another who exuded that air of certainty that everything would be alright on the night.

A great deal of the time, though, was spent in sweat and dust. We would slog our way up through those zig-zag Italian mountain roads, except when a Polish regiment was on the move. We thought very highly of the Poles as super fighting men, but they were regarded by us as lunatic drivers who whizzed about those Italian tracks and roads like Grand Prix drivers. So, whenever a Polish regiment was on the move the rest of us, where possible, stayed where we were until they had reached their new positions.

Winter was brutal at times, and all of us had miserable experiences of trying to get our vehicles and guns out of knee-deep cloying mud with rain beating down. Sometimes you would waken with your backs in your camp-bed under water. I have lain in my camp-bed and had boat races with matchsticks as the water poured through. My batman was 'Penny' Singleton, a well-meaning lad who was a touch accident-prone as when, on one occasion, he was tidying my bivouac whilst smoking a fag and set fire to the lot! But he was keen and dedicated and we had quite a good understanding – that soon was to include a ban on smoking when he was tidying my bivouac! The end of the campaign was greeted by us with mixed feelings because, whilst the slog was over, our regiment had to stay in action at Santa Croce, not far from Trieste, because Marshal Tito in Yugoslavia was making threatening noises about reclaiming certain territory that had been annexed to Italy much to the annoyance of the folk in the area who were very much Yugoslavs and who used to sing a song which sounded like 'Zivio la Svoboda,' (Long Live Freedom). Where have we heard that before? So there we were, stuck on another mini-mountain top with guns in action, this time pointing towards the Yugoslavian border, whilst the rest of the victorious forces were celebrating. It wasn't easy to keep chaps occupied during that frustrating spell and one of their little entertainments was to make a ring of petrol on the ground, set it alight and put two scorpions inside and bet on which one would win the battle. All very uncivilised and no doubt if the Friends of the Earth had existed at the time, they would have had something to say about it. But the lads seemed to enjoy it. Scorpions and evil-looking black snakes were a bit of a hazard in the intense heat, and one of the prime requirements before bedding down was to check inside the bed to make sure that a scorpion had not made its home there. Field-Marshal Harold Alexander, Supreme Allied Commander of the Mediterranean Theatre, was very popular with all who served with him because he struck everyone as being without show, but quietly efficient and one who could bring the best out of others. We all got a great kick out of his order of the day which everyone in his command received at the end of hostilities: 'You have won a victory which has ended in the complete and utter rout of the German armed forces in the Mediterranean . . . you may well be proud of this great and victorious campaign which will live long in history as one of the greatest and most successful ever waged.'

There followed a most enjoyable spell during which I was Battery sports officer, for which I had to go on a brief course at Benevento where I came across the silken skills of George Hamilton, the Aberdeen and Scotland footballer, a modest, likeable lad who made quite an impression. Perhaps it was partly George's influence, but when I was a student of physical education at Woolmanhill College in Aberdeen in 1947 and 1948, in a class comprising mostly football men, I surprised everyone, and not least myself, by coming out on top of the football examination which had been set by the famous Scottish football referee Peter Craigmyle. It surely was a feather in the cap of us rugby yokels! In January 1946 I was sports officer when we were stationed at Bolzano in the Dolomites and our regimental side achieved a 100 per cent record at football – played 10, won 10, 48 goals for and 6 against. They beat local town sides such as Rovereto (6-2), Merano (4-2) and Bolzano (4-1). That Bolzano game ended in controversy. Bolzano were area champions and when we led 4-1 at half-time they took such a dim view of being outplayed that they all left the pitch and didn't come back. Later, in the officers' mess, Colonel Hayes received a deputation from the Bolzano club, who offered abject apologies for the behaviour of their players, which 'Crusher' accepted with tact and understanding in light of the fact that we had won by playing football and not by the unsavoury tactics that had marred the previous occasion which had resulted in me being hauled over the coals.

At that time we had several super players. Sergeant George Hepplewhite hailed from the north-east of England and had played for Newcastle. He was a giant in midfield as an old-style centre-half. A stocky, little chap called Bagley had played first division football in London. He was a tricky ball-manipulator, so much so that once in a trial match when I was deputed to mark him, he beat me on the outside, the inside, over the top and through the middle. I could have killed him but my rugby training was of no avail. I couldn't get near enough to him. Half-back Stan Earl was a splendid captain and there was a lad, Prior, who was devastating on the wing and another called Wilkins who had played for

Brentford. I was very proud to be associated with that side, not that I did much else other than arrange for them to get leave to train and play, arrange matches and training spells, kit, etc. Hepplewhite, Prior, Bagley, Wilkins and Gunner Fisher all were promoted to the 59 Area eleven where they were joined by, among others, Bryn Jones of Arsenal and Wales. On one celebrated occasion Hepplewhite asked me to keep goal whilst he and the others practised their shooting. I should have known better. Hepplewhite's first shot almost took my head off. The next hit me in the lower regions like a steam-hammer, whereupon I decided that good sense and life-preservation were the better parts of valour, and hastily retired. I was just taken aback at the power and speed that professional footballers could generate and that experience has given me a much keener appreciation of the likes of Peter Shilton and Jim Leighton in lasting out so many internationals.

In April 1946 I had leave to go from our base in Milan to Trieste to join the Combined-Services, Central Mediterranean Forces rugby group to play matches against other groups: the British Army of the Rhine fifteen, British Troops Austria and a UK Forces fifteen. The BAOR side was particularly strong, including as it did, the inimitable Cliff Jones of Cardiff and Wales, R.H. 'Dicky' Guest of Waterloo and England, and Howard Campbell of Cambridge University and London Scottish, who was later to play four times for Scotland in 1947 and 1948. We played BAOR in the San Sabba Stadium, Trieste, on a boiling hot day and on brick-hard ground. Cliff Jones played full-back for BAOR and because of the hard ground he wore sandshoes. As he punted clear I jumped high to try and block the kick and landed right on his foot. He was in considerable pain and clearly also took a pretty dim view. Perhaps as he played his rugby in Wales he reckoned that his injury had been deliberately perpetrated! Not so. It was a pure accident and I felt thoroughly ashamed at having thus hurt a rugby legend. Some time later, when Cliff was president of the Welsh Rugby Union and I joined him for breakfast on the morning after a Welsh international, I reminded him of that incident. 'Don't worry, Bill,' he said, 'I've long since forgiven you ... although my foot was bloody sore.' 'Dicky' Guest was clever and very quick, and unless I am much mistaken, I believe he kicked a couple of goals in that match.

The Central Mediterranean Forces fifteen had some very useful citizens. Major J.H. Bevan was a 1946 Oxford blue, Captain Syd Harris played for Neath, Captain Forrest McLelland played for Glasgow Academicals and eventually became their club president. There were also C.W.A. Falconer (Edinburgh Academicals), Captain G.L. Davies (Cardiff), Captain Peter Lambert (Leicester), Captain E.J.H. Edwards (Cambridge University and England Services), Captain P.J. McConchy (Oxford University) and several powerful South Africans from their armoured division that played such a big part in the campaign: Lieutenant G.D. Shaw, Corporal J. Wood, and a big, rangy wing-forward, H.A. Spies. Even our referees were men of some fame – Lieut-Colonel W.V.H. Robins DSO, and Major A.I.S. Macpherson (Edinburgh Academicals), brother of the legendary G.P.S., captain of Scotland's first Grand Slam team in 1925. We beat the BTA side 39-6 in the Alexander Stadium, Milan, and had a trip to Vienna for the return match which we also won. We didn't know it then, but the member of our squad who was to gain most fame was Corporal Stan Adkins, our lock-forward who played for Coventry. Stan was big, modest and amiable and he could play all right. Little did I know then that the next time I would come across him would be at Twickenham in March 1953 when he gained the last of his seven caps. This was against Scotland. England won 26-8. I was in the radio commentary box and only a fortnight previously I had seen Scotland thrashed by the same score by Ireland at Murrayfield. So they were sad days for Scots. At Twickenham, Stan and his pals looked far bigger and heavier than the Scottish forwards. Not only that, but Stan scored one of England's six tries. That England side won the Championship outright for the first time in 16 years. They were great times those post-war months.

Back with the regiment I used to referee football matches – warrant officers and sergeants versus other ranks – and I was responsible for training a boxing team but having had an earlier experience at the hands of one J. Dempsey, I made sure that I was not a participant. It was when I was stationed with a field regiment at Harrogate that I was persuaded to take part in a boxing contest. Boxing was another favourite sport of mine. My hero was the 'Brown Bomber', Joe Louis. I remember once, as a child, shedding tears on the way home when I had collected the family paper and read in the 'stop press' that Joe had been beaten by the German, Max Schmeling. My joy was unconfined later on when Joe gained his revenge.Boxing gloves were among my Christmas presents, as was a punch-ball. I used to organise contests against school colleagues in our garage.

My interest in boxing had been stimulated by a friend of my father's, Andrew Pennycook, a local builder who had spent some years in

America and had been one of Jack Dempsey's seconds. Indeed Andrew had been in Dempsey's corner when he had fought Louis Firpo and Gene Tunney for the World Heavyweight Championship and I remember once on our High Street pavement, just outside East Bank Church, when we met Andrew and he demonstrated how Dempsey would throw a punch. In seeking to avoid it I finished on the pavement! What a character Andrew was. He played low handicap golf with just the stumps of two fingers left on one hand. I just loved his stories about Dempsey. He always claimed that in the first fight with Tunney some substance on Tunney's gloves affected Dempsey's sight. I was open mouthed at such drama. By curious coincidence those Dempsey stories were to find an echo in my own boxing experience at Harrogate. I had no particular desire to risk having my features rearranged even if that might lead to improvement! But when a great lump of PTI Sergeant tells you to report to the gym, you report to the gym. I skipped and punched the bag and tried to look fierce. I must have succeeded because not long afterwards I was told I would be boxing for real.

On the evening of the tournament I took one glance at the programme and almost tottered into a faint. It showed Private J. Dempsey v Private W. McLaren. I couldn't believe it. I thought that surely it couldn't be him, not the real 'Manassa Mauler'. Happily it wasn't. He was an ex-Navy man with tattoos all over him; his name was J. Dempsey all right and he looked mean. He was too. He knew all the wrinkles not least that of finger in the eye, but apparently he lost so many points for fouling, that I was declared the winner on points. In the showers afterwards he growled that if the fight had gone on for one more round, he would have killed me. I was in no mood to argue. He could have been right!

There was just one blot on this enjoyable landscape. Whilst our regiment was billetted in Milan one of our tasks was to run the Milan City Guard Room which really was being used as a jail but which, in fact, was just a converted reformatory. Among the prisoners were some extremely dangerous individuals either serving sentences or awaiting trial. One or two were charged with attempted murder and armed robbery. It was alleged that two of them had robbed several army vehicles and sold the contents on the black market. They had bank books covering many thousands of lire in the Bank of Italy and they had private villas and mistresses. They had lived the life of Riley and now we had to keep them under guard until their cases were called. Here was I, who knew nothing of prisons and had only an untrained staff, being asked to cope with cunning and desperate men. It was a miserable time. I worried every day about the possibility of escape. Actually three did get out but a 'trustee' to whom I had given a pleasant job in the cookhouse, came to me and provided information as to their whereabouts and in no time the Military Police had gathered them in and returned them to us. One big scare was when an Italian, reckoned to be guilty of ill-treating British prisoners, was brought in. We knew that we would have to guard him carefully because word gets round a prison very quickly. Unfortunately, our inexperienced guards were caught out. They were taking him out for his exercise, which he did on his own for safety, but this time, by mistake, before another prisoner had been returned to his cell. This other was a hefty, muscle man of oriental descent and as they passed each other he attacked the Italian with his fists before he could be restrained. The Italian, much the worse for wear, with a black eye and bruising, was due to leave the next day for his trial in Naples. I had visions of being called before a court of inquiry to explain this failure in my duty. I hurriedly sent for a medical officer to try and erase some of the damage but he was still marked when he left. No one really had any sympathy for him but I was very relieved when nothing more came of the incident.

It was with a certain amount of regret that I took my leave of the 5 Medium Regiment and the Army. I was grateful to both for many things – so much so that I almost signed on for 21 years of service. The pen was virtually poised over the paper but I was homesick and so 281771 Lieutenant W.P. McLaren was released from service on 12 May 1947. My 'demob' leave had begun in February 1947 and news of my rugby form with the CMF fifteen must have percolated through to the Scottish selectors because I was chosen to play for a Scottish fifteen against the Army at Murrayfield on 15 February 1947. There were some renowned, or soon to be renowned, players in that side: D. McIntyre (Glasgow High School FP), E.C.K. Douglas (RAF), C.W.R. Andrew (Glasgow Academicals), W.H. Munro (Glasgow High School FP) and D.D. Mackenzie (Edinburgh University); L. Bruce-Lockhart (Cambridge University) and E. Anderson (Stewart's College F.P.); H.H. Campbell (Cambridge University), S. Millar (Kelvinside-West), T.P.L. McLashan and D.T. McLean (both Royal High School FP), A. Fraser (Glasgow Academicals), W.P. McLaren (Hawick), J.B. Lees (Gala) and W. Elliot (Edinburgh Academicals).

The Army side also had some outstanding players. Major Roy Leyland already had played for England against Wales, Ireland and Scotland in 1935; T.G.H. Jackson and Frank Coutts had just been capped by Scot-

land and Don White had played for England; Grahame Budge became a
British Lion in New Zealand and Australia in 1950 and David Valentine,
a Hawick team mate of mine, gave such an outstanding performance in
the match that he thoroughly earned his first cap against Ireland a week
later. David played part of the game on the wing when Jackson was hurt
and even there he showed dash and skill, and there is no doubt that he
would have gained many more caps had he not opted for Rugby League.
The other wing-forward position against Ireland was given to the young
Royal High man D.T. McLean. Actually I had done quite well in the
match against the Army, although I got off to a humbling start. There
wasn't much in the way of team-talks in those days but there had been
reference to the danger held out by Roy Leyland and of how important it
would be for our loose-forwards to get out and about among the rival
backs as quickly as possible. So from almost the first scrummage of the
game I hurtled out in the approved manner with the aim of making an
early mark on the proceedings, whereupon I was adjudged by referee
Malcolm Allan to have been offside. The Army kicked the goal and led
3-0 thanks to my over-eagerness to carry out instructions. But I recall
that splendid Gala forward, Jim Lees, saying to me at half-time that if I
carried on the way I was going, I would get a cap. Even so I do not remember being desperately disappointed at not making the Scottish side
then because I was still on my demob leave and had been playing only
brief services rugby on the continent.

  Two big disappointments did follow, however. The South of Scotland
were due to play the touring Australians in October 1947 and I was being
tipped for a place in the South team as a wing-forward (flanker nowadays). Shortly before the South team was to be selected the Hawick
selectors asked me to play centre against Kelso as the regular centres
were unavailable. I wasn't too keen to do that because I had been playing
at wing-forward for the Combined Services team representing the
Central Mediterranean Forces. I hadn't played centre since the beginning
of the war, and I knew that whatever chance I had of playing for the
South against the Wallabies was as a wing-forward. However after two
phone calls from 'Pud' Miller, the Hawick Club secretary, I agreed to
turn out at centre against a strong Kelso side who went on to share the
Unofficial Scottish Championship with Aberdeen Grammar School FP.
Whether that, allied to the fact that I was now resident in Aberdeen
whilst studying physical education at Woolmanhill College, had any influence on the South selectors, or whether they felt that my form just

wasn't good enough, the result was that I wasn't picked for the Australian match. I remember the big headline in Jock Wemyss's article in the
Daily Express saying 'McLaren omission South team surprise.' I've still
got that cutting, and I feel the same pang of disappointment whenever I
see it. Then, about Christmas 1947, I was called down from Aberdeen to
play in a Scottish trial at Murrayfield. On the eve of that trial appearance
I was summoned to the home of W.E. 'Bill' Kyle, one of the most revered Hawick stalwarts, who had played 21 times for Scotland in days
when you really had to be outstanding as a Borderer to break through
the 'old school tie' barrier. I remember being ushered into the great
man's study, there to be told in no uncertain terms that I must make sure
during the trial that I showed the selectors that I could do a bit at the
lineouts as well as performing the other wing-forward duties. Unfortunately our trial captain H.H. Campbell (Oxford University and London
Scottish) decreed that I would operate from the very back of the lineout
and was not impressed when I suggested that I could win some ball
nearer the front. So I was stuck at the tail and the only time the ball was
thrown anywhere near there and I got it I found myself enmeshed in a
vice-like grip. The feeling was one of having two iron bands imprisoning
my arms. The bands belonged to Douglas Elliot, one of the greatest Scottish wing-forwards, whose strength had been developed in his every-day
life as a son of the soil. I was much impressed by the form of temporary
paralysis he imposed on my arms and it did not surprise me that he remained Scotland's most capped wing-forward with 29 appearances until
John Jeffrey of Kelso gained his 30th cap in the second Test against the
All Blacks in Auckland in June 1990. In any event, I was replaced at half-
time in the trial by an Anglo-Scot. The selectors apparently wanted to
have a closer look at him. From photographs of about that time, however, there was evidence that, unknown to me, tuberculosis was beginning to take a stronger hold for I looked thinner and a bit drawn. The intense physical pressure of a compressed course in physical education
could have been a factor in this deterioration although I did finish that
season and played the opening couple of games as Hawick vice-captain
in season 1948-49 before realising that something serious was wrong and
starting that heart-break spell during which the awful truth was revealed,
and with it, came the realisation that all hope had gone of my ever finding out if I could have made it to the promised land of a Scottish cap.

Life has its rough and smooth, and whilst the rough sometimes can be
hard to thole, the smooth offers much compensation. Playing for Haw-

ick in itself was a great thrill, and although we did not have a particularly memorable season in 1947-48 – there was a particularly enjoyable occasion when, in March 1948, we met Kelso at Mansfield Park in a vital Championship and Border League game. Kelso had a very strong side and were heading for both titles but we had the better of a 3-3 draw. Kelso had a key man in stand-off Archie Ferguson, and before the game it was brought home to me by Andrew Bowie, another remarkable Hawick servant, who won more than fifty seven-a-side medals and became an SRU committee-man, that my primary function was to try and upset Archie so that the Kelso backs wouldn't function effectively. I was chuffed afterwards when 'Border Callant' in the *Bulletin* newspaper wrote: 'McLaren did not push much in the scrummages but his swift breaking forced Ferguson into some thoroughly slipshod play.'

We had another memorable meeting with Kelso. It was at the Kelso sevens tournament in 1947 when we met them in the semi-final. At the end of the 7½ minutes each way (with no rest at the interval, as at Middlesex sevens) we were still locked at 0-0. We then changed ends five times before Sandy Charters scored the sudden-death winner. 'Sudden' was hardly the word. They reckon that the tie lasted some 50 minutes. It was the only time that I can recall a Hawick team being almost relieved when the opposition scored! Once when Kelso hacked the ball back into our '25' I managed to get back to kick it dead but got a roasting from Jimmy Lumsden for not running back quickly enough. Run? I could barely walk! When we took our boots off on the field our feet were red raw and we had to walk on our heels up to the hotel in the town where we changed. Not surprisingly, Kelso could hardly raise a gallop in the final and were well beaten by Melrose.

You can be so exposed in sevens; once we were playing Gala in the semifinal at Hawick and I heard the call to kick so I kicked. Unfortunately it landed in the arms of Gala's fast wing J.A. Caskey and he scored. What a blazing rocket I got from the Hawick selectors on leaving the pitch! On another occasion at the Gala tournament I caught a glimpse of our big wing, Wattie Scott, a big farmer and a tremendous force, out on the left, unmarked. So I punted across field and Wattie gathered in full stride and ran fifty yards for a try. When we came off the field I got another rocket for punting. But we scored and it was deliberate, I protested. That didn't matter. You did not kick in sevens. You handled. Some time later I heard of the Hawick scrum-half Jackie Wright, a tough, gnarled little nugget who called a spade a spade, and was playing for a composite seven that included the legendary Irish and British Lions wing Tony O'Reilly. Having just made two long runs for tries O'Reilly got the ball again and tried a drop-goal whilst he got his breath back. Whereupon Jackie trundled over to him and snarled: 'Hey, yow O'Reilly, oo dinna drop goals in seevins, oo score tries!'

Two games for the South stand out. We played the Co-Optimists at Netherdale and I was in direct opposition to Mickey Steele-Bodger who was studying at Edinburgh University. He was a nippy little operator and I took it as a personal failing that he scored a try and I didn't. Then we met the North of England at Carlisle and I remember that our team talk centred around the lineout ability of H.F. Luya of Waterloo and Headingley, an England international lock. So big Adam Crawford of Melrose was deputed to mark him. 'Mark' was the word. Adam, a super guy who gave his heart and soul in the cause of Melrose and the South, played the game of his life in giving Luya a very difficult passage. It was on that occasion that Bob Hogg showed the South of Scotland tie to those players who wanted one. It was some tie. It incorporated every one of the colours of the seven senior Border clubs and it was really like a drunken rainbow, a kind of forerunner of the current technicolour ties with which sundry television performers bedazzle their audiences. It wasn't the kind of tie you would wear to a Royal Garden Party but I was proud to have mine and I sometimes saw Adam wearing his. It certainly should have reminded him of one of his great performances.

Mention of the Co-Optimists reminds me of Selkirk sevens in September 1947 when Hawick reached the final against a Co-Optimists seven of mature talent. Tom Wright, our Captain, had been injured and as vice-captain I was in charge in the final. We ran away with a quick ten points and even when Co-Ops got back to 10-6 I was already thinking of my cup acceptance speech. But 'Copey' Murdoch of Hillhead High School, captain of Co-Ops, who had the distinction of playing for Scotland before and after the second world war, got the ball twice and each time dropped a goal. He was a drop-goal specialist and they were each worth four points in those days. Co-Optimists won 14-10 and 'Copey' made the speech. I felt like saying to him: 'Oo dinna drop goals in seevins, oo score tries!' But they were beautifully struck goals. And to think that the presentation honours were conducted by Willie Bryce, Selkirk Club president and one of the Border district's most famous internationals, a scrum-half, who also represented Scotland at hockey. Rough and smooth indeed.

5

A Real Hospital Pass

It never really dawned on me in those early days as a schoolboy when I used to do my own written reports on rugby internationals, golf matches and the Olympic Games from my own imagination, but using the names of all the great sportsmen of the day, when I would write screeds and screeds in my ledger and then would do commentary from them, that I would eventually become a radio and television rugby commentator. No such thought ever entered my mind. All I wanted to do was play rugby for Hawick and Scotland. Gradually, there developed a desire to become a games master and eventually I did qualify from Woolmanhill College up in Aberdeen with my Diploma of Physical Education, my swimming certificates, my dancing certificates, etc. I'd already started teaching in Hawick and in the villages surrounding it, travelling to some seven or eight schools during the week, and I was enjoying every moment of it. It was a real thrill for me to be starting to establish myself as a teacher of physical education and I was looking to a very long and enjoyable career – because in those days teaching really was enjoyable. The children were disciplined, obedient, pleasant and enthusiastic and teachers were just full of the love of the job they were doing.

Teachers in those days, it seemed to me, did regard teaching as a calling. They simply revelled in it. I came across some super headmasters who were strong on discipline. Some might regard them nowadays as hard men indeed, but they created a fruitful environment. I'm not saying that there aren't dedicated teachers today but there is an aura of resentment in the profession. So much is demanded of them and without that plank of strong discipline to help them it surely is an indictment of the system that so many teachers complain that they spend too much time on guidance and dealing with trouble-makers to the detriment of teaching time. When I started out in August 1948 it was so enjoyable and I have to say that the enjoyment continued until I retired in 1987.

I'd been teaching for only about six to seven weeks when tuberculosis was diagnosed and I had those near two years in hospital.

It came home to me forcibly as soon as I was admitted to hospital that it was going to be hard to accommodate myself to such a change in situation. Already, aspects of my health were worrying. I was coughing blood, which indicated the extent of the damage to my left lung. They reckoned there was a hole as big as an old half-crown and clearly that had been a problem for some time, although I hadn't known it. As I looked back I could remember little things which would have been tiny warning signs, had I known anything at all about the disease. One was when I organised a friendly rugby match on a gun position during the battle for Cassino. Whilst we were building up for the next attack that, just to break the monotony, I arranged a rugby match on a bit of grass by the gun position, with a ball made out of waste paper and bits of string. We played three or four-a-side much to the merriment of the gunners and I thought I'd got a knock on the nose as I had slight blood traces from the back of my throat. I thought nothing of it but the M O checked me over and said that he was pretty sure it had been caused by the rugby, and indeed that was my opinion. Then, before going to college up in Aberdeen, I had to pass a fairly rigorous medical examination, and there was no problem so I forgot all about it.

Yet, as it turned out, from the amount of damage done to my lung, I had almost certainly contracted tuberculosis during the war years. When I was demobilised, and went on the physical education course – a very intensive course, because some three years of learning were being compressed into fourteen months – the physical pressure began to have an effect. We were out in the swimming pool at 8 o'clock in the morning and practising our Scottish country dancing at half-past nine at night. It was that kind of time-table, a very tough programme indeed. All that probably caused an escalation of the disease. And so, by the time I'd come to the end of my course, quite a bit of damage must have been done.

I think the most interesting and frightening aspect was when I was told what treatment I would be given. It was called pneumoperitoneum and involved sticking a needle, about four to five-inches long, right into the tummy, on the right-hand side, and to pump air through that needle under the diaphragm to lift the lung. When Dr R.W. Biagi first described the treatment. I said to him: 'You're not going to shove that thing into my stomach?!' He replied: 'Indeed, I am.' I can't remember whether I actually got a local anaesthetic with the first one or not. On seeing the size of the needle, I thought a general anaesthetic would have been justified! I still have umpteen little pin-pricks on my skin because we had this treatment once a week and, for something like four years from the time I was cured in 1950, I had to return to East Fortune, and then to Galashiels Hospital, in order to get a refill once a week. When we were 'up-patients,' allowed to get up for a limited period each day, we all used to walk there quite naturally but when we came out from the treatment room, with all this air pumped under our diaphragms, we came back with cheeks blown out like moving balloons. It was an extraordinary feeling, and very uncomfortable.

Another part of the treatment was what was called a phrenic crush. The idea was to crush the phrenic nerve near the collar bone and that had the effect of lifting the diaphragm and so resting the damaged lung. The effect lasted quite a while so that you didn't need another crush for over a year. It was all fairly painless except for that moment when the nerve was crushed. It was rather like having a giant hiccough. But it seemed to do the trick of providing a restful position for the lung that needed repair.

There was something else! We slept outside! All you could see of most of us were red noses – and sometimes not even that. Fresh air was regarded as a very important part of the healing process. We virtually lived on the open-air veranda, even in rough weather. Indeed I can remember waterproof covers being put over the bottom of our beds as protection against snow! Some mornings I woke with six inches of snow on that big waterproof cover. It was perishing cold at times. On one occasion my mother came to visit me. She was tall and slim, with not an awful lot of flesh on her bones. She had to sit outside at the side of my bed until I asked the nurse if she could push me back in for just half an hour so that my mother could enjoy the warmth of the ward. What a relief that was – for my mother and me!

The aspect of treatment which really hastened my progress was the discovery of the drug called streptomycin. It was very new at the time and I remember Dr Biagi coming in to talk about it. I got the impression that we were, in a sense, guinea pigs. The streptomycin made an almost immediate impact on the extent of the disease in my lung. Instead of four years in a hospital bed, I was up and about and ready to go home in about nineteen months. You can imagine the joy that brought.

If streptomycin was the medical reason for my recovery there can be no doubt as to the personal reason. One of the great factors in my recovery from what was then a wasting disease was Bette, who has been my wife now for over forty years.

Bette and I had actually met first when I was on demob leave in March 1947. I was a bit fed-up because I'd been away from home for about four or five years and you know how difficult it is to rekindle friendships. Since a lot of fellows were still in the forces, I was at a loose end. My sister Kit had a couple of tickets for a dance in the Town Hall, for which the music was being provided by Oscar Rabin and his band, one of the great big bands of the time, and it was a big thing for them to be playing in Hawick, a town of just 16,000 folk.

As I walked into the dance hall the first person I saw was this lovely girl, dressed all in white, at the other side of the hall. The next dance was a tango so I asked if I could dance with her. She accepted and I immediately realised she was a magnificent dancer. I could tell right away she was good fun and sensible and lovely. People tend to laugh about love at first sight but there has never been any doubt in my mind that from that very first moment that I saw Bette I was in love with her.

We were courting for about seventeen months, and when I went into the sanatorium at Bangour we faced another problem because we had intended to get engaged two months later, at Christmas 1948. When I realised the seriousness of my situation and the length of time that I was going to be in hospital I really didn't want to subject Bette to that long, long trail of hospital visits and doubts about the outcome of my illness. At that time I didn't even know whether I would ever be cured but Bette never had any doubts and she was the one who said: 'No, we're going to see this thing through together. We're going to face it and we're going to take whatever is in store.'

Bette came in to see me every weekend. It was a long trip, an hour and a quarter on the train up to Edinburgh, and then bus, either to Bangour or, once we'd got back to East Fortune, the one hour ride away down to East Lothian. Not only did those visits keep up my morale and confidence but Bette always brought in food of all kinds – steak and stews and tripe and onions in casserole form, half-a-dozen or a dozen eggs every week – and all this when rationing was still in force and it was very difficult indeed to obtain any extras. We were lucky in that Bette's uncle,

Watt Hogarth, was manager of the Hawick Co-operative Society's fish and poultry department and he was an absolute gem in getting little extra titbits in addition to the rations.

Sometimes there was an unexpected and heartwarming bonus; one of the bakers in Hawick, R.T. Smith ('Firpo' Smith, as he was known), had played for Scotland as a prop-forward out of the Kelso Club. R.T. was standing at the entrance to his bakery and he asked Bette to wait for just a second. He disappeared and returned with a huge fruit cake. 'Take this in to Bill and wish him well from me,' he said. I didn't know R.T. Smith personally. I knew of him because I knew about all the great rugby players who had played for Scotland out of the Borders – Jimmy Graham, Jock Allan, Jack Waters and others – but that wonderful gesture was typical of the acts of kindness that kept Bette and me going through those very hard times during which we had to wait quite a long period before there was any sign of improvement at all in my health.

I became an up-patient, and that was an absolute treat. To be able to go on even short walks just about the hospital and to visit people in other wards really gave you a feeling of progress, whilst also breaking the monotony of a long day.

As an up-patient, I took on the business of organising competitions at putting, table tennis and darts and there may have been a billiard table there. I helped to create our own putting green on the patch of grass outside our ward.

East Fortune Hospital was the place where I first started out as a commentator, because when there were table tennis and other competitions between up-patients I used to do commentary for patients in the wards via the P A System. I was a bit of a D J as well because I used to pipe music and play records to the wards for patients who had made requests. You can imagine what a 'guddle' I made of doing a commentary on a table tennis match with the ball flitting about like a bit of shrapnel, but the bed-patients seemed to enjoy getting a bit of a giggle out of it and that was really what we aimed to do. It gave patients confined to bed, some for many months and, indeed, years, a little bit of added interest. So those were the first commentaries I gave to live audiences although as a very young boy I used to do fictional commentaries by impersonating the great rugby commentators of the day.

It was a coincidence, too, that when I was playing records for the patients in East Fortune, Bette, who was the Lyle and Scott mannequin and receptionist, was playing music over their P A System for all the

workers in the factory. Our favourite song at the time was Ella Fitzgerald's 'My Happiness.' We loved that song because it seemed to be so
appropriate to our own situation. I got moaned at in East Fortune for
playing it too often and Bette got the same from the Lyle and Scott
workers with their 'Oh, hell, no' that yin again!'

So there were laughs and moments of fun among the pain and bore-
dom; but it was still a year and a half of my youth wasted and a cruel and
premature curtailment of what might well have been a promising sporting career.

6
The World of the Microphone

When I was declared cured and fit to work again, I was hoping for a vacancy in teaching. I was fit to teach again, but my desire was to stay in my own home area rather than to seek a post elsewhere because Doctor Joe Tyrie and my tuberculosis records were all in Hawick, and I just thought it would be a good thing to stay close, just in case anything did go wrong. Doctor Tyrie was the TB physician for the Borders and I have fond memory of the care and comfort provided by this gem of a man. In order to fill in a bit of time until a teaching vacancy cropped up, I took a job as a general reporter with one of the two local papers in the town, the *Hawick Express*, whose owner-editor was Mr John Hood, a vastly experienced journalist, a real professional and a man of high principle and integrity. I had the deepest respect for him apart altogether from the fact that over the next eight or nine years he brought a new shape to my life. I shall be forever grateful to Mr Hood who was a strong task master, who drove you hard, made sure that you did the job well, but always was fair and consistent – and kind too. The job with the *Hawick Express* entailed being responsible for the sports pages, which included all the rugby matches, junior, semi-junior, school (and, of course, the Hawick 'Greens'), football and other sports; but in addition, I had to attend local Town Council meetings, meetings of the Education Committee and of Roxburgh County Council as it was in those days. I had to attend the local courts and report on all the cases that came before the Magistrates and the Sheriff. If there was a fire I had to report that and anything that cropped up in the way of sensational news. Mr Hood was the kind of man who expected you to be the eyes and ears of the *Hawick Express* and to be right on your toes. That was a wonderful experience for me because, apart from having to work very hard indeed, including and over weekends and during holidays, Mr Hood himself was a fine example of a journalist and taught me a lot that was invaluable later. I can remember him, for instance, throwing one of my reports back at me with bits of paper floating all over the office, telling me that he wanted his readers to be able to understand everything I wrote and he didn't need a clever dick of a reporter trying to show how superior he was in the use of fancy words! Secondly, he said, would I kindly make sure that I didn't use thirty-five words if eight would do! He was a past master at cutting out all the words that weren't necessary and leaving the paragraphs still saying exactly what was meant in the first place. Now you might think he failed completely to impress that upon me but it still was good training because when, eventually, I had to do radio and television reports for the BBC in which I had to squeeze stories of six club matches into maybe one and half to two minutes on the air, there was no place for spare words. So his training helped me to get what I wanted to say into the time allotted.

Not only that but Mr Hood was the one who launched me, screaming, virtually screaming, into my radio and, eventually, my television commentary career. He was the local correspondent for the British Broadcasting Corporation, reporting any items of news from Hawick, including reports from racehorse owner Ken Oliver's Auction Mart, showing the average price of sheep and cattle being sold and so on. Unknown to me, he'd written to the BBC and said that he had a young fellow on his staff who was very keen on rugby football, who reported games, who kept statistical details and generally was very interested in the game in its entirety. If they had any vacancies, he suggested, they might find some use for him. I didn't know this, of course. The first I knew about it was a letter asking me to attend a commentary audition at the South of Scotland versus South Africa match, featuring the famous 1951-52 Springboks, Basil Kenyon's great lot, that was to be played at our own home ground at Mansfield Park. I chucked the letter in the bucket. I thought somebody was having me on, maybe the other lad in the office, and it was only some time later that Mr Hood asked if I had heard from the BBC. Then all was revealed. He said: 'Well, you'll be going.' I said: 'No fear, I'm not going to do an audition, I don't know the first thing about commentary work.' Well, he was a strong personality and he persuaded me to go despite my lack of enthusiasm.

There were six of us there and each did commentary for ten minutes. I was invited up to Edinburgh to hear my ten minutes-worth being played back and I must say I was pleased at the way I mentioned players. That came over reasonably well. But I was appalled that I hadn't mentioned which area of the field the play was in so that the listener had no idea whatsoever of whether it was the South African '25' or near touch or what. That was the first real lesson: the radio audience had to be regarded as totally blind, every single detail of the picture had to be painted in, otherwise the listeners couldn't really get the complete story. The thing just developed from there. The BBC then asked me to do another test commentary for three-quarters of an hour at a Heriot's F.P. versus Watsonians club match in Edinburgh, and shortly after that I was asked to do Glasgow versus Edinburgh, the inter-city match, then regarded as a very important trial for the Scottish team. That was in Glasgow in December 1952; 55 minutes live radio on the Scottish Home Service. I'll never forget that day because I missed three meals over it – breakfast turned to ashes in my mouth, I didn't even think about lunch, I was so nervous, and I was so relieved to get the thing over and done with that I didn't have dinner either! I remember that terrible feeling in the pit of the stomach, in the commentary box, maybe a couple of minutes before I got the cue to start. That was a dreadful time, and I thought, 'If I have to go through this all the time, I'll be absolutely shattered.' I remember Peter Thomson, a good friend of mine who was then Head of Sport in Glasgow BBC, telling me that nervousness was a good sign, that when you didn't feel sick, when you didn't feel that stomach churning, that would be the time to stop. Peter told me that, before his first live commentary, he went outside the commentary box and was physically sick, and I haven't come across anyone, even among the finest professionals, in all those years of broadcasting who doesn't experience stomach butterflies just before they start. In my case, on that first live commentary, my butterflies were clamping about in hob-nailed boots!

It was actually during that first live commentary that a Scottish international player took a penalty kick to touch and actually missed the ball. That was such a shock that I almost came out with something along the-lines of 'Well, I'll be damned!' I remember the hairs sitting up on the back of my neck at the thought of what I'd almost said, and it brought home to me how careful you had to be so as not to offend people with bad language!

In 1953 I was asked to provide ten minutes of commentary at the Scotland v Wales match at Murrayfield; I was sandwiched between Rex

Alston and G.V. Wynne-Jones who were the established radio rugby commentators. They were super fellows and Rex Alston was a great help to me in those early days. I remember G.V. Wynne-Jones telling me that in his first commentary at the France v Wales game in Paris, Rex had done the introductory bit about the weather and the conditions and the changes and then handed over to 'Geevers' to do the first twenty minutes. As he did so 'Geevers' leaned on the table and the leg gave way and his very first words to the waiting audience were 'Oh, hell!'

That Scotland v Wales game in 1953 was another nerve-racking occasion. In those days we did radio commentary from the back of the main stand with the result that you seemed to be miles away from the play, and identification was very difficult indeed – no such thing as television monitors to help you along then! In the 1955 game against Ireland on a dull, overcast day and near the end of the match I described a run by Robin Charters from the far side, and it was only when he had gone some twenty-five yards that I realised it was not Robin but Ian Swan, whose running style was somewhat similar. For years after that old guys would stop me on Hawick High Street and remind me of 'yon day when ee got Chairters wrong.' You see, I had played in the same Hawick team as Robin. That taught me just how hard it can be in certain conditions to spot players correctly in the instant. Getting back to Murrayfield in 1953, I remember vividly the anxiety I felt at having to do ten minutes alongside two experienced men, recognised as excellent commentators. The idea was simply to see how I would react to the big occasion. I managed to muddle through. I suppose I was glad, in a way, that it was only ten minutes but I must have done reasonably well because that led to me getting a bigger share. I cannot remember if there was any scoring during my commentary stint, but I can still see the great Bleddyn Williams running thirty yards for his second try in that 12-0 Welsh win. It was the first time also that I had seen Cliff Morgan and Rex Willis in action as Welsh half-backs; Morgan, crafty as a bag of weasels and with scuttling pace and superb balance like a kind of flying Charlie Chaplin, Willis, barrel-chested and so strong he had to be nailed to the floor.

I was thrilled at being asked to share commentary at Wales v Scotland, in 1954, the last international match played at St Helen's, Swansea. It was my first broadcast from Wales, whose folk have been so kind to me over the years. Ken Jones, the great Welsh wing, equalled the Welsh record of caps on that day and I seem to remember that the Welsh went out of their way to give him a try. Wales won 15-3 and although Ken didn't score it didn't matter because he was recognised all over the world as a truly great sprinter and a great wing, and he was given a great ovation at the end of that memorable day – memorable for Ken and certainly for me, too.

I recall, too, how helpful Rex Alston was. We shared a France v Scotland game in Paris in the early 1950s and I was travelling from Scotland by train. Of course I was travelling third class because I got my expenses from the Scottish Programme Executive and they were pretty tight in those days. Indeed, I think for my early commentaries I got a fee of four pounds! There I was, sitting in a crowded compartment when Rex appeared at the doorway. 'My dear chap,' he said, 'you can't travel in third class, you're BBC. Come and travel first class with me.' When I told him I couldn't afford to do so he insisted, and I found myself 'howking' my luggage out from amongst the other occupants and making my way up the train. Rex arranged it all and from that time onwards I was always able to travel in more comfort.

In the hotel, too, on the eve of the match, Rex ran over the French pronunciations with me and I can recall spending some time trying to get the pronunciation of Dufau, the French scrum-half, absolutely right for Rex. That brought home to me very early on how important it was with the BBC hierarchy to get things right. I've done my best to do so since then although Ian Kirkpatrick, the New Zealand captain here in 1972 – 73, told me that the whole of New Zealand was convulsed once when, during a television commentary, I spoke of a player from Manawatu and got it all wrong with the emphasis on the 'Wat' bit instead of the 'tu.'

Once, when Scotland were playing England at Murrayfield, the English were based at the Marine Hotel down in North Berwick which, incidentally, has almost since then been a favourite watering hole for Bette and myself. (We go down for a couple of days and have some golf there – I'm a country member at the Gullane Club which has three courses). Rex said it would be helpful to preparations if I went down and had lunch with the English team, then watched them training. Well, I wasn't all that concerned about having lunch with them. I'm kind of shy and modest (as everybody will have noted from this book!) but Rex was the BBC staff man and so I agreed and drove down in my old Morris 11. Rex met me and took me in first of all to have a refreshment with the English committee men. He introduced me to the RFU secretary, Robin Prescott. By coincidence, he had been the Weapons Training Officer at Wrotham in Kent when I was doing my OCTU. Prescott had taught me how to put a sticky bomb on a tank. So when I was introduced to him, I said how delighted I was to meet him again, that he wouldn't remember me but he had shown me how to put a sticky bomb on a tank at Wrotham. I remember him giving me one of those old-fashioned looks then saying, 'Oh really, did you kill anybody?' 'Not so far,' I replied.

So we had lunch with the English party, met the players and went to Carlkemp Priory rugby pitch just along the road from the hotel and watched the training session. From that day I found the succeeding English officials and players friendly and helpful. I remember, too, that Rex and I had a drop-goal contest which ended in a draw. Having a friend and colleague of the old school such as Rex Alston, with his high standards of attitude and performance, was immensely beneficial to me when I was just feeling my way along. I owe a great deal to him.

By 1954 I was becoming established as the Scottish radio rugby commentator. I remember being at the Ireland v Scotland game in 1954 at Ravenhill in Belfast. It was the last international played there and that was the first time I shared commentary with Sammy Walker. I was excited about that, too, for Sammy had been a great Irish and British Lions forward who had captained the Lions in South Africa in 1938. He was a big, bluff, happy-go-lucky character and I enjoyed very much working with him because of his tremendous enthusiasm and commitment. But that first of several broadcasts with Sammy didn't set any heather on fire. Ireland won 6-0, both tries by Mick Mortell of Bective Rangers, Scotland having lost hooker Bob MacEwen in the second half with a damaged knee, but I remember Sammy saying that he'd seen and played in a goodly number of internationals but that was the worst he had ever seen. That match brought home to me how hard it could be to make a dreich game interesting for the radio listener unless the commentator could embellish the picture with some tactical points.

Another great character I worked with a lot was Andrew Wemyss, known to all as 'Jock,' who had played for Gala and Edinburgh Wanderers and who did summaries with me in those early days. They say that once (I wasn't there at the time), in a radio broadcast from Paris, 'Jock,' when describing Scottish pack play, had said 'the Scottish forwards are just rotten!' He got quite a bit of stick after that! He was inclined sometimes in fun I believed, to mispronounce French names. He would call Jean Prat by the woman's name, Jean, and one big fellow, J.P. Saux of Pau, he always called 'Socks.' I've heard him refer to Pierre Albaladejo as Pierre Alphabet! I think Jock did it with a twinkle in his eye; he was a wonderful character and in those early days he helped me a lot. There was I, a youngster, wet behind the ears and with my number nothing like dry and Jock would introduce me to folk in the game, Rugby Union officials and others and that helped me to become established and to boost my confidence.

Jock was a wonderful story-teller. I travelled to Ireland matches on the Glasgow-Dublin boat with Jock when we used to take off from the Anderson Quay in Glasgow and sail overnight and Jock would regale us with a whole series of anecdotes about the great days, both before and after the first world war, in Scottish rugby and, indeed, in British rugby. He knew all the great players and all about them, and I remember once being absolutely fascinated just listening to him on the Dublin boat coming home, over the Saturday night and the Sunday morning. Suddenly I realised that it was about twenty-to-four in the morning and there I was still absolutely enchanted and sore with laughing.

Jock actually had played for Scotland before the first world war as a forward, and then after it with just one eye because he'd lost the other in battle. He told a lovely story about the France v Scotland game in Paris in 1922. Apparently, he'd found out that there was a French forward playing in the same match who also had lost an eye in the war. His name was Lubin-Lebrère, and he played for Toulouse. So they got together before the game and arranged to mark each other, and because each had only the one eye they tended to feel for each other at the lineouts; and on one occasion the referee, H.C. Harrison of England, who was nick-named 'Dreadnought,' was going to penalise them when Charlie Usher, the Scottish captain, ran past and said, 'Oh, come on, ref, for God's sake leave them alone, they're both half-blind!'

In those early days commentators had to be sort of jacks-of-all-trades, capable of doing scene-sets before kick-off, commentary and sometimes summary as well, and Jock was a most entertaining and informative summariser. When Sammy Walker and I shared matches, each of us would take twenty minutes of commentary in turn, and the one who was off had to be handy to come in with analytical points. I used to enjoy that, because during the time when you weren't actually doing commentary, you could assess the trend of play, watch individual players and see the whys and wherefores of what was happening on the field. Sometimes, at the end of the match you had to keep the broadcast going for anything between two and fifteen minutes until told to hand back to the studio. I used to have a little list of areas of the game, scrummages, lineouts, loose,

ABOVE In the Hawick Seven as a 17-year-old (on right, back row), alongside Scottish cap Rob Barrie. Also in the back row, from left: Wallis Heath, Rob 'Tough' Robson. Front row, from the left: Will Richardson, Jimmy Lumsden, John Hall

Captain of the Hawick Seven, beaten in the final of the Selkirk Sevens by the Co-Optimists, 1947. On the right is Scottish international W. C. W. 'Copey' Murdock (Hillhead HS FP)

RIGHT A member of the Combined Services XV, Central Mediterranean Forces, 1946

BELOW The *Hawick Express* staff. Mr Hood on the extreme left, next to me

FAR RIGHT The Combined Services XV, Italy 1946. I am fifth from the left, back row. Stan Adkins (Coventry and England) is fifth from the left, front row

BELOW RIGHT Combined Services, Central Mediterranean Forces. I am third left, back row; the legendary Cliff Jones (Cardiff and Wales) is third left, middle row: Dicky Guest (Waterloo and England) is fifth left, middle row

A.

LEFT In the BBC studio, Edinburgh

Bette and myself and the view from our hilltop home

RIGHT With the Scottish Sevens squad at our 40th wedding anniversary celebration in Hong Kong. Left to right: James Smith (hotel manager), Scott Nichol, Janie, Tony Stanger, Derek White, self, Scott Hastings, Bette, Ron Kirkpatrick, Greig Oliver, Linda Craig Chalmers, John Jeffrey

BELOW RIGHT Three generations of rugby men. Left to right: me, Rory and Gregor Lawson, our grandsons, and son-in-law Alan Lawson (15 caps for Scotland)

FAR LEFT With SRU President Adam Robson and BBC chief Alasdair Milne at the 1984 Grand Slam reception

BELOW LEFT Stop me – if you can! Another of Hawick's favourite sons in typical pose – Hugh McLeod, 40 caps and a double British Lion

LEFT Andy Irvine (Heriots FP and Scotland) about to tilt his lance . . .

. . . and having another 'go' with colleagues Alastair McHarg and Mike Biggar (second and third from left) about to lend support – once they've discovered exactly where he is going!

ABOVE Jim Renwick (Hawick and Scotland), who survived being a pupil of mine to become Scotland's most capped back! A rare talent who had the distinction, among others, of scoring a try in each of three consecutive internationals against Wales at Cardiff

ABOVE RIGHT Myself as seen by caricaturist John Ireland

Tony Stanger (Hawick and Scotland), hero of Scotland's Grand Slam win over England in 1990, crosses swords with Patrice Lagisquet and with the Hastings clan providing back-up

dribbling rushes, handling, full-back play and so on so that, at a glance, I could remind myself of another aspect of play. That was a help if you had to keep the broadcast going for a while until they were ready in the studio to take over. It was a very good training ground in that you not only had to be the commentator who dealt with the thing as it was happening on the spot, but also had to be able to bring to the attention of listeners little points which perhaps hadn't come out in commentary, but which you'd been able to note, during your twenty minutes off.

It was in the early fifties that I came across, for the first time, the famous New Zealand radio commentator, Winston McCarthy. The BBC decided to send me down to Cardiff to watch, in the commentary box, the Wales v New Zealand game in December 1953. It was part of my training to see a real expert at work, and Winston McCarthy certainly was that. I remember standing behind him in the Cardiff commentary position at that historic game which Wales won by 13-8, and being absolutely amazed at the outpouring of words from this little New Zealander. He was really like a verbal typewriter, a machine gun, and he was as knowledgeable of tactics as you would expect of a New Zealander. He got quite excited, too, and he had that distinctive way of building up a kick at goal. He used to work up the tension as the kicker made his preparations, then he would say 'Listen, listen, the crowd will tell you,' and as it went over, he'd shout 'It's a GOAL!' Listeners in this country really warmed to him.

Once Winston and Kevin Skinner, the New Zealand prop-forward, had a night out on the beer before, if I remember rightly, the South v New Zealand game in 1954; but whatever condition they might have been in the night before, it made no difference to their performances. Winston was a little red of eye but he was still on the ball with that tremendous rat-tat-tat of description. Skinner, of course, was one of the great strong men of New Zealand rugby football, renowned for his front-row play. The 1953 Wales v New Zealand game was memorable for, among other things, an All Black try by Bill Oliver at which Winston got so excited that we had to grab his coat-tails to prevent him disappearing over the balustrade into a forty-feet drop. There was, too, one of the most famous cross-kicks of all time when Welsh wing-forward, Clem Thomas, hemmed in on the South touch-line, kicked the ball far across into the midfield, and there Ken Jones, the famous Newport wing-threequarter, scooped up the ball and scored the winning try. The 56,000 crowd, as you can imagine, just went potty and Winston, to his credit, described the move beautifully despite his natural disappointment. I've never come across anybody who could rattle words together quite like Winston.

I've since come to know that same Clem Thomas well as a rugby correspondent of very keen perception and of many brave comments over the years. He is another of the characters in rugby football with a distinctive guffaw when something really amuses him. That is something you just have to hear to have lived! I often pull his leg about the time when Wales played Scotland at Cardiff in February 1958 and John Collins, the Welsh wing, was given the ball near the right tough-line but Adam Robson, the Hawick and Scottish wing forward, had him absolutely covered. However Adam's jersey stretched out like a rubber band and there was a very large butcher's hand attached to it, so that Adam couldn't get at Collins who went and scored the vital try in the Welsh 8-3 victory. Whenever I remind Clem about that, he just gives me a look of innocence accompanied by that great guffaw, like, to quote P.G. Wodehouse, 'a bull pulling its foot out of a swamp.' That was one of the occasions when Clem was captain of Wales. On a boat trip during my first visit to the Hong Kong sevens in 1989, Clem got his own back with several pointed comments about my food intake! I certainly was hungry on that trip! Clem is good company and like many other people in the Rugby game, I was delighted when he was given an award for his services to journalism at the 'Whitbread's Rugby World and Post' award ceremony in 1990. That was thoroughly well deserved.

7
Sound and Vision; Tricks of the Trade

When I was asked to switch more or less permanently to television commentary in, I think, 1960, I wasn't all that keen because I was so used to radio. For instance, there was Scotland v Wales at Murrayfield in 1963. It had 111 lineouts and is engraved on my memory as one of the most testing undertakings any commentator could have to face. An irate lieutenant-colonel wrote from his Highland fastness to tell me I was 'a bloody fool' and there couldn't possibly be that many lineouts in any match. He was wrong; there were. It really proved just a matter of kick to touch, lineout, kick to touch, lineout, almost throughout the match which was, moreover, conducted in rain and sleet. Clive Rowlands as captain and super tactician, was the key man in the Welsh side that day. They won 6-0 against the odds, their first win at Murrayfield for ten years. They reckoned that Clive had six different signals for the Welsh team and every one meant kick to touch! Clive himself says that, in his family, when they're having a meal, they don't say 'pass the salt, please,' they say 'kick the salt over, please!' I've often pulled his leg about those 111 lineouts, and the fact that his drop-goal from a lineout actually passed a yard outside the post (10,000 Scots positioned behind the posts will confirm that!), but he just gives me the same answer each time: 'Well, you know who won, don't you?'

The switch to television had its problems in commentary technique. The contrasts of obligation as between radio and television commentary became very clear. In radio, you simply got a tap on the shoulder from your studio manager to tell you when you were 'on the air' and you knew that you were then on your own, that you had to get on with it and give every single detail, paint every bit of the picture. You kept on going until he passed you a little note which told you how long to keep talking before you brought your commentary to an end and handed back to the studio. That was pretty straightforward. Television wasn't as simple as that. For one thing, you could watch part or all of the game on a monitor, a television set in front of you. The picture was there that the viewers were seeing and the first problem was to decide when to look at the monitor and when to look at the pitch. Obviously the monitor gave a very clear picture of what was going on in the close-quarter exchanges. The camera can get in very close indeed to, for instance, scrummages and rucks and mauls and lineouts. On the other hand, the monitor itself might not show the positioning of all the players. It might be in close at a scrummage, and so the formation that the back divisions have adopted isn't always evident. Striking the right balance isn't easy between watching the pitch for any changes in positioning, perhaps a full-back moving up on the blind-side, that you could draw the viewers' attention to as being significant, and on the other hand, keeping an eye on the monitor so that you could interpret the close-quarter situation the viewers were seeing. Another pitfall was that, in radio, you just got on with it and there was nothing to distract you or disturb you, apart from the crowd. The people in the stand at Murrayfield in the old days when we broadcast from the press box at the back of the stand, could be a little off-putting when they were cheering and so on. But in radio, generally speaking, you just kept talking all the time without too much disturbance.

Television provides a marked contrast. For one thing you have to keep earphones on in case the producer, in his scanner-van, wants to communicate with you. The trouble is, you can hear lots of other things as well – the producer talking to the studio, to 'Grandstand,' to his camera crew, to the studio manager . . . You can hear the production secretary as well. At first, I found it quite hard to concentrate on describing the play with all those distractions in my ear. In fact, one time I took the headphones off and put them aside, whereupon the dialogue went something like this: Studio manager (sitting beside me): 'Bill, would you mind putting on your earphones as your producer, Bill Stevenson, has a message for you?' Bill Stevenson: 'Bill McLaren, we do not, repeat not, remove our earphones until transmission ends and permission is given. Is this clearly understood?' McLaren: 'Yes, sorr, whatever you say, sorr!' So I just had to get used to doing commentary with various other sounds in my ears.

Clearly, the producer has to be in immediate contact with his commentator. As half-time approaches, for instance, the producer can warn the commentator to provide a brief thirty seconds half-time wrap-up and lead back to so-and-so in the studio so that he can talk about the soccer results; or the message might be for the commentator and his summariser to keep things going right through half-time.

The biggest problem for radio commentators switching to television is knowing when to talk. Some folk reckon I haven't solved that problem yet! On radio, you had to paint the whole picture so you spoke all the time, on television the viewer can see much of what is going on on his screen. In my early TV commentaries, I spoke too much (some reckon I still do). Perhaps, as a school teacher, I wanted to explain things too much and too often. The problem was, and still is, that there are two kinds of viewer – one, the rugby specialist who knows quite a lot about the game, the other, the non-rugby man probably waiting for the football results or the next horse-race to come along. I have always felt that we should seek to stimulate his interest as well. So there was that difficulty of talking enough to try to sharpen the interest of people who knew nothing about the game and, at the same time, trying not to irritate the specialists who knew exactly why the French were running out the back of the lineout, why Doug Hopwood, for instance, of South Africa, was picking up at the base of the scrummage and why he had detached from that scrummage, and so on. As a school teacher, I'd been used to describing things in detail and I was keen to help people to understand the game better. To the uninitiated, Rugby is a mysterious game with 42 players (including replacements), complicated laws, various set positions, and varied tactical possibilities. In trying to help viewers to understand more about the game and to share my own intense love of Rugby Union, I certainly did speak more than other television commentators did and, for a while about that time, in the early sixties, I got quite a bit of stick from irate people for talking too much. Once on the 'Points of View' programme, a viewer referred to my 'verbal diarrhoea!' Of course it was a worrying time for me. I wanted to get the balance right. I wrote to those critics who complained by letter and sought to explain that the 'Grandstand' audience was a mixed audience and not entirely a rugby specialist audience. One of the pleasures for me in rugby commentary has been the number of people, amongst them a lot of womenfolk, who have written, or who have stopped me, and said how much they had learned about the game through watching on television, and that they now enjoyed watching games whereas previously they had not been interested. That has given me a lot of satisfaction, although I can well understand the annoyance of the specialist who knows his game pretty well and doesn't need any explanations. I did try to adjust my style of commentary, to talk much less, but it was unnatural and so, over the years, I have been regarded as coming close to radio commentary during television broadcasts, although perhaps not quite so much nowadays.

I have been lucky enough to witness some of the most dramatic and historic rugby events as well as the greatest team performances during most of the post-war years. And each time I got in for nothing. And each time I had just about the best seat in the house. All the same, it has been hard work and for someone like myself, one of the world's worriers who always tried to cover whatever might go wrong, there has been enough tension and nervousness to keep anyone going for a lifetime. The business of preparing for commentaries has evolved, in my case, over the years. My early preparation was pretty haphazard because I didn't have anybody to show me how to go about it. I just worked out a system that would suit me, and, initially, all I tried to do was get a sentence or so about each player in the game so that I could fill in a little bit of background information about him in the hope that this would stimulate listener/viewer interest. The players' names were laid out in their field formation but one soon discovered that that could be confusing if they did not line up in that formation. The wing-forwards might be the other way round. But I think that the influence that wrought the biggest change in my preparatory work was the late Richard Dimbleby. The famous broadcaster came to Hawick to do a 'Down Your Way' programme and I was deputed to chat to him about the rugby scene in Hawick. As a very young journalist, I was quaking when my turn came but he was a thoughtful man, so natural and encouraging, and quickly put me at my ease. Afterwards I expressed my amazement at the sheets and sheets of notes he had in front of him, and I remember him saying that he expected to use perhaps about six per cent of his homework but that the other 94 per cent was there should he have need of it. So I determined from then onwards to elicit as much background information about the game and the players I was to cover and to have it all available ' should I have need of it.' Thus started what I refer to as 'my big sheet' – a double foolscap lined sheet with one team listed on the left (the home team), the other on the right, details about past matches down the middle: record scores in the fixture, memorable incidents and background details about the Union presidents, coaches, chairmen of selectors, physiotherapists, doctors, groundsmen, referee, touch-judges (and nowadays the replacement touch-judge) with all the replacement players' names in the bottom right corner. The details of those pen-pictures are gathered in various ways – from programmes of matches, from reliable newspapers, from players and officials themselves, often by telephone or with a request to fill in a details sheet which I have compiled and sent to them. I get irritated when programmes list only a player's age instead of his date of birth. The fellow may have had a birthday by the time of the match and some become quite niggly if their details are wrong. I like to have details of height, weight, occupation, school, college or university, clubs, representative honours, positions played and the like. Sporting achievements by other members of the family also add interest. I thought it gave an insight into the sporting nature of the Lineen family, for instance, when I was able to tell viewers that Sean Lineen, the Scottish centre, was the son of Terry Lineen who had played 12 times for the All Blacks and that Sean's mother had been a New Zealand netball international.

Some viewers do not appreciate such information but I have had many letters from those who enjoy hearing those little additional bits of background and generally the players themselves appreciate them. Curiously most players can be extremely vague about the number of caps they have won and the number of international points or, indeed, club points they have scored, so I always keep an up-to-date record of caps and points for all the countries in the International Championship so that, at a glance, for instance, I can confirm that Iain Milne, the Scottish tight-head prop, gained his 43rd cap in the first Test against New Zealand in Dunedin on 16 June 1990, and that he had not scored an international try, a point incidentally that gives much pleasure to his younger brother, Ken who, when he scored against Fiji at Murrayfield in October 1989, admitted to the thought running through his head that although Iain might have far more caps, Ken had scored one more international try than him!

Another instance: in 1971 Scotland beat England for the first time at Twickenham in 33 years. That's quite a significant little statistic with which to interest listeners/viewers but unless you look through all the fixtures and all the results and work that out, then of course at the end of the game, when the victory is accomplished, you miss out on that bit of information. I usually did much of that kind of research during the summer holidays from school.

At one time preparation for a match just concerned details about 30 players, but when replacements were introduced in 1969, it meant having background information about 42 players as well as about all the officials concerned. Referees, for instance, have become personalities in their own right. People are interested in the likes of Clive Norling of Wales and Fred Howard of England. By now, Clive Norling will have set a new world record for having had charge of international matches. Listeners enjoy hearing about that and Clive must be very proud of such a feat. He deserves a George Cross for surviving as many!

As for touch-judges I had an experience at the France v Scotland game in 1973 in Paris which really brought me round to the view that I must always have information about touch-judges as well because you never know when the referee might get injured. Folk are amused when I suggest such a thing, but I've done commentary on two games in which the referees had to be assisted from the field. At the England v Wales game at Twickenham in 1970, French referee Robert Calmet suffered a broken leg and was replaced by England's Johnny Johnson. At the France v Scotland occasion in 1973 Ken Pattinson, a pleasant, cheery fellow from the North Midlands of England, was the referee and a good one, too, but after about fifteen minutes Ken suffered knee damage and had to go off the field. Prior to the game I had sought out Michel Celaya, chairman of the French selectors, to confirm that there were no changes in the French side and, as I did so, this fellow in black shorts went past. So just by chance, I asked Celaya who he was and he told me he was the touch-judge, Palmade. When Ken Pattinson was carried off, guess who came on? None other than Palmade. I didn't even know his Christian name, but I was able to say that the replacement referee was Monsieur Palmade, a French referee, and this was his first international. That saved my bacon, because if I hadn't asked Celaya who he was, I wouldn't have had a clue and there was no way in which I could have had information like that ferried up to me, because at Parc des Princes in those days we used to do commentary from as far away from the pitch as you could possibly imagine. We were right at the back of the main stand behind the press box. Not only that, but we were enclosed in a commentary box that had 3-inch bullet-proof glass at the front. You really felt quite disembodied from the action because there was little crowd reaction in your earphones. Of course you had the monitor but it was, for me, the most unlikeable commentary position because you just felt out of touch. It was like broadcasting in a cave! The BBC have done a little negotiating with their counterparts in France and, thanks to Pierre Salviac, the French rugby commentator and a good friend of mine, we've managed to get a commentary position a bit closer to the play and out in the open.

That's a vast improvement. But in those early days in 1973, Parc des Princes was the worst place on earth to do commentary from. We've had some fun in France over the years. In the old Colombes stadium where I did my first commentary broadcasts, on one occasion, when the All Blacks were playing France, we were situated down on the touch-line, in fact on the athletics track. The effect was to be doing commentary from a foot below ground level and that really was a problem, because all you could see on looking at the pitch were a lot of hairy legs! It was a blessing that the monitor I had was a large set and the quality on it was absolutely first-class so that I virtually did the entire commentary from the monitor. It was almost impossible from that low commentary position on the running track to sort out who was doing what.

One of the other irritations in broadcasting at Parc des Princes was the fact that the only way down from the commentary position was by lift which was badly over-used, so that you could wait for ages to get yourself down to the bottom floor. I recall with some feeling the end of the France v England game there in February 1980 when England had their first win in Paris for sixteen years. The margin was 17-13. Having completed commentary, I was then asked by my producer Huw Jones, a genial, thoughtful Welshman with whom I enjoyed working, to get down to pitch-level in order to interview one or two of the English players for 'Grandstand.' We couldn't get down by the lift because there was a huge crowd there, so Huw and I started clambering over rows and rows of seats. I think we went over about forty rows, and also clambered over a safety fence which was about eight-feet high, and eventually, slightly bruised about the knee caps and ankles, we managed to get down to pitch-level. And there I remember interviewing Bill Beaumont, John Horton of Bath who, if I remember rightly, dropped a couple of goals, John Carleton of Orrell, who was one of the try-scorers and Nick Preston of Richmond who was a try-scorer too. So we did get our interview, but it was a hectic business, for we had been concerned, Huw and I that, by the time we got down to pitch-level, the players would already be in the bath and singing of their victory. Huw justifiably was delighted that we'd managed to overcome the problem and got the task done. When the interviews were completed, an English supporter presented me with a beautiful red rose. I am not sure why, unless he thought I was English too! All the same it was a real nice gesture and Bette was delighted with the rose when I arrived home that evening.

One of the commentary aids that has been absolutely essential over the years has been one to help me get players' numbers into my head so that, as soon as I see a number, I can put the name of the player to it. Rugby is an unusual game in that there can be a lot of wide spread of play in more spectacular passages, with the ball flipping along the back divisions so that you can see players clearly, can make out their features, their way of running, their build and so on – all a great help to identification. On the other hand, there are a great number of situations in which there are just piles of bodies. Consider the number of moving mauls that there are nowadays, and ruck play in which players drive in and smash forward and leave the ball behind and then, of course, there are push-over tries.

In all of those close-quarter situations it can be impossible to see players' features or even shape or a players' running style. On those occasions sometimes the only thing that can help you to identify the player is a glimpse of the number. More often than not you have just a split second to identify the player, so knowing each player's number in the instant is of crucial value. One way of ensuring this that I learned a good many years ago, is to have a pack of playing cards with the numbers 1 to 15 on them. This was a system I learned from Raymond Glendenning, the football and horse-racing commentator of the early postwar years. I remember reading somewhere that Raymond, for his horse-racing commentaries, used to have a set of playing cards with the owners' colours on them. For the race that he was going to commentate on if, say, there were eight horses, he would take out the cards with the eight owners' colours on them and he would shuffle them, turn them over and put the horse's name to the card as soon as he saw the owner's colours. So I just adopted that system and got my own home-made pack of playing cards and prior to each match, I turn them over for about twenty minutes to half-an-hour each evening of the week prior to the match. As each number is turned over I have to put the player's name to it.

Of course I make a point of finding out from the programme people exactly what numbers each player will carry, and in this regard I owe a great deal to those publishing firms who have provided me with such information over all those years – Programme Publications Ltd in London and Bill Cotton, who runs the business now, and Marjon Print up in Belfast with Will McConnell and his wife Ruth, and Jonathon their son who does those splendid Irish team pen-pictures. They have been so helpful as has been Bert Brown at the Alma Press in Broxburn and Des Donegan of DBA Publications in Dublin. The one problem is that players occasionally come out on the day of the match with the wrong jerseys on. That really does give a commentator the hump because it can prove confusing and is unfair also to the thousands of supporters who depend on programme numbers for identification. The French are the biggest pests when it comes to being incorrectly numbered but, in another regard, they were extremely helpful. I refer to their much maligned coach, Jacques Fouroux, 'le Patron' or 'le Petit Général' as he was known. For a coach who got so much flak from all quarters, Jacques Fouroux always was courteous and had a sharp sense of humour. I suppose he had to have that in light of the moans about his option for big, heavy forwards, for a scrum-half throwing in and a hooker at scrum-half at the lineouts, for playing props as hookers and for putting a damper on the flair of the French backs. Considering the success France has achieved since he became coach this criticism has seemed to me to be a bit unfair. Jean-Pierre Rives was not a big, heavy forward but there aren't many of his like about. Not only that, but the French backs have scored some quite breath-taking tries with Patrice Lagisquet and Philippe Sella, at the present time, sharing no fewer that 43 international tries and full-back Serge Blanco claiming 34.

Fouroux has not been able to eliminate from the international effort the indisciplines and violent play that sometimes scar the French club game. Even Rives himself was guilty of childish behaviour when France lost the Grand Slam to Scotland at Murrayfield in 1984. The French also give away too many penalties at breakdown points. But under Fouroux's guidance they were the team one always liked to see in action because, when they did, and still do, put it together as, for instance, when they came back from 7-21 down against Ireland at Landsdowne Road in 1989, they are a joy to watch.

I had particular reason to be grateful to Fouroux at Nantes in 1987 when I was due to cover the France v Argentina match. At the French practice he asked how many of the French side I had not seen before and promptly called each one over and introduced him to me. It was a gesture I appreciated for it helped my identification. The same happened prior to the France v Scotland match in 1989. The French were at a training camp in a big, country house some forty miles from Paris. Pierre Salviac, the French commentator who shares their TV presentation with Pierre Albaladejo, the former French stand-off (known as 'Monsieur le Drop' because of his famous drop-goal feats), drove me out to the

French practice and there again I met all the players and found Fouroux immensely helpful.

Mind you, there have been times when the French hierarchy have not been quite so co-operative. Prior to one French game in Paris in pre-Fouroux days we, the media, were all assembled at a sports complex where the French squad were billeted, with a view to watching their training session. Whereupon a committee-man, with the distinct appearance of a Mafia hit man, lumbered over and told us in unmistakable terms to push off. We protested and explained how important it was for our commentary, and indeed for the players, to be able to identify every member of their squad. To no avail. 'Push off or else,' was the clear warning. So we grudgingly toddled off, French TV and radio men and newspaper correspondents. Had Jacques Fouroux or Pierre Salviac been there, we might have been able to prevail upon them to make a plea of mitigation on our behalf. As it turned out we did see the French practise, but from a distance of some 150 yards. There we were, about twenty-five of us, all crouched behind a wall with just the top of our heads showing like so many anxious Chads and quietly hoping that the 'heavy' would not come among us.

Prior to the England v France game at Twickenham in 1983 the BBC booked me into the Heathrow Hotel where the French were staying, so that I might get up-to-date with their news and check up on the features and build of those I had not seen before at mealtimes. Unfortunately they ate privately and, on asking if I might attend their training session on the Friday morning just to sort out who was who, I was told by their official that the practice would be private. Could I then just attend the warm-up with the promise to leave before the tactical preparations started? In a word: 'NON!' I believe it is very important to the success of any commentary on Rugby Union to have seen all the players before the match starts so, I decided, against my principles, because I appreciate the wish of any squad to practise in secret, to follow their bus. I felt like Hercule Poirot and I was hopeful that the bus wouldn't stop for them to send their front-row over to point out the error of my ways. Eventually, we arrived at the training pitch at Windsor in the lea of the castle (what a back-drop to a rugby training session!) to find at least fifty of the rugby press and sundry other interested souls all awaiting the session. I did make the point to Dr Jean Pené, the squad's medical officer and a serious but very pleasant man, that I could have missed the session and how much of a blow that would have been. But the good doctor just shrugged and said that it was meant to be private but . . . .

Just how vital that session was to me was brought home on the day after at Twickenham. France had two locks new to the championship in Jean Condom and Jean-Claude Orso. It was some relief to me to discover that Condom pronounced his name *Condong* – that is after I found out what a condom was! Condom and Orso took the field at Twickenham with the wrong jerseys on. The numbers they wore did not accord with those in the official programme. If I had not attended that French session on the Friday I would have identified those two wrongly all afternoon. It was hard enough, because I had practised the programme numbers all week – Orso 4, Condom 5. When they came out Orso wore number 5. But at least I knew them, having identified them at the practice. Incidentally six players wore the wrong jerseys in that match. The French centres, Christian Belascain and Didier Codorniou, were wrongly numbered and so were the English locks, Steve Bainbridge and Maurice Colclough.

It is perfectly understandable that coaches and officials might want to keep surprise moves secret from the opposition and so arrange certain sessions that are not for public scrutiny. But it does seem to me to be an obligation on their part to stage at least one public session so that the press can get their up-to-date information and photographs, and commentators can see in action the players and replacements so as to be able to identify each one at a glance. The home countries generally are very fair and co-operative. Scotland, for instance, do have a private session on the Thursday but they also come out on the Friday morning for a brief spell that is a boon to media people. Commentators, after all have just a split second to put a name to a player. In a line-handling move by backs, or close-passing by the forwards, identification often is at rat-a-tat speed. The aim should be to name every player who makes a contribution to a move but that can be very hazardous in the early stages of a game if there are identification problems.

A Friday training session was ideal for me, a teacher of physical education, requiring leave of absence to fulfil commentary commitments, leave which Roxburgh Education Committee, then the Border Region Education Committee, were so kind to grant me. That had been one of the conditions they agreed to when I was interviewed about my return to teaching in 1959. It meant just the one day off school – that is until the Welsh changed their routine to a Wednesday training spell after which the players went back home and did not report to the team hotel until Friday evening. I couldn't understand the reason for this. Apparently their fitness and health experts felt that training on the Thursday and Friday was not conducive to maximum performance on the Saturday. Yet Wales had enjoyed their second 'golden era' with three Grand Slams, eight outright or shared Championships and six Triple Crowns between 1969 and 1979, during which time they trained on the Thursday and Friday. Of course I had an axe to grind in that a Wednesday training session down at the Police ground at Waterton Cross, Bridgend, presented considerable problems where leave of absence was concerned. I always had made a point of never taking more leave than was absolutely necessary for the job to be done properly. One of the main reasons why I never did cover a British Lions tour, despite having been asked to do so since 1966, was that I would be off school during the very hectic summer term when so much organising of athletics, cricket, etc., had to be done.

One trip to Wales is firmly etched upon my memory. I left home at 4 o'clock on the Wednesday morning, had a nightmare car journey in a blizzard to Newcastle airport (some 60 miles), missed the plane, got the next to Heathrow, got the airport bus to Reading station, took the train to Bridgend, where BBC producer Dewi Griffiths (how much I owe to him for his unfailing encouragement and good humour over many years) had a car waiting to whisk me to the Welsh training. As soon as it was all over I did the entire journey in reverse and arrived home at about 11 o'clock at night and was in front of my first class at 9 o'clock on Thursday morning. And they'll tell you that a commentator's life is, as my old boss John Hood used to say, 'all gas and gaiters!' Yet only once do I recall missing a training session. Prior to the Romania v Scotland game in Bucharest in 1984, I was looking forward to seeing the Romanians in practice because they had a number of newcomers whom I had never seen before. So it was something of a shock when Chris Thau, the *Times* and *Rugby World and Post* rugby correspondent, and a real friend on that trip who eased our path considerably, said that the Romanian session was private and I could not attend. Chris was Romanian and if anyone could have got that decision reversed he was the one. But the Romanian hierarchy were adamant. Romania's Mr Rugby, Viorel Murariu, an old-world type of gentleman who has done so much to bring Romanian rugby out of the shadows into the international arena, said he would bring coloured photographs of all the players to the ground on the day of the match. He was as good as his word and Mircea Munteanu and Vasile Pascu, their hooker and prop, duly delivered the photographs an hour and a half before kick-off. They were a help but no substitute for a training spell and this was brought home to me when I found that our commentary box was not much bigger than a rabbit hutch, that three of us, all extremely well nourished, Chris Thau (summariser), Nevin McGhee (producer who smoothed our path all the way) and myself, had to squash into it, that the temperature was in the high nineties and, worst of all, we were fairly distant from the pitch. That was some trip. Yet the Romanian folk we had to deal with (our troubles in trying to gain entrance to the training session apart) were kindness itself, despite the fact that they seemed to be having such a poor time in economic terms. I felt great sympathy for the Scottish team because they went out there as Grand Slam Champions and were beaten by Romania for the first time, the brutal heat simply sapping their puff.

I have always regarded attendance at an international training session as a privilege and what I see there is essentially for my own use in commentary. Obviously I might see a move being tried that is comparatively new in which case I keep it in the back of my mind so that if such a situation occurs during the commentary I might be able to alert viewers to what is happening as a stimulus to their interest in the action.

I have watched sessions in every conceivable type of weather. I once stood for an hour and a half as the Irish trained at the Old Belvedere ground in a blizzard. The snow lay four to five inches deep. No other squad would have worked outdoors in that snowstorm but the Irish did. Unfortunately (for me, at least), they were all 'happeet up' in balaclavas, rain-suits, hoods and the like. You could hardly tell one from the other! Well, you could always tell Willie Duggan because he was usually last out of the dressing room and was having a last draw on a fag and he was inevitably first back into the dressing room and first to get a fag lit up. Once I travelled from Cardiff to Reading with Willie, Phil Orr and Trevor Ringland on the train. They mauled a tin of Hawick balls (mint sweets) and a tin of shortbread like starving wolves and Willie dropped this pearl before us: 'Oi'm firmly of the view that the quickest way to take the edge off your form is by training.' What a man.

At one All Blacks training session during their 1967 tour the rain lashed down throughout. It was a real cloudburst, but they stayed out and went through their drills under the lash of Freddie Allen, their coach. No one seemed to complain which was just about par for the All Black course. I have seen some wonderful French training sessions – wonderful because players there would give full rein to their sumptuous skills. Once, they were late in arriving for their session – 75 minutes late – but the wait was worth it. Their very first move incorporated some four switches of direction, amazing sleight of hand, forwards running and handling like backs and, if I remember rightly, it finished with a drop-goal by Benoit Dauga, the huge, hawk-eyed lock-cum-number 8, which was greeted by a spontaneous round of applause from all of his colleagues. It was quite brilliant. Then they got down to the nitty-gritty.

I only wish that sides had the courage to take into the actual game the flare and adventurism that they show on the practice pitch. I have seen some magnificent practice sessions, but when the game got under way so many of the participants went into the shell of caution and did not give rein to their full capabilities. One of the few who can turn it on in both practice and game is David Campese of Australia. Jo Maso of France was another who just couldn't restrain his natural flair and there were times, too, when Andy Irvine would let it rip. Thank goodness for them. The first time I saw the French perform their 'percussion' moves from the lineout I was amazed. That was in the late fifties and the idea was brilliantly conceived. They sought to overcome claustrophobic midfield defences by engaging them, first with forward attack, thence hopefully to feed their own backs with their rivals already compromised. They were quite devastating in peeling round the back or front of the lineout. The idea is reckoned to have been formulated in the mind of the French captain, Lucien Mias, and although it is common-place nowadays it was quite revolutionary then and it gave the French a head start, not only in providing a novel method of launching forwards as the initial attack force but also as a means of breaking up the opposition's set defences which were so hard to penetrate. The French were very well equipped for the job. They had mobile tight-forwards in the likes of Amadée Domenech, Robert Vigier, René Brejassou, Michel Celaya, Bernard Chevallier and Mias himself with, later, Alfred Rocques, Bernard Mommejat and Jean-Claude Berejnoi; and very quick and skilful loose-forwards in Jean Prat, Henri Domec, Michel Crauste, Walter Spanghero, François Moncla and André Herrero. Those forwards preferred to be running about in the open, and they had among their number dependable ball-winners for the lineouts and link men rumbling round back or front who had the kind of safe hands for gathering in a deflected ball and imparting the initial thrust. The crucial aspect, however, was the practised drill which required every forward to be in close support of the initial driver so that one often had the impression of a human tidal wave rolling and turning as each forward took his turn at driving in to take the ball from his colleague before continuing the thrust at a slightly different angle. By turning their back into the tackle each forward thus hid the ball so that opponents were unaware at times which player exactly had possession. It was magnificent to watch, so precise was the drill and the order of events and, of course, if the result was to launch a forward into space the players who often had to undertake the tackle chores were the opposing midfield backs. Once they were sucked in, the French would quickly spin the ball wide into less cluttered confines.

It took the home countries quite some time to assess how best to counter such moves, which also incorporated the scrummage pick-up which I had first seen done well by the South African, Doug Hopwood. Eventually the New Zealanders found the simple answer in explosive tackling which sent the ball carrier backwards so that the move lost its momentum; another ploy was to drive in sideways to arrest the forward advance of the rolling maul. But even in modern times when many have embraced the New Zealand concept of driving head-on and shoulder-first into defenders instead of turning the back, there are still remnants of the French method in the modern game and, at the time, the French were just a bit ahead of their rivals in experimenting with ways of countering the close-lying defences that were strangling the game and that brought about the introduction of the Australian dispensation that restricted kicking on the full into touch from between the '25' lines. That also was meant to open up the game. But I feel that the French in the fifties and sixties were the more successful and they certainly showed how forwards could not only be support troops but should also be able to provide the first attacking thrusts. I recall one embarrassing incident concerned with French innovation. Some of us were discussing with Charlie Drummond of the SRU the prospects for the game and French 'percussion' cropped up. Some time later Charlie called me into a room where the Scottish party were assembled and showed me a blackboard and chalk and asked me to explain how I thought the French forwards would work their lineout. That shook me and although I initiated a discussion about French method I told Charlie, a good friend of mine, that I didn't want to be put in such a position again. Because I was so grateful for the opportunity of seeing the French players at training for my own purposes I didn't want to jeopardise that arrangement.

There! My enthusiasm for the more aesthetic aspects of the game has led me far from my original topic – the various tricks I use to ensure my commentary is as fluent and informative as I can possibly make it. You'll have gathered that I rely on three principle methods: attendance at training sessions, memorisation of players' jersey numbers with my pack of cards, and familiarising myself with the information on my double foolscap sheet.

My big sheet, incidentally, is written in four colours of ink with each line in a different colour so that the details stand out. Unfortunately, once at Leicester we were doing commentary on the top of the stand with just a tarpaulin as so-called cover. But the heavens opened and in no time my big sheet, with four colours of ink running all over the place, looked like a road map of the British Isles. I have a big sheet for every match commentary. It takes several hours to complete each one and curiously, in the early days, I very seldom referred to it during the match. Indeed once, Onllwyn Brace, the former Welsh scrum-half, reckoned that during one Welsh international at Cardiff, I didn't refer to the sheet more than half a dozen times. I think I have a wee peek at it more than that nowadays as the memory isn't quite as sharp as it used to be. The true value of the sheet is on the eve of each match, for which I have a settled routine from which I very seldom depart. Hopefully on the Thursday afternoon and Friday morning I will have seen each squad at training as an aid to identification and to being up-to-date with any fitness doubts. Friday afternoon is often taken up with a broadcast, such as a chat with Helen Rollinson on BBC Television's 'Sport on Friday,' and a visit to the ground just to familiarise oneself with the pitch and atmosphere and to have a chat with the groundsmen about possible conditions. On Friday evening I always have an early meal, often on my own, occasionally to enjoy the company of John Readon or that ebullient character, Ian Robertson, and once memorably that also of Graham Jenkins, brother of Richard Burton who, along with Ian, provided a most fascinating meal, coloured by chat and laughter. But even then, I left early for my room, there to pore over the details on the sheet for some three hours and to get as much into the memory bank as possible. On Saturday morning I would have a final check of the law book and then I would feel some satisfaction at having done everything possible to ensure a good broadcast prior to commending my soul to the Lord in the hope that He would guide me along the way. All during the week I would have been turning over my pack of 15 cards and seeking to put the correct names to each number before shuffling them again and again until I felt that my speed was improving.

Once the game is over and the job done I then get homeward bound as quickly as possible, eschewing all the post-match celebrations. I don't know how many dinner invitations I have turned down. Certainly Mickey Steele-Bodger and 'Fergie' Ferguson of the Barbarians have scolded me time and again for not accepting their most kind invitations. It isn't that I do not appreciate such thoughtfulness but I am happiest in my own hill-top home in Hawick with my feet up and with Bette by my side. Bette has been my best pal for forty years. She had been a gem through the early times, through all the rough and smooth. Although it might have caused a little offence to some, the plain fact is that I prefer my wife's company to that of any post-match dinner gathering. Indeed it might be said that I am not a typical Rugby Union type (I'd considered a variation on that expression as a possible title for this book). Apart from non-attendance at dinners I never have been one for frequenting pubs or clubs, and some of the high-jinks at and after post-match functions that one has heard of really just leave me cold. I am not a drinker. Boyhood experience of alcoholism at close-range saw to that. What passes for rugby revelry could well merit a £10 fine or twenty days inside for vandalism elsewhere.

Actually, one of the last dinners I did attend was in the late fifties. It was the Hawick club's annual dinner and as I was working for the *Hawick Express* in those days and therefore regarded as a professional, you can imagine my surprise when I was asked to propose the toast to the Hawick team at the dinner. What I didn't know was that I was about the sixth to be asked! Others had turned it down probably because Hawick had suffered, by their standards, a disastrous season with some eleven defeats. I agreed. On the night I was quaking. There was I, a professional, at the top table. Happily, I was seated beside one of the outstanding personalities in the game, Charlie Drummond of Melrose, whom I knew from my playing days and who was to become later one of the game's most popular administrators. Charlie suggested that he and I should have a gargle or two of whisky just to steady our nerves. I wasn't keen because I was not used to drinking whisky. Charlie insisted. It did help. I got my speech over quite successfully, even to the extent of almost convincing the audience that the season hadn't been so bad after all. But when the dinner was over there was an after-effect. I had arranged with a local garage to leave my bicycle in their doorway. When I came out from the dinner hotel I was slightly the worse for wear, and as there were two police officers standing on the other side of the street

outside Martin's the bakers, I deemed it politic to walk my bicycle along
the High Street. They followed me part of the way, but then decided that
I was not going to be guilty of riding a bike whilst under the influence
and so they turned and went away. Whereupon, I mounted my bike outside the Constitutional Club and fell off under the railway bridge forty
yards further on. The following day I was lying on our sofa feeling like
something the cat had dragged in, when Bette started to devour a sausage
roll. I just hear the crinkle of the pastry. Like the American trooper putting marmalade on spam as we sailed to Italy during the war, that was all
I needed.

It amused me after that Hawick club dinner to hear that the club committee had had a meeting at which there had been some disagreement
over whether a member of the press should have been invited to speak at
the dinner. I never found out what conclusion they had come to, but I
never was invited to speak at it again. I didn't think my speech was as bad
as all that!

I did attend one or two other dinners and spoke at some but frankly I
did not enjoy them at all. I die a thousand deaths at the thought of having
to make a public speech. This comes as some surprise to folk who think
that a TV person should be able to stand up and let it flow without any
trouble. Not me. Making a speech ruins my appetite until I get it over
and done with. Even when I had to make a speech when receiving retirement gifts from the schools at which I was a teacher I found it a testing, not to mention highly emotional experience. At Drumlanrig School
all the pupils and staff were gathered in the functions hall and I felt a
lump in my throat as I received a beautiful typewriter. I got through my
speech reasonably well, except for the closing sentence but the big
crunch came when Basil Deane, the headmaster, called on the entire
school to sing 'Just for Mr McLaren, "Oh God, go with you till we meet
again".' That did it! I bent down and kidded on that I was tying my
laces. An emotional moment indeed.

So, one way or another, I find the whole thing a bit of a strain. I find
that the onus of making a speech is such that the meal, as P.G. Wodehouse would have said, 'turns to ashes in my mouth.' And by the time
you could get round to talking to the fellows you wanted to chat with,
nine times out of ten they were at the babbling stage having imbibed too
freely.

The last dinner I spoke at was one some years ago, held by the semi-
junior Hawick PSA club, and that because I was asked to do so by Hugh

McLeod, then the club president, and a man for whom I always have had the highest respect and admiration. And during the World Cup I agreed to say a few words at a special night arranged by the Kaikorai Club in Dunedin, among whose members were a number of Scots and whose event organiser, Tony Kennedy, couldn't have been more kind or hospitable. I am sure that I have earned some criticism by withdrawing from rugby dinners. Folk seem to think that all somebody like me has to do is to stand up and speak. That it is nae bother at a'. But it was no pleasure for me, and all I could do was try to compensate by complying with the many requests over the years to write articles for club programmes or tour brochures arranged by clubs or schools. Generally speaking, the social side of the rugby game has never had a great deal of appeal for me despite the flattering nick-names 'the voice of rugby' and 'Mr Rugby' so often bestowed upon me.

Mind you I suppose I'll have to attend the Barbarians dinner on the eve of their match against Scotland in September. Mickey Steele-Bodger and 'Fergie' Ferguson have often invited me to Barbarians' functions and I have made my apology each time. But at the 1991 Hong Kong sevens tournament Mickey approached me with grim countenance, poked his finger in my chest and simply ordered me to be at that final centenary dinner in Edinburgh. He was, at that moment, a replica of Herbert Waddell! Not only that but he had enlisted the support of Bette and our daughters Linda and Janie. As Mickey prodded me with his finger it brought to mind an incident the late 'Jock' Wemyss, a great Barbarian in his day, told me about when he was playing. A referee admonished him whilst poking his finger at Jock's chest, whereupon Jock drew himself up to his full six-feet two-inches and rebuked the official: 'Sir, will you kindly remove your digit from my person?'

I hope I have never given offence by turning down invitations to speak at functions. Just the other day I turned down a fee of £750 for speaking for fifteen or twenty minutes at a London sporting club. I do appreciate the compliment of being invited but I prefer to leave that to those who, remarkable fellows, can bring the house down and never turn a hair. Both of those talents are quite beyond me.

Occasionally I consider it worth the agony of public speaking – as, for example, when I had the opportunity of honouring one of the giants of Scottish rugby, W.I.D. Elliot. Douglas Elliot held the Scottish record for a wing-forward of 29 caps until that mark was passed by John Jeffrey of Kelso on the Scottish tour of New Zealand in 1990. Douglas was the one

Scot named by R.K. Stent, the South African rugby correspondent, when he chose the best British players who had faced the 1951-52 Springboks tourists. I had played against Douglas a couple of times and so had first-hand evidence of his greatness. So when a lounge in the Carfraemill Hotel, near Lauder, was to be named after him, and I was asked to perform the opening ceremony, I was delighted to do so.

That Hawick club dinner was the last time that I was under the weather through alcohol. It always has seemed to me since to be a form of simple-mindedness to get all boozed up, act like an idiot and be ill the next day. And such a waste of money too. In any event, I have made some famous, thrilling journeys just to get back home on the night of the match. Once, Cliff Morgan and I left Stade Colombes at 6 p.m. French time and I was sitting alongside Bette at home at 10.45. Cliff had hired a taxi to take us to Orly airport. That was some journey. Cliff said 'Vite, vite!' to the driver but he didn't really mean him to use just two tyres all the way there. The man was mad. He tore through lights, he swung round corners like Fangio, he shot up the blind side. Cliffie got curled up in sheer anxiety until he was almost sitting on the rear window. I was just waiting for the guy to slow down so that I could jump out. But he got us there. I've never seen two men get out of a taxi so quickly – just in case he decided to take off again. I don't know if you have ever tried to keep up with a nippy Welsh stand-off along an escalator. I failed completely. But we made the plane. I've had some hairy journeys like that just to get home. Once I had to get from Heathrow to King's Cross station with barely a minute to spare. Cliff made my hair stand on end by breaking the sound barrier in his automatic roadster but he screamed into King's Cross with just enough time for me to get into my sleeper. Nigel Mansell couldn't have done better.

There was an occasion in Dublin, too, that I will never forget. The only way of getting home from Dublin in those days was to catch a plane to London in time to get on the Edinburgh shuttle. So Huw Jones, our producer and another Welshman I have a lot of time for, arranged with the manager of Jury's Hotel, where we stayed, to have a car waiting at the hotel ready to whisk us out to the airport. It still was going to be touch and go. When we arrived at the hotel after the game we were somewhat surprised to find two police motor-cyclists in attendance as well. We were even more surprised when they proceeded to set their sirens screaming to clear a path for our car driver. Mama mia, what a trip that was! It wasn't only going through red lights that made your hair stand on end. It was doing seventy up the wrong side of the traffic islands. The police riders hedge-hopped each other brilliantly but I remember wondering what kind of mincemeat we would become if one of them forgot to cover one of the crossing points. Bless the Irish. Again we got there. Our company comprised Huw, who chattered all the way to ease the strain, John Reason, who maintained a majestic calm, and Peter West who, I am sure like me, died a thousand deaths during that journey. Twice in that way I was deeply indebted to Vincent O'Hanlon and Joe Melody, the two young managers on the staff of Jury's, for arranging those journeys. There were times during them when one's life seemed to pass before one's eyes and one wished that attendance at church had been more regular. But just to get back home made it all worthwhile. You know, on the Sunday after doing commentary, which can be a wearing business, the best therapy I could get was to drive with Bette and our Basset hound, Dougal, (so named because he obviously was one who would have fallen off the magic roundabout) just a couple of miles up the road where we would be in virtual wilderness among the wild birds, the hares and the foxes. That, on a sunny day with dew sparkling and just a faint edge to the wind, after the hustle and bustle and pressure of an international weekend, was as near to heaven as you can imagine.

It always used to amuse me, and still does, that whenever I return from a commentary assignment, whether from Twickenham, Paris, Cardiff, Dublin or the Hong-Kong sevens, folk you meet on the street or on the golf course are sure that you have had a great time, a kind of weekend holiday jaunt. If only they knew. Of course, I have been fortunate in seeing some of the greatest games and greatest players on most of the best known venues in the world game. Thanks to the BBC I have been to every Championship Rugby stadium, to the famous grounds in New Zealand during the World Cup, as well as the great thrill of covering one of the most enthralling Cup games on Sydney's Concorde Oval. My one regret is that I have not done commentary from one of South Africa's famous grounds and, indeed, that the last commentary I provided with the Springboks playing was their final match against the Barbarians at Twickenham on 31 January 1970. That was the match in which David Duckham scored one of his greatest tries with a sixty-yard run up the left touchline before coming inside the South African full-back, H.O. de Villiers, like a blink of light on his way to the line. It also was the best performance by the Springboks during their tour in which they had been subjected to taunts, darts, tin-tacks, smoke bombs, open hostility and demonstrations. The South African boycott is a subject explored at greater length in Chapter 13; meanwhile I will just mention how much it saddens me that we have not seen the Springboks play in this country for all those years, not since that 21-12 win over the Baa-Baas, at the end of which two of the greatest players I have ever seen, Mike Gibson and Gareth Edwards carried the South African captain, Dawie de Villiers, shoulder high from the field. It seems to me an indictment of the sporting, and especially the rugby fraternity, that the South Africans have been left in the wilderness for all that time especially in taking into account the efforts of Danie Craven and the rugby hierarchy to come more into line with world opinion and demand. Recent events, however, do indicate that things are quite likely to change; perhaps by the time this book goes to press South Africa will have been welcomed back into the international sporting community. Certainly there is something of a hollow ring about declaring World Champions when South Africa has not competed. It's like hailing World Football Champions in the absence of West Germany, Italy and Brazil.

8

Scotland's Long Dark Tunnel

My entry into commentary work coincided with the darkest period in Scottish rugby history. Happily the two were not connected. Between February 1951 and February 1955, Scotland lost 17 major international matches in a row. My first nine radio commentaries of Scottish games were all of defeats. I had shared in the exultation as a spectator when the Scots registered that totally unexpected 19-0 win over a star-studded Wales at Murrayfield on 3 February 1951. I already had started working for the *Hawick Express* and Bette and I, who were to be married in March, were among the record 80,000 crowd and had a fairly close view of that remarkable drop-goal by Scotland's captain, Peter Kininmonth (Richmond), that ignited a memorable Scottish effort against a Wales containing famous names such as Lewis Jones, Jack Matthews, Ken Jones, Rex Willis, Roy John and the captain John Gwilliam. Wales had 11 British Lions in that side so that Scotland's triumph held out some promise for the future. Instead Scotland lost those next 17 internationals in which they scored just 11 tries and conceded 51. I didn't enter the lists until the Welsh game of 1953 but I had seen one or two of the home internationals prior to that.

The defeat that sticks in the memory is that 0-44 thrashing from the South Africans at Murrayfield on 24 November 1951. They were just awesome. It was like sevens played by fifteen men. I had never seen anything quite like them. I had never seen a prop forward run as fast as Chris Koch, had never seen such as huge a man as 'Okey' Geffin kick goals, had never seen very big forwards, such as Ernst Dinkelman, Jan Pickard, Gert Dannhauser, Basie van Wyk, 'Saltie' du Rand and Hennie Muller, running and handling with such dexterity. When they were launched it

79

was like watching a cattle stampede; with remarkable skill and ball transference they brought a new dimension to forward play. How their backs prospered – Rik van Schoor, of the crew-cut dome, Tjol Lategan, elegance at speed, 'Chum' Osche and Paul Johnstone on the wings; and then there was that combination of shrewdness and physical strength from P.A. du Toit at scrum-half and quickness of thought and action from J.D. Brewis at stand-off. Behind them was the 21-year-old Johnny Buchler, safe as houses in catch, clearance and tackle. They won 30 of their 31 matches.

At Murrayfield the massive Geffin thumped over seven goals in nine attempts from all over the pitch, with the old-fashioned style of having the ball sloping towards the goal and with a dead straight run-up. Perhaps the Scots had London Counties to thank for being at the receiving end of a South African backlash, because, just nine days before, the representative side had administered the only defeat of that South African tour by 11-9, when their hero was the Harlequins lock, Alan Grimsdell, whose second half penalty-goal was the match-winner. That 0-44 defeat stood as the biggest in an international until Ireland beat Romania 60-0 in 1986. On that sad day at Murrayfield, as the South Africans cantered away to a 17-0 margin, I whispered to Bette: 'We're going to see history made today.' We sure did! That prediction wasn't all that clever because, just a month previously, I'd been lucky enough to see those Springboks beat a combined Glasgow-Edinburgh fifteen 43-11 in Glasgow. It was a remarkable game in that their magnificent loose-forward, Hennie Muller, showed another side to Springbok all-round skill by slotting home four superb goals as well as romping in for his try. In that game their prop-forward Chris Koch scored two tries and, as he had done the same against Scotland, I had the privilege of seeing a prop-forward register four tries in two games. That was very unusual in those days when forwards still were regarded as the ball providers, the piano shifters who were expected to leave the piano playing to the aristocrats behind them. Koch not only could run about the paddock at a rate of knots, but he was a fearsome scrummager as well. My Hawick friend, Hugh McLeod, was only 19 when he played for South of Scotland against those Springboks, whose props that day were Koch and 'Okey' Geffin. The match was memorable for me, too, in that it was the scene of the audition commentary that launched me on my career in radio and television. What is more the South lost by only 3-13, in retrospect, some effort against that side.

I came into the commentary scene just as Scotland had chalked up eight consecutive defeats. My debut 'on the air' marked the ninth, Wales beating Scotland 12-0 at Murrayfield on 7 February 1953. There followed two crushing defeats, one from Ireland at Murrayfield, the other from England at Twickenham. Each was by 26-8 and although one admired the silken skills of Jack Kyle and the nippy pace of Seamus Byrne, who scored three of Ireland's six tries, and the awesome power of England's heavyweight pack and the contrasting threats posed by England's centres, Jeff Butterfield and Phil Davies, it became quite depressing to see the Scots being put to the sword. I honestly believe that Scotland's rivals genuinely felt sympathetic towards them and were hoping that the run of defeats could be ended although not against them, of course. Strangely enough, there followed three defeats from which the Scots emerged with much credit and which encouraged hopes that their dismal run might be near its end. They created for 1954 a virtual new pack with three Macs in the front row – Hugh McLeod, of Hawick, Bob MacEwen of Cambridge University and Tom McLashan of Royal High School FP; a new middle row of Ewen Ferguson of Oxford University (later Sir Ewen, British Ambassador in Paris) and Ernie Michie of Aberdeen University, later of Langholm; and a back row of Adam Robson of Hawick, and the two Richmond forwards, Peter Kininmonth and 'Chick' Henderson. At 6ft 4ins and 15st 13lbs, Ferguson was, by Scottish standards, a monster and with Kininmonth turning the scale at 14st 11lbs, there was a bit more meat to the pack although even at that they were always going to be out-weighted. It is fascinating to compare the weights of the members of that pack with the eight who came so near to toppling the All Blacks winning run in the 18-21 loss at Auckland on 23 June 1990.

1954	st lb	1990	st lb
McGlashan	14 5	David Sole	16 4
MacEwen	13 00	Ken Milne	14 3
McLeod	13 10	Iain Milne	18 3
Fergusson	15 13	Chris Gray	16 12
Michie	14 00	Damian Cronin	16 8
Robson	12 10	John Jeffrey	14 4
Kininmonth	14 11	Derek White	15 10
Henderson	13 7	Finlay Calder	15 6
Average	14 2	Average	15 13

The effects of war rationing? Modern fitness training including weight training? Whatever the reason, the 1954 pack would have had a hard time holding their own with the 1990 combine in the realms of ball-winning alone, apart altogether from the overall speed about the paddock demonstrated by those modern forwards. All the same, that reconstructed pack of 1954 did much to restore Scottish pride with fire and passion on the field. France won at Murrayfield fortuitously by a try from René Brejassou, a Tarbes prop, described in the programme as 'a bull of a fellow but gentle, a wood and coal merchant with pitch-black hair so stiff as to defy the enterprise of the most skilful hairdresser. A very charming character, popular with his fellows.' He wasn't all that popular with the Scots and his hair did stand on end as he rumbled some twenty-five yards up in front of the Murrayfield stand towards the clock end for the game's only score.

The mighty All Blacks were next – Bob Scott, Ron Jarden, Kevin Skinner, 'Tiny' White, Peter Jones, Bob Stuart and all. They came to Murrayfield having lost only to Wales and Cardiff, and having beaten a depleted South of Scotland by 32-0 at Galashiels. But Scotland, inspired by the return as captain of one of their greatest forwards, Douglas Elliot of Edinburgh Academicals, held the New Zealand forwards and the whole side tackled courageously. Ian Swan and Grant Weatherstone, the wings, came within inches of tries. A penalty for 'foot up' (it would be a free-kick nowadays) gave Bob Scott the chance to send the kick just scraping over the bar from 30 yards, again the only score of the match.

The last defeat of that 17 in a row run came from France in Paris. That was on 8 January 1955 and the match was played at Stade Colombes. It was a memorable trip for me as the first to the French capital. Getting there was hard enough. I left Hawick on the Wednesday night, got the train from Edinburgh to London to Dover and to Calais thence to Paris. I was to share the commentary with Rex Alston.

After having seen the big French forwards training on the Friday, I made the point in a preview piece for the London Home Service that 'one hopes that the French forwards will not be allowed to rumble about in the prairie as they did in practice.' Unfortunately they were. Of course they had magnificent runners in their pack in Henri Domec, Jean Barthe, Bernard Chevallier and Michel Celaya, and they were so much bigger and heavier that they were able to free that amazing wing-forward, Jean Prat to play virtually as an extra threequarter. What is more, on a firm surface the Scottish forwards persisted in trying to wheel the scrummage and take the ball away in the dribble. I was very much in favour of 'wheel and dribble' but only in the most favourable conditions. After all, I could remember Tom Wright, our groundsman and trainer with the Hawick club at Mansfield Park, making the Hawick forwards dribble up and down the terracing touch-line time and again until we had the technique and control just right. Forwards don't dribble any more because they reckon that the ball is better controlled with the hands and that, in any case, the dribble is easily stopped by an opponent falling on it. I accept the first point but sundry international forwards and club men, too, down the years could testify to the difficulty and danger of trying to stop foot-rushes, especially in sloppy conditions, and I do not know how many times I have seen a try lost because a fat-head tried to pick up a wet ball instead of keeping it going with his feet and just falling on it at the line. Once I had a lovely chat with the legendary Irishman, Eugene O'Davy, capped 34 times, about Scotland's Triple Crown win in 1933 when they beat Ireland at Landsdowne Road by two drop-goals (four points each in those days) to two tries (three points in those days). Ireland were pressing on the Scottish line and leading by 6-4 when suddenly the Scottish forwards ignited a foot-rush from their own line to the Irish '25.' Davy was one who had to go in to try and stop the rush and when he got up, there was Harry Lind of Dunfermline slotting the winning drop goal. It was some foot-rush, I remember that great Irishman saying. 'Forwards really could control the dribble in those days.' In any event, whenever Scotland tried to dribble on the firm Paris ground in 1955, the French simply scooped up the ball and launched counter-attacks. They won 15-0 and all of us began to wonder if Scotland ever would stop the slide. At the post-match dinner that mighty Scottish forward of former days, John Bannerman, then SRU president, referred to 'this long lane that seems to have no turning.' Mind you spirits were raised a bit by a visit to the 'Moulin Rouge' after the meal before catching the Golden Arrow train at midday on the Sunday to be back home by 6 a.m. on Monday morning.

Two points stick about that trip. As we made our way to the commentary box on the Saturday Rex introduced me to the French lock Bernard Chevallier. For a few moments of some pain I wished he hadn't. Chevallier was a 16½-stone railway worker who had put the shot and thrown the discus to a high standard. He had hands the size of frying pans and when he shook mine and bawled 'Enchanté' my whole arm seemed to suffer a form of paralysis. I didn't know the French for 'could

I please have my hand back?' but I knew then why they had two nick-names for this giant – 'Cheval' meaning 'Horse' and 'Carnera' after the Italian heavyweight boxer, Primo Carnera, a huge fellow said to be phe-nomenally strong. The other was that, whereas the French team were numbered in modern fashion, the backs 15 to 9, the forwards 1 to 8, Scot-land did it the other way round, backs 1 to 7, forwards 8 to 15; which made it a wee bit confusing for commentators and underlined also that the Scottish hierarchy took their time about falling into line with general practice – and sometimes didn't!

When the Scots returned to Paris two years later Chevallier had a rough time at the hands of the Scottish props, Hugh McLeod of Hawick and Tom Elliot of Gala, a tough, rugged son of the soil. Those two hatched a plot to stifle the domination of Chevallier at the lineouts. On the French throw one would grab his jersey collar and the other his feet and they would pull in opposite directions. Of course they would have to time their assault perfectly otherwise they would be penalised by the referee, England's L.M. Boundy. It worked like a charm; big Chevallier got a bit fed up with the whole scheme and Scotland won by 6-0 from a drop-goal and a penalty goal by their debutante full-back, Ken Scotland. It was a memorable day for the Heriot's FP Club in Edinburgh, for Scot-land was joined in the Scottish side by another new cap, Eddie McKeat-ing, who had shared with Scotland many sporting honours at George Heriot's School and had played with him for the Scottish Schools. They were both only twenty. That day, Ian MacGregor, the Scottish wing for-ward from Hillhead H.S. FP and Llanelli, was given a painful trampling by the French forwards; his back badly wealed afterwards. The previous season MacGregor had subjected the French scrum-half and captain, Gerard Dufau, to several punishing tackles that proved a big factor in Scotland's 12-0 win at Murrayfield. The French forwards and Dufau re-membered. They got a bit of their own back in 1957 but MacGregor, already accustomed to Welsh club rugby with Llanelli, took it without a moan. That 1957 French match commentary was shared with Bob Hud-son of the BBC with 'Jock' Wemyss doing the summaries, and after the match, Bob and I were about to have a meal in the Scottish team hotel, the Normandie, when in popped Bob Hogg of Gala, vice-president of the SRU. After enquiring why we were not going to the official team dinner, Bob, a really nice man, toddled off to it. A couple of minutes later a magnum of champagne was brought to our table. When I said that we had not ordered it, the waiter explained that it came with the compliments of Mr Hogg. That was not the only time that I experienced the thoughtfulness of Bob Hogg. A few days later I received a cheque from the BBC for nine shillings (about 45p in today's money). That was the balance of my expenses which worked out as follows: Amount advanced by BBC 12,000 francs (£12.4/11): amount refunded by McLaren 9,000 francs (£9.3/8): balance 3,000 francs (£3.1/3): actual expenses 3,440 francs (£3.10/3): amount due to McLaren 440 francs (9/-).

By then, however, Scotland had brought to an end their miserable run. That French match of 1955 was the last defeat. The next match was against Wales at Murrayfield a fortnight later. Over all the years of international rugby, Scotland have produced some totally unexpected successes but none was more welcome than that achieved against Wales in 1955. Wales came north with their famous Morgan-Willis half-back pairing, their international sprinter Ken Jones of Newport on the right wing, and what a pack – Billy Williams, Bryn Meredith, Courtney Meredith, Russell Robins, Rhys Williams, Sid Judd, Rees Stephens and Clem Thomas. When Cliff Morgan placed a deft little chip kick to perfection for Trevor Brewer of London Welsh to score within five minutes, the feeling was simply that of 'here we go again.' But I recall Scotland being inspired by that elegant wing Arthur Smith, then playing for Cambridge University. Released by a pass from Adam Robson of Hawick, Smith took off up the touch-line side, beat two tackles with a shrug and change of pace, punted over full-back A.B. Edwards's head, tapped the ball further with his foot then picked up without a break in stride for one of the greatest solo tries. Smith was a master of changing pace without appearing to change stride pattern. Once I asked Robin Chisholm of Melrose, a fine, tackling full-back, how Smith had managed to score three tries in a Scottish trial when each time Chisholm seemed to have him set up for the tackle. Robin said that he had lined him up but each time Smith just seemed to purr away as the tackle was launched like some ghostly phantom. No one who was there will ever forget that Smith try against Wales in 1955. It was worth only three points in those days but a Jimmy Docherty drop-goal and a Kim Elgie penalty-goal had Scotland leading 9-8, Stephens having converted a second Brewer try. The tension at Murrayfield that day was as tight as a drumskin and the elation and relief was unforgettable when Willis was forced into a wild pass which Scotland's scrum-half, Jimmy Nichol, pounced upon for the deciding try, converted by Elgie for an historic 14-8 win. Joy was unconfined and I must say that I felt a lump in my throat as the final whistle sounded.

Nor will I ever forget that moment when I handed over to that great
Scot, Jock Wemyss, for his summary. For as long as I had known him
Jock was almost lost for words. I remember him saying with a tear on his
cheek: 'Well I can hardly speak. It has been such a long journey but at
last we have come out of that long, dark tunnel into the sunshine once
more.'

9
Officials, Selectors and other Fearsome Creatures

Of all the many changes that have taken place in the Rugby Union game over the post-war years one of the most significant has been in the relations between the Unions and the media. Certainly insofar as the Scottish Rugby Union is concerned, the difference in attitude has been quite remarkable. It also has been to the general benefit of the game. At one time the press were treated quite abominably, partly because they were regarded as professionals who were making money out of the game, and partly because of an innate fear by officials of being quoted, that views they would prefer to remain private would be made known to all and sundry.

When I was on my demobilisation leave in 1947 the editor of the *Hawick Express*, John Hood, who then was unknown to me, asked through a mutual friend if, as I was going anyway, I would be good enough to mark on a programme the results of an Army boxing contest that was being staged in our local town hall. All I did was to mark in 'won on points' or 'KO'd 1st round' against each contest. I handed the programme into the *Hawick Express* and thought no more about it. That is, until I was called into the office of the manager of the National Bank of Scotland in Hawick, R.L. Scott, then a member of the SRU committee, later to become SRU president, and a man for whom I had much respect as one of the Hawick club's outstanding committee stalwarts.

'Billy, I hear you did a bit of reporting for the *Hawick Express* the other day,' he said. Why had I done so? Had I received payment for it? When I explained what had happened he said that I must be sure never to do anything like that again. It was not allowed. I was petrified, so much so that I did not even ask why not. You just didn't query such orders in those days. Yet all I had done was a simple favour for a friend with no thought of reward and I received no money for it.

On one of my earliest reporting assignments in the early fifties I was invited into the Melrose committee room at the Greenyards by the then secretary, Bob Brown, for a refreshment before the game. I declined because I already knew the official attitude to the press. Bob would have none of it. He was a wonderful character, strong of will, given to plain speaking and a tremendous servant to the Melrose club as have been his two equally likeable sons, Derek, now on the SRU committee, and Mac who, as club president, had the pleasure at the 1990 Melrose sevens of asking his mother, Peggy, another great club stalwart, to present the trophy and medals to the first winners from the southern hemisphere, Randwick from Sydney. Once Bob was told on the telephone by the secretary of the SRU that the Union had decided that Melrose could not hold their sevens tournament on the usual date.

'You just pop down to the Greenyards on the second Saturday in April,' retorted Bob, 'and you'll see soon enough whether the Melrose sevens are being held or not.' And the sevens did go ahead as planned. So when I said to Bob that I didn't want to accept his invitation to the committee room because of possible embarrassment if any Union officials were there he insisted: 'Come on, it's nothing to do with them,' he said. So I went and was duly embarrassed, with that feeling of being where I should not have been. Bob meant well and I always appreciated the thoughtful gesture but I didn't make the same mistake again.

For all that, I will always remember Bob as an original; Norman Mair, so highly respected for his rugby and golf writings in *The Scotsman,* has told the story of the evening on which he went to see Melrose play Trinity Academicals, a game that Melrose unaccountably lost, whereupon Norman approached Bob and asked if he could join the Melrose club as a player. 'Tonight,' growled Bob, *'anybody* can join Melrose!'

It was on a plane returning from an international match in Dublin and on which members of the press were permitted to travel that one SRU official came down the aisle and told the press group that 'you bloody people have no right to be here!' Admittedly he was under the influence. At one time it was reckoned that the Kremlin and the Scottish Rugby Union ran neck and neck in the 'niet' stakes, in the secrecy with which they surrounded their activities and their decision-making. It was generally believed that to any proposal put to them, the Union immediately said 'NO' – then proceeded to discuss the case; then they said

'NO' again! I don't suppose you could expect anything else from a band of brothers who had been brought up with an attitude as depicted by their former autocratic secretary, J. Aikman Smith, who, when it was suggested that the Scottish team might be numbered as others were, replied that under no circumstances would they number their players 'like cattle in an auction mart.'

Getting blood out of a stone used to be easier than squeezing information out of the SRU. On one occasion the Union decided to hold an experimental game at Murrayfield at which certain scrummage proposals were to be tried out. John Robertson of the *Edinburgh Evening News* and generally the press spokesmen, was deputed to enquire of a Union official just what the proposals were. The reply he received was: 'Use your bloody eyes.'

It was after a practice session at the Edinburgh University ground at Craiglockhart that I asked Alf Wilson, then a Scottish selector and later manager of the British Lions in Australia and New Zealand in 1959, if he would tell us who were the reserves for the forthcoming Scottish game with England. Alf refused. I pointed out that it gave the players concerned a real fillip for it to be known that they were so close to cap status; Alf said that they would not tell us who the chaps were because if someone called off from the national side, the selectors might not play one of the reserves. I argued that that was no justifiable reason for not announcing the names of the reserves, but to no avail.

Back in 1947, having been chosen to play for the Rest of Scotland v the Army I did not have time to see any official about a railway ticket because I was just back home after Army service. So I just bought a return ticket from Hawick to Edinburgh and travelled up on the Saturday morning to meet with the other members of the team. When I asked for a refund of the money spent on the ticket I was informed that I could not be given money but that I could have another ticket. I didn't want another ticket. I wasn't going to Edinburgh again for the foreseeable future. I never got the money. A few years back, I was tricked by Cliff Morgan into making a speech at a farewell meal for the then Scottish Rugby Union secretary, John Law, and during that I made a mock special plea for the two shillings and fourpence ha'penny (or however much it was) from John Law for that journey made something like thirty-five years previously. But John, whom I had come to like and respect, simply gave me that glazed look and slight upturn of the nostrils that spelt out in the simplest terms that I had no chance.

Perhaps I was fortunate in one respect; my early broadcasting experience was frequently in the company of Andrew 'Jock' Wemyss, doyen of Scottish rugby broadcasters and writers, who was, for many years, the *Daily Express* rugby correspondent in Scotland. Jock was one of the game's great characters. It was hardly surprising that he was on friendly terms with the rugby hierarchy for he had played for Scotland both before and after the first world war and, indeed, after it with just one eye. He had been a playing contemporary of some of the Union committee, had been one of the founders of the Scottish Co-Optimists Club, a kind of Scottish Barbarians, and he was himself a Barbarian and indeed became that famous Club's historian. Being associated with 'Jock' in broadcast work was of much benefit to me, for he was immensely helpful in providing advice and information and he introduced me to many rugby officials of differing nationalities and that enabled me to become 'accepted.' Even so you can imagine my surprise during one of my early visits to an international in Dublin when, after the Irish practice session, I and other media men were invited to 'have a jar' with the Irish selectors and players. I thought they must have been speaking to someone else. A jar with the selectors? I could hardly believe it. But right enough, we had a very pleasant half hour with them and with the players also joining in. I have had a soft spot for the Irish from that day.

It was prior to the Ireland v Scotland match in Dublin in 1960 that a bit of drama was enacted that caused quite a bit of controversy. Frans ten Bos, the London Scottish lock, had been recovering from injury but he took part in all the preparatory activities and pronounced himself as fit to play. He certainly gave it 100 per cent during a vigorous session. Yet later that evening, Alf Wilson, then chairman of selectors, announced that ten Bos would not play and that his place would be taken by Oliver Grant, one of the three Grant brothers of Hawick, the others being Jack, who had played for the South of Scotland against the 1952 Springboks and 1954 New Zealanders, and Derrick, a British Lion in Australia and New Zealand in 1966 and later Scotland's national coach. It was to be Oliver's first cap and he played an important role in Scotland's first win at Lansdowne Road for 33 years. But there was a feeling that ten Bos had been unfairly treated and the lad himself was hurt and distressed at the decision to leave him out.

Perhaps the heaviest criticism of the national selectors occurred at Twickenham in 1959. Donald Macdonald, the blond, little, tearaway Edinburgh University wing-forward, called off at the eleventh hour and instead of introducing Derek Brown of Melrose for his first cap the selectors opted for Jock Davidson of London Scottish. Jock was heavier than Derek but the Melrose man was such a wholehearted 80-minutes player, reared in the demanding environs of the Border game, that there were very strong feelings expressed about his omission. Derek never did gain a cap and remains one of the unluckiest players ever to have got so near and been so deserving. That 1959 match, at which I shared the radio commentary, was quite distinctive for the courage shown by the Fife farmer, David Rollo who was gaining his first cap out of the Howe of Fife club. Soon after the start David suffered a broken nose but, after a brief absence for repairs, he returned to play prop with undiminished fire. After that debut it hardly was surprising that David went on to gain 40 caps and British Lions selection to South Africa in 1962. That match, which was drawn 3-3, and in which Ken Scotland, one of the finest all-round backs I have ever seen, made two vital tackles on Bev Risman and Malcolm Phillips, also produced some remarkable statistics.

In one article on the game Jim Swanton quoted details that gave a very clear picture of the state of international play in those days. That England v Scotland match produced 78 lineouts, 71 scrummages, 25 penalties, 3 touchdowns and 2 marks – 179 stoppages in all. But, as Swanton pointed out, that was an improvement on the previous game, England v France, that had produced 193 stoppages. Amazingly, England finished that Championship with one victory, one defeat and two draws, having scored, believe it or not, just 9 points and conceded 11; they scored not one single try and conceded just one. The scores in that English Championship campaign were: Wales 0-5 (Cardiff); Ireland 3-0 (Dublin); France 3-3 (Twickenham); Scotland 3-3 (Twickenham). Those of us who complain about lack of widespread play and adventurism in the modern game, and with some justification, still should compare those statistics of 1959 with the 1990 Championship in which England scored a record 90 points in four games (including 12 tries with just 3 conceded).

In those early years I could not understand the SRU's suspicious approach to the media. Most of the Scottish rugby writers I have known have had the game and its personalities very much at heart. Writers such as John Robertson, Reg Prophit, the late Hugh Young, John Downie, Peter Donald and Walter Thomson were not headline-hunting newsmen but writers who loved the game and who wanted to see it put its best foot forward whilst, at the same time, accepting fair criticism that they might offer. For myself, I would rather miss a good sensational story than cause embarrassment or distress to anyone in the game. I have been stopped in Hawick High Street and been given a right dressing down by the former Hawick club secretary, 'Pud' Miller, for something I wrote in criticism of the club in the *Hawick Express*, but I thought it was fair and right and we had some argument to the great interest and pleasure of passers-by. Once, in the Union's committee room in the Normandie Hotel in Paris, to which my wife and I had been invited for a night-cap, I was upbraided by Alf Wilson and George Thomson for suggesting that it was high time that Scotland had a proper league set-up rather than the haphazard unofficial newspaper championship which had been run for some years. Alf and George then were completely against any such development. I recall George asking what would happen if his club, Watsonians, had both a first and second fifteen in the top division. So what? I argued. If they were good enough, good luck to them. There was quite an argy-bargy and at one point they had me pinned up against the wall so forceful were their arguments. Norman Mair and myself were going to be responsible for ruining the whole spirit of the Scottish game, they alleged. However national leagues did come to Scotland in 1973-74 and they have since been the envy of others, who have since introduced the same kind of set-up in their countries. Of course, there are still refinements required in the Scottish league structure and the intensely competitive nature of league games is not everyone's cup of tea but something had to be done to replace a system in which not all clubs played the same fixtures. Some Union folk were against the whole idea of having champions, but my view was that any championship had to be won on a basis fair to all.

How things have changed. Nowadays the relationship between Union and media is near ideal. Regular press conferences are held for the dissemination of information and Union officials are extremely helpful. All have realised that co-operation between the two branches is essential for the general benefit of the game, especially in these days when sponsors put so much into the game and naturally want as much media exposure as possible. Sometimes my heart bleeds for the representatives of a beaten team who have to face the battery of press and their questions at aftermatch sessions. It can't be easy to avoid 'faux-pas' in the immediate after-math of a crucial match. Geoff Cooke, the England manager, may have regretted making the 'scavengers' reference to Scotland's play in the 12-12 draw with England at Twickenham in 1989. Big Rhys Williams, whom Hugh McLeod always regarded as one of the strongest and toughest locks he had ever played with, once lost his cool when faced with an impertinent query about Welsh spirit and ambition. Perhaps the most effective performances I have seen have been by Bob Munro, the manager of Scotland's World Cup side in 1987, Ian McGeechan, Scottish and Lions' coach and Finlay Calder, Scotland's captain. Calder is a joker who could provide an amalgam of fun-poking, often at himself, and reasoned judgement. McGeechan was always in control of his thoughts and a master at keeping things in perspective and at game analysis. Munro was an honest soul, eminently approachable, with an impish sense of humour and a deal of common sense. As a former Leith Academicals and Edinburgh prop-forward, Munro might not have been everyone's choice as manager of the World Cup party, especially after serious illness, but he did a splendid job and grew in stature as the competition progressed. I was also impressed by the confident responses by England's captain Will Carling to any and every question after one training session. Carling, in my opinion, was the most penetrative centre of the 1990 Championship and a joy to watch in sevens with his explosive pace and strength.

Rugby Union, generally speaking, has been fairly fortunate in its press corps. They are, in the main, a well-meaning group with the interests of the game, as well as of their newspapers, very much at heart. I enjoy reading David Hands in *The Times* because he is so fair and factual, a good judge of play and players. *The Times* also provides reports, teamlists and names of referees of matches played in other parts of the world, a very important service for folk like myself who are very interested in what is going on elsewhere. John Mason, also, is a very dependable rugby journalist and a nice man with it. I always have had a high regard for the coverage by Norman Mair, formerly of *The Scotsman*.

Norman never was *persona grata* with all members of the Scottish Rugby Union because he wrote what he felt and had the ear of some very influential people in the game. There have been times when I have had to read one of Norman's sentences two or three times over in order to get the gist, but he has been one of the most perceptive of analysts and his articles have been both enlightening and enjoyable – especially the little humorous stories that were so often his punchlines. I liked the one especially about that renowned after-dinner speaker, Lord Birkett, who was a trifle long-winded, but didn't take umbrage if his audience began to look at their watches but did take a very dim view when they looked at their watches, shook them, then held them up to their ears.

   Norman and Chris Rea were hard acts to follow at *The Scotsman*, but
I admire the way Graham Law has set about his task in his own style that
is at once distinctive and informative. Bill McMurtrie of the *Glasgow
Herald* is a very sound rugby and cricket journalist, brought up in the
faith by his father, John, editor of the *Border Telegraph* for many years
and one of the outstanding journalists of his time. Bill keeps the most
meticulous records and his factual reporting is decorated with interesting
statistics from his extensive collection. Bill often produces a telling statistic that no one else has and, in addition, he is one of the journalistic fraternity who sticks to his word and always does what he promised to do.
Another who gives a first-class service is Bill Lothian of the *Edinburgh
Evening News*. There isn't much going on in Scotland or Edinburgh
rugby that Bill doesn't know about and his writings mirror that gathering of intelligence. I enjoy, too, the press box company of John Smail,
editor of *The Southern Reporter*, a sound rugby journalist who played
fullback for Selkirk. He produced a fascinating 'Story of Border Rugby'
in cassette form and takes a dim view only of the fact that instead of buy-
ing the informative *Southern Reporter*, I get my mother-in-law's copy
second-hand! Things have improved for rugby's press corps. There were
no press conferences at all in olden times and information was in very
short supply, but now part of the Sunday and Monday newspaper copy
is based on post-match conferences at which the chairman of selectors,
the coach and the captain of each team is available to answer questions.
Nor are players as frightened as they used to be to have a chat with a
journalist. There was a time when they weren't allowed to do so but
there is a much more lenient view nowadays and that is all to the good of
the game. Players should have some licence to air their views about the
game although there have to be guidelines, and players have to beware of
bringing the game into disrepute. Rugby Union administrators, in the
main, seem to have come round to the idea that they and the media must
work together as a kind of partnership into which each makes a fair contribution to the general benefit of the game. Certainly most of the reporters I have come across do a very important service and seem
genuinely concerned to help the game to put its best foot forward whilst,
at the same time, proferring criticism when they think that is fair. Nor
are the modern Union men as prickly when hearing criticism as their
predecessors were. After all, even Unions, not to mention the International Board, don't always get it right!
   Although in the old days it was very frustrating to find the Union so

lacking in co-operation they did have some very strong men at the helm who left one in no doubt as to where the dividing lines were drawn. The likes of Herbert Waddell and Alf Wilson were strong defenders of the amateur faith, and autocratic as well, but you knew exactly where you stood with them. There were not then the fuzzy areas that abound today, where it seems that the same rules and approaches do not apply in the member countries of the International Board. In playing practices, in refereeing interpretations and in what many regard as forms of 'shamateurism' there are considerable differences between the home countries and the southern hemisphere and France. It would have been interesting to have seen the reaction of Messrs Waddell and Wilson to the current moves to allow players to be paid for interviews, for opening shops, for writing books, for making speeches. I can almost see the steam coming out of their ears.

Down the years there have been sarcastic references to the 'gin and tonic brigade,' meaning the Union officials. There certainly have been some doughnuts among them. At the same time it is not generally realised just how much work and travel a Union committee man has to put in. I remember Scotland's World Cup Manager, Duncan Paterson, in one interview, saying that he had received quite a shock when he first went on the Union committee as a South representative to find just how many meetings and how much travel were involved. The current Scottish Rugby Union committee carries mostly very sensible, sound citizens who have served their time as players, committee-men at club and district level or coaches and, in the case of Alan Hosie, as a much respected international referee.

The search for excellence in performance and for success has placed immense pressures on all concerned, most especially players and, even more-so, coaches, and none of them should be out of pocket in their devotion to duty. Nor will the game ever return to the happy-go-lucky days of 'train on Tuesday and Thursday, play on Saturday and the rest of the week is your own!' It takes more than that to reach the top rung these days. But Rugby Union never was intended to be a seven-days-a-week job and that is what it is in danger of becoming if fixtures continue to proliferate and more squad and mini-squad sessions are demanded. One wonders where the pursuit of excellence will take us to. Hopefully, not to the extremes that so disgraced that great sprinter Ben Johnson. Rugby Union always has prided itself on being just different and, because of the standards set by stalwarts of old, of having personnel who were just different. But all are subject to human frailty like the rest of mankind and it is important that the problems that have afflicted other sports, such as bad on-field behaviour and crowd trouble, not to mention pursuit of the buck, should not be allowed to damage the greatest of all team games.

10
All-time Greats:
Teams and Players

It has been my good fortune through the auspices of the BBC, who have treated me with much fairness and understanding over some 39 years, to have seen many of the most thrilling games, great teams and world-class players that have been an adornment to Rugby Union. There have been numerous occasions when I have watched in sheer delight as players have demonstrated a marvellous grasp of the fundamental skills under high pressure and teams have put together such wonders of interplay as to make one suck in the breath in amazement. The first international side to make a big impression on me were the 1935 New Zealanders. They were the first touring team I had ever seen when they played the South of Scotland at our home ground of Mansfield Park in Hawick. I watched with awe from the enclosure seats down at pitch-level as they walked on to the pitch led by Jack Manchester, who held the ball in one hand the size of a bucket lid. I had never seen such big fellows and their all-black uniform made them look even more formidable. Yet they weren't a great side. The South lost by only 8-11 and they lost three and drew one of their 28 games, their defeats including those by Wales and England, but I recall being impressed by a big, blond full-back called Gilbert and by the speed of their threequarter T.H.C. Caughey of Auckland.

The 1938 Scottish side left an imprint because I was lucky enough to be at Twickenham as a 14-year-old schoolboy sitting in the East stand as Scotland scored five tries to one in beating England 21-16 to win the Triple Crown and Championship. That was Wilson Shaw's match, for the Scottish captain scored two cracking tries and he had his famed centres with him then, Charles Dick and Duncan Macrae. Once I had to interview Duncan for a chapter in a book on rugby greats by Cliff Mor-

97

gan and what a personality Duncan turned out to be. He was in every sense the proud, kilted Scot, born and bred to a love of Scottish life and tradition in Kyle of Lochalsh in the far north-west, and totally unafraid both on and off the rugby field. That great Welsh midfield player, Wilfred Wooller, described the Shaw-Dick-Macrae combination as the greatest midfield trio he had ever played against, and I recall the 1938 British Lions captain, Sammy Walker, saying that Macrae, a great success on that tour, would be in his world best side for 'he had everything – acceleration, immaculate hands, split-second timing of the pass, baffling body swerve and attacking flair and a bone-crushing tackle.' Ironically, Macrae's final rugby appearance had that element of robustness about it for when asked to say a few words after a rugby film show at the Highland Club in Inverness, the rival club to his own outfit, Ross Sutherland, Duncan waxed eloquent about being fearless and resolute in the tackle. That weekend, Highland met Ross Sutherland and Duncan's farewell appearance was marred by his being carried off unconscious. When he came to he asked his friend, the late Dr Aymer Wilson, what had happened and the blunt reply was: 'Well, Duncan, that'll teach you to go and open your bloody mouth about going in hard to the tackle. Someone took you at your word!'

An indelible impression also was made by the 1951-52 Springboks because they were the first really big men that I ever saw who could run and handle like backs. Their Test pack was something else: Geffin, Delport, Koch, Dinkelmann, du Rand, Van Wyk, Muller and Fry – huge fellows who thundered about the paddock like mad rhinos and who simply ran amok at Murrayfield when Scotland were beaten 44-0, a record margin that stood painfully to Scottish eyes until Ireland beat Romania 60-0 at Lansdowne Road in 1986.

Just about the greatest all-round side I have seen were the 1967 All Blacks who married massive forward power to clever and robust back play and finished their tour of 15 matches unbeaten, with 14 wins and a 3-3 draw with East Wales at Cardiff. That was in the days when the wings threw in to the lineouts, and those All Blacks used the over-arm method that has now gone out of fashion but certainly worked well for them, when allied to the quite unceremonious approach by their forwards to the simple business of ensuring that their jumper would be comparatively unmolested in going for the ball. I never saw Colin Meads, for instance, as a great lineout jumper but he won a lot of ball with a little help from his friends and by his own totally committed approach to the process. If New Zealand needed ball then the mighty Meads was prepared to die in the attempt to win it. He was a magnificent work-horse, a frightening sight at full charge with ball in hand, a man intensely proud of being an All Black and who saw to it that younger players were made aware of their responsibilities to the silver fern.

On rare occasions Meads got carried away amid the intense pressure of the international game and one has heard him on television admit that he did some things that he was not terribly proud of. I was doing commentary when he was ordered off by Kevin Kelleher, the Irish referee, in the Scotland v New Zealand game at Murrayfield on 2 December 1967. It was the first time I had had to deal with an ordering-off in an international, and it took me a bit by surprise, for the last player to have been ordered off in an international had been Cyril Brownlie of New Zealand and that some 42 years previously. Meads had already been cautioned for trampling on bodies in a ruck, so that when he swung his boot dangerously near the bending David Chisholm, the Scottish stand-off, Kevin Kelleher had no option but to dismiss him. It was still a brave decision by Kelleher because it was near the end of a game which had been comparatively free from nastiness, but it did show that he was not prepared to turn a blind eye and it is a matter of some regret that other referees did not follow his example and deal bravely and strictly with dangerous play.

Brian Lochore was another outstanding forward and much respected captain. He developed that move in which he withdrew from the scrummage to a fine art and perfected the variation in which, instead of detaching and picking up the ball himself, he broke wide and received the ball from his scrum-half Chris Laidlaw. It was a productive move in that Lochore, a big, hard farmer, never failed to take out opponents whilst handing on to a colleague in support, and was always prepared to provide a juicy target for the thundering buffaloes in his wake. And there always were thundering buffaloes in the wake of any All Black leading the charge! It was just such a move that produced a delightful try against England at Twickenham. From a scrummage just outside the England '25' on the left side, Lochore broke to the right, took Laidlaw's pass, cut inside England stand-off John Finlan, crashed into England's breaking loose-forwards and at the same time, released the burly Hawke's Bay centre, Ian MacRae, who was just made for running at defenders. Ruck ball then was popped back like a hen laying an egg, Laidlaw swept the ball to the left and Earl Kirton scythed through a fractured defence for his second try of the game. The vital ingredients by which the All Blacks

proved so devastating at that time all were there – a simple ploy that
launched a big forward over the advantage line, a further dent in the
defence line by a big centre who set up the target for a typical New Zealand ruck, 'spines in line, all together and keep the legs pumping!' Then,
almost without fail, beautifully manicured ruck ball was switched the
other way, this time towards the left and when Kirton scored he had two
pals loose outside him.

   MacRae, who had scored three tries for his province, Hawke's Bay,
against the touring England in 1963, set a new fashion that was copied by
big centres at every level of the game. This was in using formidable physique to take a pass running dead straight and so commit one or two defenders into the tackle. He never shirked this form of intensely physical
contact and if he did not manage to break through or get his pass away,
he still set up an inviting target for his forwards upon which to create a
moving ruck platform at which those All Blacks were streets ahead of the
home countries in terms of body position, cohesion, driving momentum
and always leaving a tunnel open through which the ball would appear
like a chocolate bar from a slot machine. Indeed, when their type of
rucking was first seen here in the sixties, some folk were horrified at the
sheer ferocity of the combined action. There undoubtedly was an intimidatory aspect to it for those All Blacks were quite prepared to ruck-
out with the ball any opponent foolish enough to place his body on the
wrong side. Indeed, as I remember it, this unceremonious approach led
to the first caution given to Colin Meads at the Murrayfield international
when he 'walked' over bodies in order to get to the ball. That was part
and parcel of the New Zealand game at home, but to innocents over here
it looked very rough and dangerous. Now, of course, players do not
object to being walked upon but they object to being trampled, raked
and kicked. At the same time there was some method in the New Zealand passion. It took a brave man to fall on the wrong side of the ball
against any side from New Zealand, since their rucking not only produced some choice possession, but frequently left opponents on the
floor, having been deposited there by the sheer drive and momentum of
the All-Black's technique. The point about MacRae being used as a ruck
creator was that New Zealand at that time had one of the great loose-
forward combinations in Waka Nathan, Brian Lochore and Kel Tremain, and they had in their wake Colin Meads, Sam Strahan (from Manawatu and then only twenty-two years of age) and the speedy prop Ken
Gray. All of those forwards had characteristic New Zealand physique.

Most were farmers or agricultural types. The other prop, Brian Muller, was a freezing company worker who weighed over 17 stones. He was enormous. Nathan, Lochore and Tremain were arguably the most effective breakaway trio ever to represent New Zealand. Each was a mature forward with lots of experience. Nathan was called 'the black panther.' He was quick and strong. Tremain was a big flanker by the standards of those days – just over 6 feet 2 inches, over 15 stones, with raking stride and absolutely lethal from close range. Lochore was just Lochore, a tremendous all-round forward. There were also a very fast, young flanker from Wellington called Graham Williams, just twenty-two, who had some great moments on tour, and a hooker, Bruce McLeod, who could shift as well and was quite a bulky 14½ stones plus. They were a superb pack, all apparently made out of corrugated iron and extremely mobile. Gray was one of the first prop-forwards in the modern game that I had seen who also was a genuine lineout jumper. He was 6 feet 2 inches and had sound timing and hands. Of course, in earlier days, before specialisation, every forward in the lineout was regarded as a potential catcher, but by the sixties the key lineout men were at front, middle and rear. In the New Zealand case that meant Meads, Strahan and Lochore. But Gray gave them an extra dimension as indeed did Tremain near the back. I've already mentioned Lochore's scrummage detachment and how it sparked off a try for Kirton against England. They used it as a decoy move as well and never to more crucial effect than against the Barbarians in their last match at Twickenham on 16 December 1967. The Barbarians were leading 6-3 with just two minutes to go. The All Blacks' unbeaten record seemed about to fall. The match had gone into injury time when Tony Steel shot into the centre line from the left wing to provide a try for MacRae. So it was 6-6. From the last scrummage Lochore broke off and went left but this time Laidlaw went right and punted. Barbarians fullback Stewart Wilson slipped as he put in his clearing kick and who should be standing on half-way to collect the ball, but Lochore. He charged forward then fed Kirton and from his pass Steel scored for Fergie McCormick to convert, and the All Blacks had won 11-6, four minutes into injury-time. That spoke volumes for New Zealand's spirit and commitment and their all-consuming desire to win. Even when they had drawn level they were not satisfied.

That was the first time that the BBC had transmitted a live rugby match in colour and after the game I interviewed Colin Meads, Tony Steel and the coach Fred Allen for BBC 2. Meads had just been restored to the side after his two-match suspension but I thought it prudent not to ask him about that! Close at hand he looked like King Kong! That was only the second time that the Barbarians fifteen had played at Twickenham, the previous occasion having been against London in 1935. The match with the All Blacks had been hurriedly arranged to compensate for their two-match tour of Ireland having to be cancelled because of the foot and mouth disease outbreak.

Two other points about those 1967 All Blacks. They had seen the effect of French 'percussion,' in which big forwards charged round back or front of the lineout, and they incorporated that into their own strategy. In the Scotland international Lochore deflected a throw perfectly into the hands of Meads who went out the back like a bull elephant. When half-checked he passed to Gray who had come all the way from the front and at such pace that he tore the Scots defence apart to lay on a try for MacRae. It was as easy as that except that it was timed and executed to perfection. Even Lucien Mias and his French bulls couldn't have put it together any better. The second thing is the satisfaction I found in the fact that Earl Kirton scored two tries against England and had a good tour. He hadn't been so successful when he came over first with the 1963-64 party as a 23-year-old student, and I'll never forget the traumatic experience he had at the hands of Ron Glasgow in the match against the North and Midlands of Scotland at Linksfield, Aberdeen, on 14 January 1964. Glasgow then was thirty-three and already had played six internationals for Scotland. He was a hard, very fast teacher of physical education who saw his first obligation as a wing-forward, or flanker, as being the total destruction of the entire opposing back division. That day at Linksfield he gave the New Zealand backs and especially young Kirton a torrid time. John Downie, then rugby correspondent for the *Glasgow Herald* and much respected for his fairness and knowledge, wrote that 'none had more spectacular success than Glasgow who wrought havoc among the tourists' backs from start to finish.' But Kirton survived and played a big part in the success of the 1967 party. Today loop moves are fairly commonplace but none that I have seen have excelled for sheer pace and execution the loop achieved by Kirton in the Scotland international. It was from a scrummage and direct feed from his scrum-half, Laidlaw. MacRae tore in dead straight and close, took and gave in a blink of light to the looping Kirton who tied in the Scottish wing and sent Bill Davis of Hawke's Bay roaring in for a great score. Yes, they were something else those mighty All Blacks of 1967.

The next time I came across Brian Lochore was at the World Cup when he was New Zealand coach. He didn't smile a lot. Once, after a very impressive All Blacks training session, I said to him that the All Blacks would win the Cup with a bit to spare, that they played a different kind of game to the rest of us, and he came very close to smiling but satisfied himself with the observation that they had still to do the business. He seemed a quietly effective and yet quite demanding coach. One All Blacks scrummage session that he conducted was just about the fiercest that I have ever seen. It lasted for about an hour and the two packs gave the impression of having a total hate relationship. Time and time again they crashed together with perspiration spraying everywhere. No quarter was asked or given. It really made you boggle at just what the human frame could stand. It also represented one of Lochore's biggest successes in the World Cup. Many of the pundits believed that the scrummage would be the New Zealand Achilles' heel. They had been out-scrummaged in defeat by the French at Nantes just six months previously. In the World Cup, however, the New Zealand scrummage was a powerful attack weapon. It was another example of how New Zealanders learn their lessons quicker than most and that is why tour sides in New Zealand reckon that it is vital to win the first Test before the All Blacks find out exactly what they can do and how they will do it, and that is why the All Blacks seem always to become more formidable as a series unfolds.

The touring side, however, who gave most pleasure, when it was a privilege to provide commentary on their matches, were the 1984 Australians coached by Alan Jones (sharp as a tack and never lost for a word), and captained by that rumbustious centre, Andrew Slack. They were a treat to watch whether the weather was fine or dreich. They brought a new concept of back play, with their flat alignment that enabled them to breach the gain line quickly, and with their wonderful pass improvisation as they ran through a repertoire of miss-moves, loops, dummy-loops and intrusions, all at high speed and with incredible skill levels. They flicked the ball about with such dexterity that even spectators, far less opponents, weren't quite sure who had the ball. They were masters of counter-attack and their 14½-stone fullback, Roger Gould, was a formidable figure, whether initiating attack from the deep or augmenting the back line. There was, too, the swashbuckling cavalier, David Campese, who rang down the curtain on their Grand Slam of the four internationals with a typical flourish at Murrayfield when he took off from

Mark Ella's pass on his own '22', released their 21-year-old number 8, Steve Tuynman, then looped him for a forty-metre scoring sprint that brought the house down.

Campese proved a host in himself on that tour and Mark Ella was another massive talent with his sleight of hand, deceptive change of pace, adhesive palms; he had the distinction of scoring a try in each of the four internationals, as well as two drop-goals against Ireland when the Wallabies were finding difficulty in transforming their superiority into points. The Australian forwards didn't do a lot of initial attack work on their own, apart from occasional scrummage pick-ups when required, but they appreciated the value of tidy set-piece delivery, and they had a powerful corner-stone to their scrummage in the former Argentine Test loose-head, Enrique Engardo Rodriguez, so much so that they astonished the rugby world, and not least the Welsh, by scoring a push-over try through Steve Tuynman in the Cardiff international. Every forward was adept at picking the most effective lines of support running and at providing linkage or regeneration in broken play, but Tuynman was a revelation and Simon Poidevin also enjoyed a memorable tour.

As with every successful side they had goal-kicking expertise, too, from the boot of Michael Lynagh, also twenty-one, who played as inside-centre on that tour and who broke Scottish hearts at Murrayfield with eight goals from nine attempts to equal the Australian record for an international of 21 points held by Paul McLean. Those Wallabies were the most innovative and entertaining tour side I can recall, and it was hardly surprising that their final match against the Barbarians at Cardiff spawned eleven gorgeous tries and victory by 37-30. It was a special triumph for their coach Alan Jones, among whose several telling quotes were two of particular note. After the 6-9 defeat by the South of Scotland in atrocious conditions at Mansfield Park, Hawick, he referred to being 'cocks of the walk one day and feather dusters the next'; and once on the subject of foul play and violence: 'It is possible to have civilised rugby. It is up to those in charge of young men not to allow the animalistic spirit to dominate.'

It was my good fortune also to have been doing television commentary during the second 'golden era' achieved by Wales when, between 1969 and 1979, they won three Grand Slams, six outright Championships and six Triple Crowns.

I was lucky enough to be 'on the air' when Maurice Richards scored his record-equalling four tries against England in 1969; when Wales were

3-13 down to England at half-time a year later and fought back to win 17-13 thanks to a debut try from Ray 'Chico' Hopkins of Maesteg; when Gareth Edwards scored his famous touch-line chip-and-chase try against Scotland at Cardiff in 1972. I saw Wales trounce England by thirty points to nine in 1969 and by twenty-seven points to three in 1979. I saw them beat Scotland 35-12 in 1972, Ireland 32-4 in 1975 and France 20-16 in 1972. The Welsh contribution to the game at large during that era was massive, which is why the Scots took such pride in only losing to Wales 19-18 in that memorable match in 1971. It was a dream period for all Welshmen as their players set new standards of fitness, teamwork and skill-levels and a pace of play that enabled them virtually to carry all before them. Changed days now, when one considers that first-ever Welsh wooden spoon white-wash in 1990. That was even more difficult to understand when one took into account the high quality of so much of the Welsh club game as seen every Sunday on 'Rugby Special'. At one time or another during that glorious decade they put all of their Championship rivals to the sword.

Wales remained unbeaten in the Championship at Cardiff from the French game of 1968 (9-14) to the Scottish match of 1982 (18-34) – 27 Home Championship games in which they never were beaten. Television commentary was a joy because every game involving Wales seemed guaranteed to produce quick-fire rugby with all fifteen players involved at high speed, and with each section of the team complementing the others as players exchanged roles as the situations demanded. The Welsh, of course, had stolen a march on their rivals as the first to appoint a national team coach and to have special squad sessions aimed at bringing organisation and a high degree of efficiency to a standard of teamwork not previously achieved. The effect was to lay before their fascinated audiences an amalgam of set-piece surety, initial forward probes, swift transference of ruck-maul delivery, massive support for the ball-carrier and the devastating introduction of the powerful J.P.R. Williams as an attacking full-back. It was significant, too, that a number of mighty Welsh talents came together at the same time – Williams, Gerald Davies, Barry John, Gareth Edwards, Denzil Williams, Brian Price, Brian Thomas, Delme Thomas and that superbly balanced breakaway trio of John Taylor, Mervyn Davies and the under-rated human dynamo, David Morris. There were too, the superb vision and timing and weighting of the pass from John Dawes and, later in that decade, Phil Bennett, that puff-puff wing, John Bevan, Steve Fenwick, Ray Gravell, J.J. Williams, and the Pontypool front row of Charlie Faulkner, Bobby Windsor and Graham Price, and Alan Martin and Geoff Wheel, Terry Cobner, Derek Quinnell and Jeff Squire. What a host of talent. They were virtually all the products of the Welsh club system with its fierce local rivalries – including London Welsh who, in the seventies, became the outstanding club side in the British Isles with a free-flowing style based on attacking with the ball in hand and on using all fifteen players.

I felt a very enjoyable rapport with those Welsh lads which had its basis in the deep appreciation I had for the style of play they embraced. Commentary work depends to some extent on the quality of play in each game. A 'war of attrition,' such as the Scotland v Wales match at Murrayfield in 1963, is heavy going and difficult to make interesting for the viewers. On the other hand, most Welsh games in that successful spell were full of movement and skill and you just could not help being stimulated and motivated by what was happening on the pitch and communicating this enjoyment to the viewers. Once, at Murrayfield a group of Welsh supporters carried a huge banner proclaiming that 'Bill McLaren is a Welshman.' I was not amused by that because I am a Scot and very proud of it. I came to realise, however, that in a way the Welsh lads had associated me with the thrilling play of their national teams because my enthusiasm for their method was there for all to see and hear.

Gareth Edwards was a most likeable personality. He developed a taste for 'Hawick balls,' a mint sweet manufactured by the Hill family in Hawick and now by Billy Smith of the bakery shops, the former Hawick Trades stand-off whose father, R.T. 'Firpo' Smith, played seven times for Scotland as a tight-forward out of the Kelso club in 1929 and 1930. I used to tease Gareth that most of his twenty tries for Wales were scored because he had a Hawick ball prior to the match, but I always made a point of not offering him any at all before a Scottish match!' It obviously didn't do a lot of good because six of his international tries were against Scotland, although he found it tough going at Murrayfield in 1973 and 1975. Edwards brought another dimension to the international game with the length of his pass, especially off his right hand. It spun for miles and, because of its length rather than its speed, it gave his partner extra time and room in which to choose his option. His partner being none other than Barry John made for a formidable liaison and they were at the very hub of the Welsh machine for some 23 internationals. Edwards also was the most athletic scrum-half one can remember and possessed of the strength of a young bull. He was positively lethal from close range, and although his natural instinct was to take on the opposition to the detriment occasionally of those outside him, his scoring record speaks for itself, not to mention the many other tries he created simply by engaging the opposition in his distinctive physical manner.

I remember Gareth once saying that he would rather reel in a big salmon after a good fight than score a try for Wales. He just loves his angling. Once he told me about a catch he had made: 'I tell you, Bill, it was fully seventeen pounds. It was bigger than Barry John.' Prior to one Murrayfield international he had a couple of days fishing on the Tweed at Kelso. There he was up to his waders and just under the main bridge at Kelso when three beery faces appeared on the bridge all festooned in the red and white of Wales. The three Welsh supporters gazed down, then came out with the 64,000-dollar question: 'Hey, Gar boyo, what you'm doin' down there?' Gareth thought of saying: 'I'm signing bloody autographs, in I?' – but instead he passed the time of day and got on with the lure and the contest with the inhabitants of the deep. One of the television delights that comes to mind was an interview conducted by Cliff Morgan with Gareth at the side of a river as Gareth plied his wand. Cliff was a master at letting the scenery tell its own story but, with just a little cajoling question every now and again, he painted the picture of a great international rugby player, accustomed to the idolatry of thousands, but utterly contented in the quiet rippling beauty of the riverside; Cliff elicited from Gareth a recollection of his father's admonition that 'you'd score a lot more tries for Wales if it wasn't for those rusty kneecaps of yours from all that fishing!'

Barry John cut a jaunty figure, cocky even, but with acceptable arrogance. He was just so confident in his own ability, a confidence thoroughly justified by events as this slim, wraith-like fellow wove his magic patterns with special instinct and feel. He just seemed to materialise then drift like some boyish phantom through space even where no space seemed to exist. It once was said that Barry John never seemed to leave a room by the door, he just drifted through the wall. He could torture opponents with the pin-point accuracy of his punting, and although he made no bones about his belief that tackling bigger fellows was for bigger fellows, he yet made his contribution when the call came, once notably sinking that mighty Frenchman, Benoit Dauga, in a crucial Championship decider when Barry John's unique gifts carried the day. Yet he often took an indifferent attitude to the serious business of preparation and motivation. Clive Rowlands told me that even as he was giving one of his last-minute calls to duty to the Welsh team with a stirring demand for all of their traditional national pride to rise up in the cause, Barry would be sitting at the back quietly whistling away to himself almost oblivious to what was going on in the still drama of the room.

I well recall the first international appearances of J.P.R. Williams and Mervyn Davies. That was against Scotland at Murrayfield in February 1969. J.P.R. simply oozed aggression as he was to do throughout his career, but Mervyn looked like a very slim, moving coat-hanger, a lanky drain-pipe, who nonetheless immediately showed his bravery by falling on or over the ball on numerous occasions. Brian Price said after the game that the Scots had killed the ball all afternoon but Mervyn certainly did his whack as well! He didn't have to do a lot at the lineout, where he was later to prove a dependable ball-winner, because on that afternoon Brian Price, the Welsh captain, simply dominated the middle of the line. He was a super specialist and Bill Hunter, the Hawick and Scotland lock who knew his way about the lineout as well, once named Price as one of the most effective lineout men he ever played against. J.P.R. made a quietly efficient debut by performing the orthodox full-back chores without blemish as he was to do for 54 of his 55 internationals - remember he once played as a flanker in an international against Australia in Sydney in 1978. In that first international, J.P.R. was expected to come into the attack line a lot as he had been doing to such effect for the London Welsh side who were putting together some marvellously fluent play with Williams a key figure. But after the game the famous Welsh writer, Vivian Jenkins, expressed his disappointment that only once had Williams ventured forth. 'It looked,' he wrote, 'as if J.P.R. Williams had been told to tone down his normal game.' Whether that was so or not, it certainly did not apply to his subsequent appearances for Wales in which he was to prove one of the most deadly of intruding full-backs, such was his sense of timing, his skill level and his total commitment to getting over the line or helping someone else to do so. J.P.R. surely was more responsible than anyone for the Grand Slam that Wales won in 1971, for in the game that Wales should have lost to Scotland at Murrayfield with Scotland leading 18-14 with time almost up, it was the perfect intrusion by J.P.R. that won the game for Wales. The other thing that always struck me about J.P.R. was his complete confidence in his own ability. Before the 1970 Wales v Scotland match in Cardiff the Welsh players were out on the pitch checking the conditions. A buffeting wind was sure to be a factor. As they came off the pitch I said to J.P.R. that it would be very difficult to deal with the high ball in the wind. 'Difficult perhaps, Bill' he said, 'but if someone drops a high one you can be sure it won't be me.' It was said in a matter-of-fact tone without apparent bombast. He just was so sure that his technique and powers of concentration would hold up under any pressure and he was right. And yet Andy Irvine was the most exciting full-back I've ever seen and he would be the number one choice for any World fifteen I had to select, because when he tilted his lance from the deep or as a decoy runner or in intrusion play, he just made everyone sit up and take notice. It was a wee disappointment for me that I was not doing commentary at the Scotland v France match at Murrayfield in February 1980 when the French led Scotland by 14-4 with only 12 minutes left. Irvine had missed several kicks at goal and had been given a bit of stick from the crowd. Then he scored two tries and two penalty goals as well as one conversion, 16 of the 18 points that the Scots scored for an astonishing victory by 22-14. That was Irvine at his exciting best, recapturing the form he had shown scoring five tries from full-back for the British Lions against King Country/Wanganui, coached by the legendary Colin Meads, in 1977. But if your life depended upon someone to catch a high garryowen in a stiff breeze and to stay on his feet until help arrived, J.P.R. would be your man. Nowadays, Gavin Hastings is the one you would select for that onerous task.

Had I been a winger the one player I would have least liked to mark was Gerald Davies. He was the greatest winger I ever saw. I first came across him when he was a student at Loughborough Colleges in the early sixties. They had a very good seven about that time, full of extremely fit, young students of physical education who could run all day, and they competed with success on the Border circuit, winning the Gala tournament in 1965 and the 'Blue Riband' Melrose event in 1968 and 1969. Thomas Gerald Reames Davies played in the winning seven at Galashiels on the wing, he was just turned twenty and he exhibited the side-step, change of pace and transference skills and timing that were to mark him out later as a truly great international player, even by the demanding standards of the Welsh game. He was the greatest at making a little go a long way, especially where space was concerned and I, like most others, boggled in amazement at the television screen one Sunday when it showed him scoring four tries against, of all people, Pontypool when at the height of their powers. In each case he seemed to be hemmed in with nowhere to go but such were his powers of observation and deception that he found a way to the line.

There have been some highly gifted wings in Rugby Union during the post-war years but if I was to select a Best-Ever fifteen Gerald Davies would be the second name I would write down, the first being Andy Irvine. The other wing would be David Campese of Australia because I would want my team to have a fair whack of the adventurous spirit and Campese was one of the most swashbuckling of Rugby buccaneers. He had a gift, too, for putting the finishing touch with a magical sequence. Two such situations come readily to mind. The 1984 touring Wallabies were going for their first ever Grand Slam against the four home countries at Murrayfield, having already beaten England (19-3), Ireland (16-9), and Wales (28-9). Campese had already scored an early try against Scotland and admittedly Australia were ahead by a fairly comfortable 31-12 when he drew down the final curtain with panache but, even so, the score was in every sense typical of his approach to the Rugby Union game. Keith Robertson had made a curving incision in his characteristic style, but when Iain Milne's pass was intercepted by Peter Grigg and Mark Ella fed Campese there was no thought in the Campese mind of booting to touch and stabilising the situation. He counter-attacked, ignited Steve Tuynman, one of the finds of the tour, and then looped him to gather in his pass and run fifty metres pursued by John Beattie for a try that brought the Murrayfield stand to its feet. Four years later in the Barbarians v Australia game at Cardiff, Campese once again rang down the curtain on another wonderful match with a late try that really did bring the house down. The move leading to that score seemed to me to encapsulate almost all of the admirable features of the Australian game. It is my view that one of the most fertile areas from which to attack the opposition by handling is when they have been attacking and have lost the ball. So often in such circumstances the defending side get such a shock at suddenly finding themselves in possession, especially in club play, that instinctively they hoof it away in a kind of panic rather than consider their options. The Wallabies didn't. Barbarians were on full flow attack. Rory Underwood had scissored inside off Mark Ring when he was floored with a copybook tackle by Steve Tuynman. There was one aspect of the Australian game that pointed a simple lesson – opponents put on the floor are momentarily out of the game. When Underwood's pass ricocheted to Nick Farr-Jones on half-way, it just never entered his head to put boot to ball. Instead he gave a typical demonstration of Australian ball manipulation with a low-swung, one-handed flick pass to Jeff Miller who, like the dynamic flanker he is, was right at the

perfect support point on Farr-Jones's left. Miller then took out an opponent before launching Tuynman who had shown another crucial aspect
of Australian play. He, after all, had just put in a scything tackle on
Underwood and had been on the floor too. Yet here he was, seconds
later, in perfect position to carry on the move. When Tuynman created a
ruck target, superb lay-back led to three inch-perfect passes – Farr-Jones
to Lloyd Walker to Michael Cook to David Campese. Each of those
passes was a spin-pass which brought to mind that I had spent some time
discouraging my Hawick primary schoolboy players from spinning their
passes because of the delay they created in getting the ball into the correct position in their hands in order to spin it. There was simply no delay
in those Australian passes and the effect was to provide Campese with
several options in quite a bit of space. He had stand-off Michael Lynagh
outside him (what was he doing in the wing position? Answer - playing
it off the top of his head with an astute feel for where to be and when)
but Campese then put together just about every aspect of fair deception
that the game has to offer. His change of pace took him outside Gavin
Hastings. He then veered inside Matt Duncan, came off his left foot,
then off his right foot, to leave Jonathan Davies in his wake, before
cantering in at the posts. It was a marvellous example of body control
and balance at speed and it drew from the Cardiff crowd one of the fon-
dest tributes I have ever heard from them. You could have been excused
for thinking that Gareth Edwards had just scored a last-minute try to
win a game for his beloved Wales. The Welsh can be intensely parochial,
sometimes patronising, unfailingly confident, but at that moment they
responded to individual brilliance in the most sporting and heart-felt
manner, as indeed one had heard them do on other occasions when
opponents touched the height of individual or collective genius.

Campese is just about my favourite player. He ranks alongside Andy
Irvine for providing that element of uncertainty, at times of apparent
eccentricity, within the framework of a keen sense of adventure that
would seldom be stifled even in the red-hot, competitive atmosphere of
an international. One of my regrets is that I never had the chance of
doing commentary on a seven-a-side tie in which Campese and Irvine
were in the same side. Put Gerald Davies outside them, give them three
ball-winning forwards and a quick scrum-half and then just sit back in
delight. My heart bled for Campese when his pass to full-back Greg
Martin didn't go to hand and Ieuan Evans scored the crucial try for the
British Lions in the third Test at Sydney in 1989. Of course, a relief punt

would have served Australia adequately just to give them the chance to re-marshall their forces at a lineout and perhaps even win the ball back. But if the pass had gone into Martin's mitts, he would have been off up the touch-line with Campese in support. It could have been interesting. There was a point too that Evans, in his anxiety to get the ball first, did impede Martin. But there is so much illegal impeding of opponents going on unpunished in the game nowadays that it is hardly surprising that referee René Hourquet did not blow.

Campese has played over a dozen times at full-back in Australia Tests and he seemed ideally suited to the modern role of last lines of defence. One of the most stimulating developments in the game has been the emergence of full-backs as key players in attacking moves, because this has given an added dimension to attack ploys against well-drilled and determined defences and also because it has spawned several outstanding personalities as full-backs who fitted the new bill to perfection. The change was brought about by alterations to the law concerning offside lines behind the scrummage rear feet and ten metres behind the line of touch and, even more significantly, by the introduction of the Australian dispensation under which no player was permitted to gain ground by kicking the ball directly into touch from outside his own '25.' Backs found that they had a bit more space in which to run and the effect was to produce, in 1971, one of the most attractive Championship campaigns anyone could remember and a match between Scotland and Wales at Murrayfield that incorporated just about every enjoyable aspect of the Rugby Union game, including a closing try by the inimitable Gerald Davies that owed much to that typical timed intrusion by full-back J.P.R. Williams and that historic touch-line match-winning conversion by John Taylor that won the game for Wales by 19-18. That certainly was one of the truly memorable internationals that I have been fortunate enough to see.

Not that full-backs hadn't played some part as attackers. Indeed I was surprised to hear on a New Zealand video the legendary George Nepia, full-back in all 24 games of the 'Invincible All Blacks' tour in 1924-25, saying that even in those early days he had been keen to run out of defence and come up and help his colleagues in attack but was discouraged from doing so by the great centre-cum-five-eighth, Mark Nicholls, whose reason was that 'you may come up three times and score three tries but the fourth time you could drop it and the opposition could score a winning try; so stay where you are.' Vivian Jenkins, then of

Bridgend, scored an international try from full-back for Wales against Ireland at Swansea in 1934, the first to do so as even the Bancroft brothers, Billy and Jack, with 33 and 18 caps respectively, failed to score a try between them – from full-back. It just wasn't the done thing in those days. Full-backs were there to defend and clear their lines. But the seventies saw a marked change in full-backs' obligations. They were given a part to play in augmenting attack lines in rehearsed moves but also were given licence to attack 'off the top of their heads' with uncommitted wings given the job of covering the full-back position until the lad himself returned.

The three most outstanding attacking full-backs over the last twenty years, Campese apart, undoubtedly have been J.P.R. Williams of Wales, Andy Irvine of Scotland and Serge Blanco of France with John Gallagher of New Zealand challenging for a place had he not been enticed to the professional code when at the height of his powers in the Union game. Williams was the safest defensive full-back I have seen. In the basic chores of catch, clear, tackle, fall, call and cover he had no peer because he was so totally competitive and utterly fearless with a good, strong physique as well. But he also was a formidable force whenever he joined the attack, and apart from scoring 6 international tries from full-back, he was an artiste at timing his intrusions and his passes to the frequent effect of creating tries for others. He also was a past-master at fielding an inaccurate opposition punt and starting to run one way before cleverly switching the ball to a colleague running on another path altogether. Andy Irvine, more than others, seemed to have the forest animal's instinct for when to take off, so that he would suddenly erupt from a deep position and, with his mazy running, spawn the most thrilling counterattacks. He proved at one time slightly vulnerable under high-level bombing because he was inclined to be thinking too far ahead about what he was going to do before he had caught the ball, but he was sharp in recovery and when he had to tackle, he would do so without hesitation. But to see him field a loose punt and take off at whatever level of the game was one of rugby's joyous sights and in part explains why he held the world record for international tries from full-back with ten until Serge Blanco surpassed that mark.

Blanco has re-written the record books for tries in internationals from the last line berth with 31 at the time of writing as well as four others from the wing. Indeed, his second cap for France was against Scotland in 1981 and his position then was right-wing. So he promptly scored a try in the left corner. That was typically Blanco. He could be rattled into error although, when he was, he seldom failed to compensate with some subsequent spark of genius because he was a superb tactician and judge of exactly what was possible. He was sharp as a tack, too, as when he scored a decisive try against Scotland in the World Cup qualifying tie at Christchurch. Pierre Berbezier was injured and some of the Scots seemed to be awaiting his recovery when Blanco took a quick tap-penalty to himself and ran forty metres for a crucial try. Sharp practice? Referee Fred Howard was satisfied that it was fair. Even on the doorstep of thirty-two, Blanco remains a massive force and a source of confidence to his colleagues, as when he gathered the ball on his own line against The Wallabies at Brisbane in 24 June 1990 and ran the entire length of the field to dot down his second try in one of the great matches which Australia won 48-31. It seemed just impossible for him to have got anywhere near to scoring for he had David Campese, Ian Williams and Greg Martin as his close and constant companions. But the old guy made it, to a tremendous ovation. It is a point that those prolific try-scoring full-backs all have played far more games than the international full-backs of old. J.P.R. Williams, it has already been mentioned, played 54 of his full internationals in that position, Andy Irvine had 47 cap appearances for Scotland as full-back plus four as a wing and Serge Blanco now holds the world record for caps for his country with 88, of which 76 have been as full-back and 12 as wing. Even the feats of those three remarkable players might have been surpassed by John Gallagher, formerly of Askeans and London Irish, who burst on the scene as New Zealand full-back at the 1987 World Cup with four tries in the second game against Fiji and another against Scotland in the quarter-final. He proved one of the quickest full-backs ever seen with a well-developed instinct of where and when to materialise. There are those who point a finger at his defensive capabilities as having barely been tested, such has been the command and control exerted by the All Blacks sides in which he has played, but I have no doubt that Gallagher would have been equal to any task. Certainly his try-scoring record from the back berth is quite amazing – 13 tries in just 18 internationals, top try-scorer with 12 on the 1988 tour of Australia, and in all games for New Zealand a haul of 30 tries in 40 games. No wonder the Rugby League boys were willing to pay out what he wanted for his signature.

It saddens me that a country like France, capable of such heights of brilliance and handling play, should also have a poor record of discipline.

Every country has its hard men, some more than others, but the French have played some very mean guys indeed, if one is to believe the stories of very nasty acts, especially in scrummages, that have been perpetrated. Of the twenty-three players ordered off in cap internationals, eight have been French, and there is no doubt in my mind that indiscipline cost France the Grand Slam at Murrayfield in 1984. It was equally surprising that the French captain that day, Jean-Pierre Rives, a quite remarkable flanker for one of his slight physique, should be as guilty as his colleagues and fail completely to bring the right kind of influence to bear upon them. Penalties were even conceded a further ten metres forward and Peter Dods kicked beautifully, even with one eye completely closed. The French should have got the message early in the game that Winston Jones, the Welsh referee, wasn't going to stand for impudence from players.

But when they concentrate on the jewels of their game the French sparkle as no others can and one of the joys of the 1991 Championship was to see the French taking risks again, giving it a twirl by playing it off the top of their heads and setting aside any apprehensions about committing errors. Jean Trillo has had a lot to do with this. That is not meant to be a criticism of the style of Jacques Fouroux who proceeded him and Dubroca as coach. Fouroux split the French rugby support, half of whom thought he was too dependent on massive forward strength to the detriment of traditional back play, the other half pointing to his record as coach of two Grand Slam sides and of five which either won or shared the Five Nations Championship. Trillo certainly has given the French backs licence to keep the ball alive, to trust in their 'feel' for what is on, to believe in their skill levels, to attack from anywhere on the field and to be unafraid of error.

Perhaps the best example of this style at work was against Wales in Parc des Princes on 2 March 1991. Wales had just gained some extra confidence from a thrilling 21-21 draw against Ireland, who themselves had had the beating of France but let them off the hook. But the French simply took Wales apart. They beat them everywhere, but especially in the intricacies of their back play, which bedazzled the Welsh and yet were based on simple fundamentals – crispness, variety and split-second timing of passes, straight, direct running and instant bracket support for every ball-carrier. It was a wonderful game for a commentator: sweeping moves, players appearing like jack-rabbits in places where they weren't expected, six marvellous tries and a fairy-tale ending for Serge Blanco in what was to be his last Five Nations Championship match at that venue. With the last kick of the contest he converted from the left touch-line, with a perfect strike, a sizzling try by Jean-Baptiste Lafond to which Blanco himself had given final impetus with a meticulously timed pass. His performance had been one of dazzling skill and sheer elegance, and although there have been times when he has play-acted his way through injury like so many foreign soccer stars, the idolatry in which he is rightly held by the whole of French rugby can be measured by the mighty ovation he received. What a way to ring down the curtain. Yet in his moment of greatest triumph as captain and inspiration of a French team who had beaten Wales by a record score, Blanco ran over towards a little boy in a wheelchair and presented him with a gold statuette – a delightful gesture of kindness and compassion. Only a day before, Blanco had interrupted his training to be good enough to accede to my request that he autograph a message to our grandsons. What a talent. The only trouble with French men flicking the ball around like that is that it leaves commentators breathless and trying desperately hard to keep pace with the dazzling action.

11

All-Time Greats: Matches

It is impossible to select 'the greatest ever game' from all those I've covered for the BBC. There have been so many wonderful matches incorporating all the good things that Rugby Union has to offer, including a spirit of adventurism that isn't so common nowadays when the need to win is uppermost and teams tend to play safe, percentage rugby, or, as they always claim, 'play to our strength.' Almost without exception the strength referred to is the forwards, and the method of playing to them is to turn the ball back to them, to punt so as to keep the ball in front of them, to pick up and drive off the scrummages and to peel and roll out of the lineouts, all of that fascinating enough. But I wish more sides had been pledged to play to the strength of their backs as well.

The England side of 1991, for instance, had one of the most formidable packs I have ever seen and quite rightly used them a lot. But they also had the fastest backs in the Championship – Nigel Heslop, Will Carling, Jeremy Guscott, Rob Andrew and Rory Underwood, each a lethal runner and it really was disappointing that, in their opening games against Wales and Scotland, when England had established a comfortable lead on each occasion, they adhered to their percentage formula and hardly ever used their backs as an attacking force. Of course England can point to the success of their strategy. They won. And they are not alone in having adopted a safety-first cause. But with backs of the quality they possess they still would have won if they had given them their heads and the game as a spectacle would have benefited enormously. England had shown against Wales and France in 1990 just how devastating a style of total rugby they could embrace. In those games they touched a pinnacle of team play that none of their Championship rivals could attain, not even France. That is the England that supporters wanted to see. That is the England that could have enlivened the 1991 Championship and their thoroughly merited Grand Slam. They were a very good, competent side who could have been hailed as one of the greatest all round outfits of all time if only they had let their hair down more often.

In a way it is strange that a number of the most memorable matches I have covered have involved Scotland and Wales as opponents. Over the years those two countries have produced some magnificent contests, full of movement, skill, passion and commitment. I have mentioned the ten minutes of commentary as a trial run at the Scotland v Wales match at Murrayfield in 1953. Scotland felt that they could win. Wales had omitted their famous captain, John Gwilliam. Bleddyn Williams took over and, indeed, captained Wales five times, every time to victory. It was the first time I had seen Bleddyn in action. He celebrated his elevation to captaincy with two tries at Murrayfield and I remember thinking what a good player he was, armed with all the essentials of balance, running and elusiveness. Rees Stephens led the Welsh pack and on the previous day when they had a training spell, he didn't mince his words. Boy, did he tell them! Motivation methods nowadays are sophisticated and varied but there wasn't much wrong with the way Rees got home to his disciples exactly what he wanted from them. Quite a few Celtic oaths floated across Edinburgh that day and it worked. Wales won 12-0.

It was the first time also that I had seen the twinkling deceptiveness of Cliff Morgan. Little did I realise then that this little Welsh genius was to become something of a thorn in the side of the Scots. Certainly in following seasons Scottish team talks simply revolved around trying to curb the Morgan menace. He was so astute, so quick into his running with intuitive judgement of what was on; and he could play any type of game, although I always felt that he was happiest tilting at opponents with that scuttling action of his. On that day in 1953 his burly scrum-half partner Rex Willis was hurt and Cliff had to move to scrum-half and another favourite Welshman of mine, Clem Thomas, moved from wing-forward to the wing. It didn't make any difference. They fitted in as to the manner born. After all, a few months later Clem was to produce a historic cross-field punt from the left touch-line for Ken Jones to score a crucial try when Wales beat New Zealand 13-8 at Cardiff Arms Park. It was some cross-kick.

Rees Stephens once gave me a lift in his Landrover to Bray in Ireland so that I might see the Welsh team at training. I'll never forget that ex-

ABOVE Bette and I

ABOVE RIGHT Bette and I with 'Hitler Youth' grandchildren! Between us is Gregor. Front row, left to right: Rory, Lindsay, James and Alex

At an Air France evening at Hopetown House. Left to right: Alan, Linda, Bette, self, Janie, Derek

ABOVE Three Scotland breakaway forwards who have caused me some difficulty in identification. Left to right: Derek White, John Jeffrey and Derek Turnbull

With Nigel Starmer-Smith, Gareth Edwards and the late Bill Taylor

ABOVE LEFT David Leslie (Gala) was a key figure for Scotland at the lineout tail in their 1984 Grand Slam

ABOVE RIGHT Moment of triumph – Chris Gray (Nottingham), David Sole (Edinburgh Academicals), number 1, and Finlay Calder (Stewart's-Melville FP) celebrate Scotland's 1990 Grand Slam win over England at Murrayfield

Alan Tomes (Hawick), Scotland's most capped lock with 48, wins lineout ball against France in the 1984 Grand Slam decider, aided by a secure block from number 1, Jim Aitken (Gala), and Jim Calder (Stewart's-Melville FP) and with Alister Campbell (Hawick), number 4, on the peel

ABOVE With Bill Beaumont at Murrayfield

ABOVE RIGHT Our World Cup squad – producer Brian Rogers, director Dewi Griffiths and Nigel Starmer-Smith

Bette and I at Eden Park, Auckland, prior to the World Cup final

perience. Rees did not seem to me to have much in the way of road discipline. He drove on the theory that everyone else would get out of his way. When he found that he had missed a turning he didn't go along the motorway to the next exit; he simply wrenched the wheel round, churned straight across the central reservation and, in about two seconds, we were going the other way! More than once I found my right foot pressing on the floor boards on an imaginary brake during that trip. But the 'crack' was good even if I did arrive in a cold sweat. I was grateful indeed for the offer of a lift but relieved that Rees was not going back to Dublin. I felt ever so much safer on the bus going back!

Cliff Morgan has been a true friend of mine for many years and it is a friendship I have always treasured. An inspiration to me in many ways, he is a delightful companion, intense, dedicated and yet full of fun. He has had me in stitches with his fund of amusing stories and is always prepared to poke fun at himself. We always have been on the same wave-length in our love for the Rugby Union game and our desire to see it maintain a clean image. Like me he detests vicious play, longs for a return to the old days of true sportsmanship and worries about attitudes and the effect of commercialism on the true spirit of the game. He is one of the kindest persons I have ever come across. I owe him a lot. We joined forces first virtually at the outset of 'Rugby Special' on BBC Television. And it was all so enjoyable with Alan Mouncer as producer, Cliff as presenter and interviewer and me doing most of the commentaries. It was a privilege to work with two such gifted professionals. They taught me a lot.

My first away match in Wales as a commentator in 1954 provided another happy memory – except that Scotland lost! You may have heard stories of my reluctance to leave my house. I'm a very domesticated animal, never happier than when at home with Bette or in the company of our family, and readers will, I hope, understand if I digress for a paragraph or two. One of the joys for Bette and me has been the great affection that our two daughters, Linda and Janie, have always had for each other, even though they have set up their own family homes as far apart as Dollar in the Scottish Midlands and Chalfont St Giles in Buckinghamshire. Linda's husband is Alan Lawson who played 15 times for Scotland as scrumhalf and is now managing director of an international firm based in Kirkaldy, and Janie's husband is Derek Thompson who is presenter and interviewer for Channel 4 Racing. Linda and Alan have three children, Gregor (12 years old), Rory (9) and daughter Lindsay (7) who revels in country dancing and swimming. Janie and Derek have two sons,

Alex (9) and James (6). Gregor plays stand-off and full-back for Dollar Academy, Rory has been scrumhalf in a very successful Stirling County mini team and James, who lost a kidney when he was just 18 months old, is keen on all sports too. Alex and James are following in father's footsteps as keen horsemen. Alex, so far, hasn't shown any great interest in sport, but he will mend your Flymo and seems very interested in anything mechanical. His feeling about rugby could be summed up in one conversation I had with him. 'Do you take part in sport at your school?' I asked. 'Oh, yes, we have football, cricket, athletics and rugby.' 'What do you do when the ball comes towards you on the rugby pitch?' I queried. 'I go to the toilet,' was the forthright reply. Alex may not play for England or Scotland at Rugby Union but he won't be lost for an answer!

Although I refer humorously to our grandchildren as 'The Hitler Youth,' much to the annoyance of their parents, Bette and I are very proud of them all and delight in their company, after which we retire quietly to recharge our batteries. Mind you, it gets a bit wearing when grandsons regularly beat you at snooker. Once I actually considered cheating just to win but the sporting spirit forced me back from the brink and I lost again!

To get back to that first trip to Wales in 1954, it gave me a first taste of the new demands of a new interest but it was a thrilling venture and I remember feeling terribly excited, a bit concerned to do really well and, after it was all over, an all-consuming desire to get back home to hear what Bette thought about my performance. In those days I was working on the *Hawick Express* just waiting for a teaching vacancy to crop up so I had no problem about getting time off work to do the job. The paper editor, John Hood, who, as I related in Chapter 6, had persuaded me into doing that first audition commentary was very helpful with time off, with sage advice and with constant encouragement. How fortunate I have been in the good folk who have taken an interest in my welfare. I wish John Hood were alive today so that he could appreciate the great feeling of gratitude I have for all that he did for me in those early days.

That 1954 match was memorable in other ways. St. Helen's in Swansea had been a venue for Welsh internationals since the very first home game against England in 1882, but this was to be the very last time that famous ground would be used for a Rugby Union international. Since six weeks previously I had shared commentary with the inimitable Sammy Walker at the Ireland v Scotland match at Ravenhill in Belfast, I can claim to have been present when the last internationals were played at these two legendary grounds. I don't believe that my presence had anything to do with those decisions! The Welsh Rugby Union knew that revenue at Cardiff Arms Park would be greater because of larger seating capacity, hence the need to move. In that 1954 game, which had been postponed in January because of a big freeze and was played in the most delightful conditions on the 10 April, the legendary Ken Jones was given captaincy to mark his equalling the then Welsh record of thirty-five caps held by Dicky Owen. The Welsh lads did everything they could to provide Ken Jones with a try – he scored seventeen for Wales and was one of the fastest men ever to pull on a rugby jersey – but he didn't manage to leave his mark on the game in that way. Despite that, they won 15-3 and I still can see Cliff Morgan scooting in for a typical try.

The 1956 game at Cardiff provided a remarkable pre-match ritual. The ground was frozen so the Welsh committee decided on a repeat of their success of 1893, the match with England, when they burned eighteen tons of coal during the night to soften the pitch. In 1956 they didn't have quite as many braziers (referred to in a radio broadcast by the then president of the Welsh Rugby Union as 'dozens of brassieres') but the match went on and it produced a classic Welsh try out of the then innovative ploy by which Onllwyn Brace, the Welsh scrum-half, ran laterally from a scrummage across the field and his partner Cliff Morgan did a perfect scissors at high speed and sailed in at the post untouched for a cracker of a try.

I have vivid recall of the 1962 Wales v Scotland game at Cardiff - because I wasn't there! Scottish BBC wanted me to do the TV commentary on the game; London BBC said Peter West would be doing it. London won. Before the game I wasn't particularly upset about that decision. BBC Scotland arranged for me to watch the match on television and then give some comments on it in their early evening programme. Not only that, but I always have had a high respect and admiration for Peter West. We worked together on several matches, sharing commentary, and I did enjoy that. Peter was the complete professional with a delightful turn of phrase and sense of fair play. Once, with rain battering down into the sea of mud and water that was Cardiff Arms Park prior to a Wales v Ireland game, he and I sang a verse of 'It's a great day for the Irish.' It wouldn't have got to first base in the Eurovision Song Contest but it was thoroughly appropriate because the Irish revelled in such conditions, which were very much against traditional Welsh back play, and as we sang, our producer Dewi Griffiths, another out of the top drawer, had his cameras start at our feet, which were under water, and work upwards to our battered golf umbrella and the West-McLaren choir in full voice. Actually I felt a bit of a 'wally' but it went down quite well although Peter and I were not invited to cut a disc.

Working with Peter was a pleasure, not only because he is one of nature's gentlemen but also because having two commentators meant you could use the system of having twenty-minute breaks in which to stand back and form a deeper analysis of the game, just like Sammy Walker and I used to do on radio. So when the BBC decided to have just the one voice in commentary I wrote to Peter Dimmock, then Head of Sport, expressing preference for the two commentators arrangement and how much I enjoyed working with Peter West. To no avail.

Of course in retrospect I was disappointed not to have been in Cardiff for that 1962 match, partly because Scotland won 8-3, their first win in Wales for twenty-five years, and their first win in Cardiff for thirty-five years, with that fire-brand Scottish flanker, Ron Glasgow (Dunfermline), scoring the first Scottish try in Cardiff for twenty-seven years. It was a historic victory that ended with Hugh McLeod of Hawick being chaired off the field to mark his new Scottish caps record of thirty-eight, to beat the thirty-seven of that other great Scot John Bannerman (Glasgow High School F.P.). The other Scottish try was by the big London Scot Frans ten Bos. Hugh McLeod, who led the pack on that occasion, is just about the most honest and forthright person I have ever known. As a player he never backed off. As a person he doesn't back off. He was at the heart of one of my favourite stories. He was asked to lead Scotland's pack but turned it down on the grounds that he wanted to concentrate on his own job as prop. Alf Wilson, however, a Scottish selector of strong character, insisted that Hugh should take on the leadership of the pack. Reluctantly Hugh agreed but, at the Friday training session, when several of the pack were voicing opinions about what they should do and how, Hugh made one of his most memorable speeches: 'Come here, my wee disciples,' he said. When they all had gathered round he continued: 'Now, ah want tae tell ee that ah've been asked ti lead this pack tomorrow, that ah'm no very keen on the job and if any of you lot want to be pack-leader, just let me know and ah'll put a word in for you at the right place. Meanwhile, the next one who opens his trap will get my boot bloody hard at his arse.' They reckoned that one of the Anglo-Scots said to a pal 'Well, I didn't understand a word of that but it all sounded dammed impressive!' It must have been because, on the morrow, the

Scottish pack went like bombs, claimed the two Scottish tries and won the day. That was one of the most effective Scottish packs I can remember. Hugh McLeod (Hawick); Norman Bruce (London Scottish); David Rollo (Howe of Fife); Frans ten Bos (London Scottish); Mike Campbell-Lamerton (Halifax); Ron Glasgow (Dunfermline); John Douglas (Stewarts College F.P.) and Ken Ross (Boroughmuir).

That wasn't the only inspirational speech Hugh Ferns McLeod delivered at the pithead. I think it was in 1963, on the eve of the France v Scotland game in Paris, that Hugh and I went out for a quiet meal on our own as neither of us was very keen on going to the casino. On our way back to our hotel we came across Frans ten Bos who invited us to join him for a cup of coffee in a wee cafe across the road. So in we went. I could see that Hugh had something on his mind and I didn't have long to wait. He took a sip of his coffee, then looked the giant Frans straight in the eye before delivering this broadside: 'Frans, ye think ye're a guid forrit but really ye're jist a big lump o' potted meat. Ah'm goin ti tell ye somethin'. If ah was half yer size ah'd pick up the first two Frenchmen that looked at me the morn and ah'd chuck them right ower the bloody stand.' As we left the cafe big Frans tapped me on the shoulder and said; 'You know, I'd follow him anywhere.' The following day Frans had his greatest game for Scotland who won by 11 points to 6, with a late try from Ronnie Thomson (London Scottish), the right wing, who scored in the left corner after appearing like some friendly genie to gather in an evil bounce from a mishit drop goal attempt by Iain Laughland (London Scottish). It was prior to that match that the French groundstaff took startling action to ensure that it would go ahead. The pitch was frozen hard in patches under the uneven straw covering so they simply put a match to the whole lot. It looked as if Colombes stadium was on fire, but it did the trick. The pitch had a grey, grassless look to it at the kick-off but the game went on.

A match I wish I could forget is the 1963 '111 lineouts' Scotland v Wales game at Murrayfield mentioned in Chapter 7. I'll never ever forget it. I've pulled Clive Rowlands' leg about it several times as having given me the toughest commentary job I have ever experienced. The weather was poor, sleety slosh, and Clive, as the Welsh captain, had decided that the Welsh pack would take on the big Scots eight in a head-to-head confrontation. So the game became a war of attrition up and down the touchlines. That victory for Clive's team broke a run of four consecutive Welsh defeats at Murrayfield. The irritating point was that, towards the end, the Scots, in desperation, began to move the ball wide and suddenly they had Wales in trouble. Too late. But surely there is a lesson there. Time and again in recent seasons I have seen teams play to a tight, safety-first format and then, late on, when they see defeat staring them in the face, they open out with some delightful handling play. The point is: Why not *early* in the game? Why wait till the writing is on the wall? The game would benefit in so many ways. Incidentally, shortly after that match, Hawick met Melrose at Mansfield Park in an important mid-week Border League match. There were 108 line-outs!

Ten years before that, in 1953, I had a new experience – my first away assignment as commentator when England were going for their first Championship for sixteen years and they did it in style with a 26-8 win over the Scots at Twickenham. Only a fortnight previously Scotland had lost to Ireland at Murrayfield – by 26-8! They were dark days indeed. The English players always looked far bigger and heavier than the Scots who always were out-played in the frontal exchanges, so that the Scottish backs had very few opportunities to shine as attackers and spent most of their time chasing and tackling.

It was one of my ambitions before I handed in my dinner pail to be doing commentary when Scotland won the Triple Crown. I had been present as a school-boy when they last did so at Twickenham in 1938, and I think the disappointments I had experienced each time Scotland failed to clinch the Crown merely heightened my desire to be there when eventually they did so. I did have that satisfaction. That was in Dublin in 1984 when Scotland scored five cracking tries in beating Ireland 32-9. What is more, they went on to beat France at Murrayfield to gather in the Grand Slam – and I was delighted to have been commentator for each one of their four games. But there were disappointments prior to that achievement. In 1955, 1961, 1973 and 1975 Scotland went to Twickenham requiring victory over England to win a Triple Crown. Each time they were thwarted.

The biggest disappointment was in 1955 because, with England ahead at 9-6 the Gala prop, Tom Elliot, a son of the soil and as honest as the day is long, had no doubt whatever that he scored a try under the English posts that would have given Scotland an easy conversion and victory by 11-9. But the Welsh referee, D.C. Johnson, disallowed the try. I don't remember a lot about the game except that there was one excellent head-on tackle by the Melrose full-back, Robin Chisholm, that prevented a certain score by Jeff Butterfield of Northampton, a world-class centre of vast talent. And I remember the inspiring example set by the Scottish captain. Angus Cameron (Glasgow High School F.P.) who added to his early penalty goal a fine try stemming from his own up-and-under. No-one could hoist a garryowen any more effectively than Angus. He was a past master and, with his powerful frame, a hard man to check when on full throttle.

In 1961 the Scottish selectors, in my view, were in error in changing Scotland's very successful loose forward trio of Ken Ross (Borough-muir), John Douglas (Stewart's College F.P.) and Ken Smith (Kelso) by moving Douglas to lock in place of the injured Mike Campbell-Lamerton, switching Smith to number eight and introducing John Brash (Cambridge University). The feeling was, and I agreed with it, that Scotland should have gone for an out-and-out lock for Campbell-Lamerton's place because Brash, a good footballer, played very loose but, on this occasion, not too effectively, and England's stand-off, Phil Horrocks-Taylor was permitted to take a commanding role in England's 6-0 win.

In 1973 there could be no complaint. England's pack were dominant and I remember one grand forwards' try scored by Peter Dixon from one of the most copy-book, high-speed line-out peels you could imagine, with Fran Cotton in a key link role. I was grateful to Fran that he took no exception to a comment of mine in a 'Grandstand' preview of a Twickenham game. I had been invited to have dinner with the English party on the eve of the game. When I was asked, I think by David Coleman introducing 'Grandstand,' what I thought of Fran Cotton, I said that I hadn't yet seen the big lad play but that I'd seen him deal with a five course dinner and that had been very impressive indeed! Fran took it in good spirit. I think if asked to select the best English side in the post-war years Fran would be one of the first names I would pencil in.

Finally we come to 1975. I have a painful memory of that one, and not only because Scotland lost a game they should have won – and deserved to win. I made a mistake in commentary that worried me for quite some time because I couldn't understand why it had happened. Scotland were leading 6-3 when Peter Warfield of Cambridge University made a harm-less-looking punt which Scottish full-back Andy Irvine had covered. But a cruel bounce enabled Alan Morley to be awarded a try. What con-cerned me was that I initially gave the try to England's other wing Peter Squires of Harrogate. I couldn't fathom that because I saw Alan Mor-ley's number – 11. I had had no trouble with identification all afternoon. Of course I corrected the error right away although, in such a situation, you tend to fear the worst, that you have taken ages to get it right. In fact there were only a few seconds in it. I was so upset that it almost (not quite) spoiled the dinner in an Italian restaurant that I had arranged for Bette and our daughters, Linda and Janie aged 23 and 21 respectively. A good friend of mine, John Downie, a much respected rugby correspondent of the *Glasgow Herald* and BBC radio commentator, reckoned I had suffered a 'juxtaposition of thought.' That was a bit technical for a mere PE teacher! I hoped, however, that it wouldn't happen again. I heard later that when I said that Peter Squires had scored, Alan's mum leapt to her feet in her home and shouted; 'That's our Alan, you fool!'

Well, it did happen again but, fortunately, it took a further sixteen years to do so. At the Wales v England game at Cardiff Arms Park in 1991 the ball came to Ieuan Evans of Llanelli. It was on the right wing and the number 14 was clearly visible. It was late in the game. I said it was Steve Ford, the other wing. Again I corrected it within seconds – or, at least, as soon as my producer, Dewi Griffiths, steeped in the rugby game, bawled into my earphones: 'Evans! Ieuan Evans!' I got the message. Juxtapositions, or whatever, can be very trying. They even can put you off your food. I must take this opportunity of saying that I enjoy broadcasting from Twickenham. It was the first of the current away International venues that I ever saw – on a visit with my father in 1936. I was quite over-awed at the sight of those three big, brooding stands. And the commentary position is first-class, giving a great view of the proceedings. There is no more invigorating sight in Rugby union than that of Frenchmen, with sun on their backs, giving full expression to their adventurous spirit and flair, and I can think of no better examples than two matches against England that I covered at Colombes stadium in 1970 and 1972. England were just unlucky on those occasions to be at the receiving end of some of the most wonderful rugby you ever could imagine. France won those two games 35-13 and 37-12. Fifteen tries were scored, twelve by France. In the 1970 match England's threequarter line read: Keith Fielding, David Duckham, John Spencer and John Novak and among the forwards were John Pullin, Keith Fairbrother, Peter Larter, Tony Bucknall and Bob Taylor.

Yet they were put to the sword. French tight forwards had begun to get their priorities right by doing the graft first and not seeing themselves as fly-by-night 'loosies!' They had genuine donkeys such as Elie Cester and wonderfully versatile big men like the number eight-cum-lock, Benoit Dauga. What a forward he was, a huge, dour, glowering lump who could win lineout ball and knew how to use it in the open play. And the entire back division comprised express trains, among them Jean Trillo who, in 1991, became the French backs' adviser under Daniel Dubroca's coaching and who had some harsh words to utter about the modern Frenchman's lack of style and handling expertise. Behind was the complete full-back, Pierre Villepreux who, in 1970 against England, scored four conversions, one penalty-goal and one drop-goal and in the 1972 game, five conversions and a penalty-goal. Believe it or not, for that 1972 match the French selectors, goaded by the newspaper critic who wrote 'our rugby is at the gates of hell,' made ten changes. Jo Maso, Jean-Pierre Lux, Bernard Duprat and Jean Sillieres provided a threequarter line of scorching pace and guile and the Spanghero brothers, Claude and Walter, were in the pack.

Those Frenchmen played spectacular fifteen-man rugby at blistering speed and their skill-level was so high that England, despite their admirable spirit and resilience, were simply out-played and out-run. That 1972 match was the last Rugby Union international played at Colombes stadium. In view of the facilities for commentators there, I wasn't all that sorry. It never stood comparison with those at Twickenham, Murrayfield, Lansdowne Road and Cardiff.

One of the most frenzied matches I ever attended was when Wales met Ireland at Cardiff in 1969 with the Triple Crown at stake for the Irish. That was the famous occasion of the Brian Price punch. Brian was another of those outstanding Welsh lineout exponents, rated by my Hawick friend, Billy Hunter, as just about the best he had ever played against. Brian also was pretty fair and not one you would expect to see throwing punches about. But this time he hit Noel Murphy, the Irish flanker, a rare old lick. Brian was reported afterwards as claiming, 'a pair of hands clawed at my head and went for my eyes and I had no idea who did it so I just swung round.' The Scottish referee Douglas McMahon, was quoted as saying that 'there was a lot at stake and some of the fellows got a bit excited.' The comment I enjoyed the most was by Uel Titley, the *Times* rugby correspondent, when we discussed the incident whilst waiting for the London train at Cardiff station. Uel was an old school southern gentleman type, always impeccably dressed and a gifted rugby correspondent. Since the young Prince of Wales had been at the game Uel's summing-up comprised: 'It was awful. I felt ghastly for the Prince.'

12

Fine-Tuning The Laws

I have already referred to the dire 1963 match between Scotland and Wales, in which there were 111 lineouts. That appalling statistic gave many people the feeling, as it did me at the time, that the Rugby Union game was dying on its feet because the laws favoured defences, and backs wishing to attack by handling were subjected to the most claustrophobic pressure. Once, in a Scottish trial George Stevenson of Hawick, capped 23 times as a threequarter, a strongly built extrovert, known affectionately to all as 'Stevie' and a rare character, subject on occasions to outrageous eccentricity, said to his stand-off: 'Look, son, will you stop putting the ball out and try a wee kick or two because we are being murdered out here?' The general effect on the game at all levels was to discourage backs from handling attack in case the intense pressure forced them into errors that would be exploited by their opponents. So there was a rash of punting, mostly to touch as there was no restriction then on putting the ball out of play from any part of the pitch. Hence a century of lineouts.

It was desperate viewing and it spoke volumes for the enthusiasm and love of the game that supporters still turned up at all levels. Happily, laws were altered. The Australian dispensation, limiting direct touch-kicking to inside the '25' areas (now the '22-metre' areas), and the introduction of the scrummage rear feet and lineout ten-metres offside lines did help. All the same, gifted players have now mastered the art of bouncing their kicks into touch and when this is coupled with a plethora of up-and-unders, the game is in danger of going back to those days when even talented players were afraid to spin the ball in case mistakes resulted. In the England v Scotland match at Twickenham in 1991 Rob

Andrew, who has developed into the complete stand-off, gave a superb exhibition of bouncing kicks into touch from inside the Scottish half, but how much more entertaining it would have been had he moved the ball by hand to his backs even just occasionally. There are so many up-and-unders kicked in the modern game that full-backs spend much of their time looking skywards, risking cricks in their necks, all the while offering up silent prayers to the Almighty to see them safely through each ordeal. Full-backs nowadays have to be strong in character and courage especially when they stand under a garryowen that seems to take ages to come down as the pounding of enemy hooves grows ever closer. Insurance premiums on full-backs are naturally quite expensive! Hence the value of having a big chap of 15 stones like Gavin Hastings, who has impressive static strength and can stay upright when the hordes arrive. Then, of course, you have a contrast in the slightly-built Simon Hodgkinson of Nottingham and England, a talented footballer, although there is a fair point to be made that he doesn't have quite so many up-and-unders to deal with because his forwards, a dominant force, don't allow the opposition enough ball with which to bombard him!

One other point about the modern game that tends to contribute to so much punting is the manner in which defence play has developed. Nowadays, through watching videos, opposition strengths and weaknesses are studied in detail by tactically astute coaches who then plan their defence strategy accordingly. Times have changed from those post-war days when, on one occasion, Andrew Bowie, a famous Hawick stalwart, asked Cecil Froud and myself, the Hawick wing-forwards of the day, what plans we had for dealing with opponents in possession. Cecil's reply was to the point: 'Oo're gawn tae tackle the bluidy man wi' the ba'.' That was the extent of our defence planning in those days, when in my view, ignorance was bliss and the game was played more or less 'off the cuff'. You made it up as you went along. Now everything is planned and perfected. Not only that, but defenders now are physically far fitter, far stronger, than in those earlier times. They are, too, far more committed to the need for knocking opponents backwards so that tackling now is very physical and bruising, as a means of thus transforming defence into attack. All of which contributes to that element of safety first that so inhibits a lot of the rugby played nowadays.

That is not to say that there aren't joyous moments from the field of play. There have been some wonderfully entertaining games. Scotland v Ireland at Murrayfield in 1989 lifted the spirit, eight magnificent tries and exhilarating flow; Wales v Ireland 1991, six cracking tries, ebb and flow, a joy to watch. But the game needs more of that style, which is why I am a strong supporter of the Barbarians ideal. Heaven help the game if ever the Barbarians go out of existence and there is nothing to remind us of the priceless gifts the game has to offer when the approach is just right.

One other aspect of the game that has been disappointing to one of my vintage is the demise of the lineout catcher which, perhaps, to some degree, has been unavoidable but certainly has had an adverse effect on the quality of play. As a youngster who saw the great Border forwards of the thirties in action, and from my own experience as a young player before and after the second world war, it seemed to me that lineout catching was a must, that a player who didn't try to catch the ball at the lineouts was liable to get a broadside from some irate former stalwart standing on the touch-line. It is true that, in olden days, every player in the lineout was a potential catcher and that the thrower, usually the wing, had licence to throw to any one of his colleagues who seemed in the best position to catch the ball. That wasn't to say that there weren't specialist lineout men. My local hero, Jock Beattie, was renowned for his lineout play. So were Jock Allan of Melrose, Jack Waters of Selkirk and other greats. But there was far more spacing in olden times and other players in the line were used as jumpers too. And the aim generally was to catch the ball. One of the great early exponents was Bill Kyle, capped 21 times by Scotland between 1902 and 1910, idolised in my home town because he gained those caps in days when the 'old school tie' counted for so much in Scottish selection. Kyle's feat really established Border players as genuine cap contenders in the eyes of the hierarchy, although the first Borderer to be capped was Adam Dalgleish of Gala. In my own brief career as a forward it would never have dawned on me to knock the ball backwards. You simply were expected to try and catch it. Nowadays, of course, lineout players are far more street-wise in the arts of obstruction in its various forms and even the introduction of one-metre spacing at the lineout has not encouraged a return to the old methods. The result is that deflecting the ball has become the norm and has placed scrum-halves especially in the danger area. They can be sitting ducks to predators getting through or round the edges of the line to put fierce physical pressure on them as they try to cope with splintered ball.

There have been some gifted lineout practitioners who could deflect a throw-in on to a sixpence. Delme Thomas of Llanelli and Wales was a notable exponent. Time and again he rose like a rocketing pheasant and palmed ball to the desired spot for his scrum-half. One recalls that crucial try by Gerald Davies at Murrayfield in 1971 which, with John Taylor's touch-line conversion, won the match for Wales. It would never have happened but for the Delme Thomas expertise that was used so effectively for Wales, not only in attack but in defence situations as well. Whenever Wales really needed lineout ball, Delme almost invariably provided it. England's two most recent jumpers, Paul Ackford and Wade Dooley, have this gift as well, allied, as it is, to impressive physical dimension and to the talent possessed by Richard Hill of Bath, their scrum-half, who has the quickest clearance hands in the business. Even so I felt that men as big as Ackford (6ft 7ins) and Dooley (6ft 8ins) and reasonably athletic with it, should have caught the ball more, so as to provide a wider variety of option and, not least, so as to check opposing predators from their spoiling operations.

One of the most effective lineout players, despite his not being of gigantic proportions, was Bob Norster of Cardiff and Wales. He was just 6ft 4ins but a super jumper and timer of his jump and he often caused bigger fellows more embarrassment than anyone else. In the unexpected Welsh win over England at Cardiff in 1989 Norster was at the very core of that triumph by having the better of his lineout duel with Dooley. Another who jumped higher than anyone had a right to expect was the South African Frik du Preez, capped 24 times between 1960 and 1971. He was a magnificent lineout forward who also could scorch the grass with remarkable pace for a bulky man. Of course, in modern times, lineout specialists have to cheat if they hope to survive, because virtually everyone is out to gain every advantage in the cluttered confines. A little nudge here, a pull on the jersey there, a climb up an opponents shoulders somewhere else, an opposing prop driving in as well.

Lineout specialists have to look out for themselves and are cunning operators, using their knowledge of how differing referees will interpret the lineout law provisions. The International Board are really the governing body responsible for setting the laws and the tone by which the game will be played and administered worldwide. They haven't done a very good job of that. Some of their proposed law alterations over the years have confused and confounded referees. And although there have been meetings between top international referees and IB representatives, there still is no general uniformity in the way the laws are interpreted and administered. The lineout is a good example. Southern hemisphere and French referees tend to let the players referee the lineout. With some, anything goes. Referees from the home Unions have been inclined towards a stricter implementation, but some seem to be leaning more than ever to the Southern hemisphere style. I have to admit that I have come round to agreeing with this approach. If referees were to blow for every lineout offence they see, the game would barely get off first base. Good referees can sense when they have to take a firmer line to avoid a bit of knuckle developing, but some of the most entertaining games have owed much to sensible refereeing of the lineouts. What does irritate is when a referee blows for a long throw-in that is fractionally off the straight and yet permits squint putting-in to the scrummages. At least a lineout player can adjust his line of jump to cope with any deviation. A poor hooker is just stuck there and simply hasn't a hope if the opponents' put-in favours their own hooker. Once, Peter Brown of Gala and Scotland, one of the most dextrous of lineout specialists, hardly won a ball in the first half of a Scottish trial and only discovered late on that his opposite number, the lofty Hawick specialist, Billy Hunter, another of the game's distinctive personalities and a lineout corner-stone to Hawick's great run of success in the sixties, had been quietly standing on his foot throughout! Billy won quite a bit of ball that day and Peter learned quite a lot about the facts of life at the throw-in. Billy used to have colleagues rolling in the aisles with his blunt views, all spoken in broad Hawick dialect; 'They're jist a bunch o' boys, wet behind the ears,' he would say of opponents he had just cleaned out. And in the dressing room at the first of his seven international appearances, he broke the tension by standing up after tying his boot laces, clapping his hands and proclaiming: 'Right, boys, this is it. Mind ye this isnae the trailer. This is the big picture now.' His habit of always trying to catch lineout ball was underlined in one of Billy's many anecdotes. He tells of once rising for a ball with the intention of catching it but it skidded off his fingers and dropped down on Hawick's side, whereupon he felt a little tug on his jersey. It was Hugh McLeod, Hawick's forty-times capped prop, who snarled at the big man: 'Hey, pal, if ye cannae catch eet, leave eet alane. Somebody else'll catch eet.' H. F. McLeod always did call a spade a spade.

One of the most startling examples of the effect on a scrum-half of failure to catch the ball at the throw-in was at the Wales v Scotland game at Cardiff in 1966. It was a foul day. Cardiff Arms Park in those days could resemble a swamp. It always was going to be difficult to catch the ball which was as easy to grasp as an orange pip, but to have tapped ball back as often as the Scots forwards did that day was injudicious, to say the least. The victim was Scotland's scrum-half Alex Hastie of Melrose, who formed a thirteen-appearance half-back combination with his club partner, David Chisholm; not one of the first ten of those internationals was lost. Hastie was one of that Border breed of durable scrum-halves, all 'shilpit' little chaps, seeming in need of a good meal and all of whom, through operating behind lightweight packs always struggling for ball, had to live on their wits and their raw courage. Roy Laidlaw and Gary Armstrong, who have given the Jed-Forest club some of their proudest moments as Scotland's scrum-halves, are others of the same type, tough as old raw-hide, alert to the main chance, abrasive predators. Hawick's Greig Oliver is in the same mould. In times past, Hawick's scrum-halves, gifted players such as Glen Turnbull and Harry Whitaker, have been fortunate in playing behind dominant packs but unfortunate in that their cap prospects have been hampered through their inability to prove that they could function just as effectively behind struggling forwards. Recently, however, Hawick have fallen from the grace of their past halycon times and Greig has had to scratch and grovel in adverse conditions and he has done it so well as to retain his place on the bench as understudy to Gary Armstrong for Scotland's side. As for 1966 in Cardiff, I have vivid recall of Alex Hastie trying to deal with all kinds of ricochets from his forwards, time and again disappearing under a sea of scarlet jerseys, looking like a drowned prairie dog and never once shirking the onerous task in hand. It was just about the grittiest performance I have ever seen from a scrum-half and I recall writing at the time that he should have taken out a court action against his forwards claiming their responsibility for him being the victim of grievous bodily harm. Alex, however, got his own back against the Welsh at Murrayfield a year later when Scotland won by 11-5 in what should have been termed 'the Melrose game'. The Greenyards club had four players in the Scottish side – Alex Hastie, David Chisholm, hooker Frank Laidlaw and number eight Jim Telfer. That quartet had considerable influence on the outcome. David popped over a timely drop-goal and the other three all had a hand in Scotland's crucial try. Frank, (it was Norman Mair who said of Laidlaw that he regarded the loss of his own ball as he would a family bereavement) had a hand in Wales getting 'dodgy' scrummage ball, Alex harassed Welsh scrum-half Billy Hullin and fed Jim who galloped over. As someone has said on occasions during TV commentary 'they certainly will be celebrating at the Greenyards tonight'.

It was in the mid-sixties that I was privileged, and that's the only way to describe it, to be at Cardiff on two momentous occasions in which the humps and hollows of rugby fortunes were stressed in a marked degree. Wales had to beat France for their first retention of the Championship for fifty-seven years. Unusually, Wales named ten forwards and it was only on the morning of the match that they decided to leave out Denzil Williams and Brian Thomas and play Howard Norris (Cardiff) and Bill Morris (Newport) as being more suited to the conditions. I hoped that this secrecy would not become the trend as has happened in football, when often teams are not announced until the last moment, causing considerable headaches for commentators in trying to ensure that they have some background information about all the players who take the field. Happily, national selectors in Rugby Union announce their teams at least a week in advance, giving everyone time in which to research background details and get names and numbers into their heads.

The match was a contest full of commitment and passion and it had moments of high elation and total anguish. It also produced one of the most spectacular tries of all time. France were leading 8-6 and were on the attack with ten minutes left when Stuart Watkins, the strapping Newport wing, intercepted near his own '25' and ran seventy-five yards for a spectacular score, handing off the diminutive French full-back Claude Lacaze on the way. The same Lacaze, who was nicknamed 'Le Papillon' ('the butterfly'), still could have compensated by winning the game for France with a late penalty-goal. He struck it clean from the touch-line and it was going over when a gust of wind swung it past the post. My heart bled for Lacaze. I can still see him, his head bowed, absolutely miserable. As Willy John McBride once said to two young new caps on the eve of an Irish international: 'Aye boys, it can be a long, hard road.' I know how Lacaze felt. Once I missed a sitter of a conversion right in front of the posts for Hawick against an Army side on our own ground at the beginning of the second world war. You feel a right twit. Not only that but I got the expected ragging from team-mates and committee men. I thought that was a bit beyond the pale. We won by over fifty points! Which brings to mind a comment made away back in the olden days when one Hawick player missed an easy conversion and, as he ran back up the field expecting to get sympathy from his team mates, instead was greeted by the Hawick full-back with the caustic comment; 'I could have kicked a chest o' drawers over frae there.'

Another memorable match was between Scotland and Wales at Murrayfield in 1971. After so many tight, low-scoring matches in the late fifties and sixties, this was a breath of fresh air rated by everyone as just about the most exciting match they'd ever seen. It certainly was the most thrilling in my commentary career up till then. A riveting affair of ebb and flow, of massive endeavour and high skill and of sporting spirit. Wales had started out on their second golden era with Barry John and Gareth Edwards playing together for the eighteenth time and with J. P. R. Williams, Gerald Davies, John Dawes and John Bevan in the backs, and in a mighty pack they had one of the most effective loose-forward trios ever fielded by Wales – John Taylor, Mervyn Davies and David Morris. In those days I did the entire commentary and summaries on my own. So different nowadays, when I have the vast experience of Bill Beaumont to call on during breaks in the play.

In that 1971 game the wingers threw into the lineouts, in which the participants were closed tight together, in contrast to modern times when there has to be one-metre spacing between players and a gap of half-a-metre down the middle. There seems a distinct possibility, however, that before very long we will revert to the tight positioning and double banking of olden times to the general benefit. When the New Zealand referee David Bishop was in the UK in 1991 to officiate at the Scotland v Wales and Wales v Ireland games, he expressed the view to a meeting of the Border referees that spacing had spoiled the lineout play by providing gaps through which spoilers could pour whereas when lineouts were tightly closed, with players cluttered together, it did perhaps make lifting more difficult to detect, but it formed a natural block and the quality of the ball was higher with less pressure on the scrum-half. I've always believed, anyway, that lifting should be legalised, that a wee 'dookse', as we call it in Scotland, helps the jumper to get higher, and the lifter at least would have to concentrate on that and not on more nefarious pursuits.

It was interesting in that 1971 game that Peter Brown, Scotland's captain, opted for a lineout instead of a scrummage. Scotland had Peter, his brother Gordon and Alastair McHarg as their lineout providers and they had been doing pretty well, whereas the Welsh scrummage was over a stone a man heavier. I remember one magnificent early break by big centre John Frame, one of the five Gala players in the side, and J.P.R. Williams being awarded a mark on the Welsh ten-metres line (you can only do that now inside your own '22'); and there were six super tries. Scotland led four times and had Peter Brown not been unlucky enough to see his conversion of Chris Rea's flaring try hit the upright and stay out, it would have been all over. Scotland's lead would have been 20-14 and as tries then counted just three points, the final score would have been 20-19 to Scotland, whose other try was by the finest tight-head prop ever to play for Scotland, Sandy Carmichael of West of Scotland. Sandy churned through the front of a lineout, grabbed the bouncing ball and took Gareth Edwards with him over the line. Gareth had the look of a chap who has tried to stop a raging bull. It also was the unusual (certainly it would be unusual nowadays) sight of J.P.R. Williams taking a penalty kick at goal with the ball placed at an angle pointing towards the posts and with J.P.R. running straight on to it and kicking with his toe. So different now, with virtually every kicker using the round-the-corner method and hitting the ball with the inside edge of his foot. As we all know, Gerald Davies scorched in for a try at the corner, John Taylor made 'the finest conversion since St. Paul's' and Wales won 19-18. What a match!

Having already talked about the inconsistency in refereeing lineouts, it must be mentioned that the same problem occurs in other areas of the game. For example, in some countries referees are very strict about blowing for collapsed scrummages or mauls with safety very much in mind. In others they are prepared to allow the collapse situations to develop if there is a chance of the ball becoming available. The belief there is that the main danger in scrummages is when the two packs clunk together so that it is preferable to give the ball the chance of emerging from a fallen scrummage than to order another scrummage. For years southern hemisphere referees permitted a fierce form of rucking in which opponents could be rucked out with the ball. That was not acceptable to referees in the United Kingdom. But there has been some coming together here. In 1991 the Scottish Rugby Union issued a directive in which the southern hemisphere method received official approval. The directive, issued on 5 February 1991, stated; 'If a ruck is created from a tackle, players on their feet must be permitted to play the ball. This will involve legal use of the foot or feet to ruck the ball for continuity of play following a tackle. The rucking may well encompass the "rucking-back" of players lying on the ground in an endeavour to secure possession of the ball. This applies equally to forwards in the ruck and to the scrum-half behind the ruck legally using his foot to obtain the ball. *It must be emphasised that "stamping" is illegal, dangerous and will not be condoned. There is a clear difference in action and intent between stamping and rucking.*'

At least in this area, there is now some uniformity of intention.

13
Barred From The
International Feast

There has always been a quickening of the pulse when an All Blacks tour of the United Kingdom is about to start. And the same can be said of a tour of the Springboks, although, because of the way their players have been treated, many of the younger generation of rugby supporters and players in this country have never had the experience of seeing Springboks playing over here. It is some experience. It seems to me to be an indictment of the sporting fraternity, and especially the Rugby Union contingent that, the last Springboks tour side was as long ago as 1969-70. Naturally, the revulsion at certain aspects of the apartheid system in South Africa found its expression in movements which aimed at stopping all sporting links with the Republic. Nor was there any doubt in my mind that the ostracising of the South African sportspeople from international competition certainly focused the minds of some South African officials towards presenting a more acceptable system to the outside world. But some of the actions adopted by those aiming to stop tours were despicable.

Bette and I were referred to as 'racist scum' on our way down to Mansfield Park to see the South African Barbarians play in 1979 – a tour party comprising equal numbers of coloureds, blacks and whites. That, said the protesters, was just window dressing. When the Springboks last toured the UK, I was asked to provide commentary on their match against the Midland Counties (East) at Welford Road, Leicester. I remember having to walk the gauntlet up a narrow channel lined on each side by policemen holding back the mob. Those policemen were covered in spittle, had hats knocked off, were kicked in places where no man should be kicked and yet took it all with stoic calm. I couldn't believe

that people in the British Isles would behave in that manner. But, come
to think of it, the same types were prepared to spread broken glass and
nails on rugby pitches so I shouldn't have been so naive. Constant noise
outside the South Africans' hotels to try and prevent them sleeping was
another unbelievable ploy that sickened decent people.

I've already mentioned the 1951-52 Springboks who made such an impression on me. A group of us, including the former British Lions forward, Willie Welsh, had quite a day out when we travelled through to
Glasgow to see the Springboks play the Glasgow-Edinburgh side, then
went on to Paisley to see Peter Keenan fight Maurice Sandeyron of
France for the European Bantam-Weight title. We had to drive home in a
pea-soup fog but it had been worth it just to see the full splendour of the
South African game even though it had been at the expense of our fellow
Scots in the Cities.

Physically, the 1960-61 Springboks were monsters, certainly by the
standards of that time, but when you compare their statistics with those
of modern players, the contrast is remarkable:

England locks and number 8 (1991)

Paul Ackford:	6 ft 6 ins 17 st 6 lbs
Wade Dooley:	6 ft 8 ins 17 st 9 lbs
Dean Richards:	6 ft 3½ ins 17 st 3 lbs

South African Locks and number 8 (1960-61)

Avril Malan:	6 ft 2 ins 15 st
Johan Claassen:	6 ft 3 ins 15 st 7 lbs
Doug Hopwood:	6 ft 3 ins 14 st 11 lbs

However, if ever a tour party were well equipped for a 'subdue and
penetrate' policy, Avril Malan's men certainly were. Malan was only
twenty-three but was a splendid forward who led by example. He was
involved in one of the most devastating shoulder tackles ever, when, in
the closing match against the Barbarians at Cardiff, he burst down the
right touch-line from a lineout, was flat out after some forty yards, then
was shoulder-charged into touch by burly Swansea full back, Haydn
Mainwaring. Malan was badly shaken but continued to play and, in true
Barbarian spirit, was chaired from the field at the end. One wonders if
such a charge-tackle would be regarded nowadays as dangerous. That
name Mainwaring caused me a bit concern once when Bill of that ilk

from the Aberavon Club was chosen to play lock for Wales. Some English folk pronounced the name as 'Mannering' so I enquired of Billy how it should be pronounced. 'For God sake,' he said, 'don't say "Mannering" in front of my mother or she will have a fit.' Mrs Mainwaring was a formidable and devoted servant of the Aberavon Club. I never did have the pleasure of meeting her but I made sure I said Mainwaring just as it is spelt.

I covered all four of the tourists' games in Scotland and was much impressed by the powerful running in the centre of John Gainsford of Western Province who was just twenty-one and scored 13 tries on the tour, and by the play of the 'middle-of-the-back-row' forward, Doug Hopwood, also of Western Province. Hopwood was one of the first to be described as a number 8 and he was the first I had seen who made the scrummage pick-up move a devastating ploy. He was so technically efficient, his timing was first-class and he took off fast and caught opposing defenders napping especially those who were coming across that move for the very first time. The South African front row work also was a huge factor in their success. When they beat the Glasgow-Edinburgh fifteen in Glasgow by 16-11, their front row lifted one side of their opponent's edifice clean off the ground. I believe that the blonde Fanie Kuhn (Transvaal) was the chief lifter! He would be penalised today. The other test prop was one Piet du Toit (Boland). He was a 24-year-old farmer weighing fifteen stones, light by modern standards but a big boy then, and I recall Hugh McLeod selecting du Toit as the one he found most difficult to scrummage against. Hugh could hold his own with any opponent. That's why he had forty caps in a row before retiring, as he put it, 'because forty is a nice roond figure'. Apparently du Toit was strong enough to take his opponent down, a practice not common in those days but one that became part and parcel of a prop's armoury, although it is against the law now. Not only that, but du Toit would pull his opponent's jersey downwards so forming a triangle of jersey that had the effect also of preventing the opposing hooker from seeing the ball coming in. I remember that in the international against Scotland at Murrayfield Abe Malan, the South African hooker, won seven strikes against the put-in, mainly because of the massive shove generated by the huge South African forwards. Seven strikes against the put-in today would cause some puzzlement because, almost without exception, the side putting in win the strike. In my opinion this is a pity and I have written before that the game would benefit as a spectacle if there was more uncertainty about who would win scrummage ball. As things are, there is hardly any doubt so that the side not putting in automatically take up defensive alignment whereas if, as in olden times, there was no certainty about who might win the ball, perhaps both back divisions would line up in attacking positions to the general good of the game as a handling spectacle. Of course it is a fair argument that, because the team putting in are virtually sure of winning the scrummage, it has been necessary for teams to have at their disposal various scrummage pick-up ploys which aim to tie in opposing defenders and so clear the way for their backs to run against fractured defences. Unfortunately there has developed an obsession with such moves, so that too much of the play is centred on the forwards and too little on providing backs with chances to run and handle. In any event, Doug Hopwood was an outstanding exponent of scrummage pick-up play, although I seem to remember a big Australian called Mac Hughes using the ploy in the tour to the UK in 1957-58 – not, however, with the same impact as achieved by Hopwood.

That 1960-61 Springboks tour also introduced to a British audience for the first time that remarkable forward Frik du Preez of Northern Transvaal. He was a 24-year-old corporal in the South African Air Force and was to become, along with another outstanding flanker, Jan Ellis, South Africa's most capped player with 38. Du Preez played against England and Scotland on the tour and was second-top scorer with 58 points from three tries and 21 goals. I remember being told that he once dropped kicked a penalty-goal eighty-five yards at the Loftus Versfeld stadium in Pretoria. That is some belt! During that tour, he certainly showed some of the qualities that were to mark him out as one of South Africa's great players, a mighty lineout jumper and one of the fastest big men the game has spawned. He toured the British Isles and France four times, initially as a flanker, later as a lock and, at the end of the sixties, if you had been asked to select two lock-forwards for a World fifteen to play the British Isles, du Preez and Colin Meads of New Zealand almost certainly would have been the names on the sheet.

In the Murrayfield international the South Africans had such control that they played it tight in the opening spell, spread play more at the start of the second half, but were able to close it up again after Scotland had cut the deficit to 6-5. Not surprisingly the South African tries (only three points each in those days) both stemmed from pick-up ploys by Hopwood who scored the first and made the second for another great South African lock, Johan Claassen, the 6ft 3in school teacher from Western

Transvaal. The Scottish try was a typical opportunist effort by Scotland's captain Arthur Smith. Iain Laughland (London Scottish), operating at stand-off, tried a drop-goal after John Douglas (Stewarts College F.P.), Norman Bruce (London Scottish) and Hugh McLeod (Hawick) had rolled out of the back of a lineout. The ball sliced off Laughland's foot but Arthur Smith, purring as always like a high-powered Rolls Royce, screamed up the wing like a shell and got the touch just before the ball rolled out of play. Ken Scotland, one of the eight Heriots F.P. full-backs to have played for Scotland, and that day giving one of his finest performances, converted from the touch-line and it said much for the Scottish effort on short rations of ball that it took two penalty-goals by du Preez to clinch a South African win by twelve points to five to ensure their 'Grand Slam' of the four home countries. The match was marked by some magnificent Scottish tackling in which the mid-field of Laughland, Eddie McKeating (Heriots F.P.) and George Stevenson (Hawick) set a superb example, that deprived a South African threequarter line comprising Janie Engelbrecht, Ian Kirkpatrick, John Gainsford and Hennie van Zyl of a try; some feat considering that those four contributed 38 tries during the tour.

In every one of their four games in Scotland the Springboks had scrummage ascendancy and that certainly underlined to Scots just how essential it had become to have a scrummage that at least could hold its own, and at best could put pressure on opponents. Curiously, the game that gave the tourists their most anxious moment was against the combined Glasgow-Edinburgh side at Hughenden. The tourist pack were two stones per man heavier, but with only ten minutes left the Cities led 11-8 and seemed capable of holding on. But they lost their captain David Edwards (Heriots F.P.) with a badly torn ear. Edwards was one of the great competitors, a human battle-cruiser who did everything with all guns blazing and who would run until he dropped, his spirit undampened. The Springboks then took the lead for the first time and the Cities lost their gallant Heriots F.P. hooker, Bob Tollervey, another rare competitor desperately unlucky not to be capped. As Tollervey went off, the indomitable Edwards returned, his head swathed in bandages and a scrum cap over his stitched ear. One newspaper picture of the time showed a very unusual situation. At a scrummage which seemed to have disintegrated, John Douglas, the Stewarts College F.P. lock-cum-number 8 was seen with a huge South African forward draped over his shoulder. John clearly had lifted him off the ground. The biter bit! But then John Douglas, too, was a player full of acumen and spirit who never gave less than 100 per cent. The injuries to the Cities players brought criticism of the Springboks as 'rugby rough-necks' but in the 'Sanderson slant', written by the famous James of that ilk in the *Sunday Express*, the view was expressed that such criticisms were quite unfair. Referring to 'some of Europe's bad-boy footballers, the kick and punch men', he said that if they could take the knocks the Rugby Union players did and without a murmur of complaint 'then our football might not descend into the fist and boot battles we see so often here and on the Continent.' Nor, he claimed, did Rugby Union produce 'the theatricals we see in our soccer.' And to think that all happened in November 1960!

When those Springboks took their leave of Scotland with a 22-9 win over the North of Scotland at Linksfield stadium in Aberdeen, they did so with hardly one punt but with a whole series of handling attacks that endeared them to the audience. Yet for all the ball they won, they were restricted to just four tries. All of us have heard of the telegrammed plea to the Springboks in New Zealand to 'scrum, scrum and scrum'. Well, where Scots have been concerned, almost since Rugby Union began, the insistence has been to 'tackle, tackle and tackle'. So often Scots have been outweighted and have just had to chase, hound, harass and flatten. They certainly did that for North of Scotland on that perishing cold day at Aberdeen with the loose-forwards, Ron Glasgow (Dunfermline), Bob Steven (Howe of Fife) and Bill Glen (Perthshire Academicals) showing a fine example. The North's nine points were from three penalty-goals by their captain Jim Craig (Harris Academy F.P.), who regularly topped a hundred points per season with his goal kicking. He would be nearer three hundred today with such a surfeit of offence awards and goals being landed from beyond half-way.

I felt desperately sorry for the 1965 Springboks who were sent on a suicide mission for goodness knows what reason. They were well out of their own season and had neither the fitness levels nor match hardness required even for just five matches in Ireland and Scotland, whereas their hosts were at the end of their seasons in April and were as fit as fleas. It was sad to see such outstanding players as Janie Engelbrecht, John Gainsford, Keith Oxlee, Dawie de Villiers, Fanie Kuhn, Avril Malan, Frik du Preez, Doug Hopwood and Tommy Bedford suffer such a shattering experience. They lost four and drew one of their five games. Tom Kiernan's late penalty-goal took Ireland home by 9-6, and a late drop-goal by David Chisholm (Melrose) gave the Scots an 8-5 margin that

compensated in part for that 0-44 drubbing at the hands of the Springboks at Murrayfield in 1951.

I've already referred to my revulsion at the treatment meted out by
anti-apartheid demonstrators to the 1969-70 Springboks. At the opening
cocktail party in their honour they made a fine impression on everyone
with their friendliness and politeness, but from then onwards they lived
an artificial existence in hotel rooms, mainly watching television to avoid
abuse and physical attacks directed at them.

There was a theory about that touring party, that they were a bit out-
dated in their approach, that they held to their old formula of having
tank squadrons up front, grinding the opposition into near submission
then shipping the ball to their backs for orthodox line-handling. By this
time, the All-Blacks had developed the technique of ruck play at the
second phase and it came home to the Springboks too late, that their
opponents in the UK knew more about that than they did. In any event,
the South Africans were well-equipped with massive forward power.
Some idea of this can be gained when their four prop forwards' details
are listed as follows:

Mof Myburgh:	33 years old	6 ft 1 in	17 st 2 lbs
Tiny Neethling:	30 years old	6 ft 1½ ins	20 st 2 lbs
Hannes Marais:	28 years old	5 ft 11½ ins	15 st 7 lbs
Ronnie Potgieter:	25 years old	6 ft	18 st 2 lbs

Once, when Martin Van Rensburg was injured in the Swansea game and
Myburgh went on to replace him a wag in the crowd shouted: 'Hey,
you're allowed only one replacement at a time, not two!' The coach of
those Springboks was Avril Malan, the former South African lock and
captain, and he seemed a bit old-fashioned in his thinking, but he certainly was a bit ahead of his time with his concept of the hooker throwing in to lineouts instead of the wingers. This allowed the wingers to
adopt an auxiliary full-back role. It didn't always work too well as, for
instance, when hooker Charlie Cockrell threw in badly when confronted
by the 6ft 10ins of Peter Stagg in the Scotland international. But nowadays the Malan idea is part and parcel of the game. Hookers do throw in
and wings do act as auxiliary full-backs. H.O. de Villiers, their full-back,
was a star on that tour, supremely safe in the orthodox full-back chores
and lauded even more for his all-consuming desire to attack from the
deep. To see him take an opposition punt on the full, high-up or low-

down, then to launch himself past or through opponents, had to be one of the great joys of a sad tour.

A Hawick friend of mine, Eric Grierson, refereed the Ireland v South Africa match on 10 January 1970. It went to eight minutes of extra-time and in that period Ireland's Tom Kiernan landed a penalty goal for an 8-8 draw. I heard afterwards that Eric had had an official reprimand from the Scottish Rugby Union for having explained to a media man his method of timing the game. Nothing wrong in that, I thought. Clearly, the SRU disagreed.

Still, one of my most pleasurable moments in commentary took place at the Wales v South Africa match at Cardiff Arms Park which was reduced to a rain sloshed quagmire. In no time, players were encased in mud, numbers obscured. In injury-time at the end of the game, a Welshman, covered from head-to-foot in mud, spurted over at the corner from a ruck despite the valiant efforts of another chap also covered from head to foot in mud. I named the scorer as Gareth Edwards and the tackler as Hannes Marais. I was correct on each count and I have to admit to a feeling of relief and pleasure at having got those two right. It all took place on the far side of the pitch furthest from our commentary box which made them all the harder to identify. I was proud of that bit of commentary which owed everything to the trouble I had taken to attend the practice sessions of both teams.

There was one final pleasure for the tourists. In the closing game against the Barbarians at Twickenham they turned on the style in the second half with exhilarating passages. There were two very special tries among the seven scored. Gareth Edwards, the Barbarians captain, sent David Duckham away up the west stand touch-line. There was no more inspiring sight in the game than the fair-haired Duckham in full flight, this time weaving past Sid Nomis and inside H.O. de Villiers over sixty yards. Then came the Jan Ellis effort. He already had scored one and had proved a lynch pin in the South African defence. Gobbling up a loose ball, he set off with forty yards to go to the line. Sundry tacklers were brushed off and with a faint veer inwards, then a swing outwards, he beat even the great Mike Gibson before breezing in for a try. Twickenham rose to him. What a forward, and what a pair of flankers he and Piet Greyling made. I was thrilled, too, when prior to that final match Dawie de Villiers, the South African captain, shook my hand and said: 'I want to thank you for being so fair to us in commentary. We have appreciated that very much.' That was the last we saw of the Springboks in the UK.

It has been a disgrace that a world Rugby Union power has been eliminated from world competition for all those years, even allowing for their country's unacceptable racist policy. The demonstrators had a right to protest – but some of the methods they used to do so could not be justified. Thankfully, the South Africans are about to be welcomed back into international competition, and when they are we will then be able to justify calling the great competition the World Cup. Without the South Africans, it wasn't. With a bit of luck too, the South Africans will be invited to host the 1995 World Cup. That they deserve.

14

An Amateur Game With
A Professional Face

At the risk of being labelled an aged traditionalist who would hold back the wheels of so-called progress, I have to admit to feelings of disappointment at the manner in which, in certain respects, the Rugby Union game has changed since my own brief playing days. What a pity that we cannot put the clock back to where it was in the immediate post-war years. Then I thought we had it just about right. The game really was just part of the tapestry of life, a joyous recreational relief from day-to-day work commitments, one that occupied only a part of the normal week. It really was fun to train and play. It wasn't ever regarded as a chore. Training took up the Tuesday and Thursday evenings, play was on the Saturday afternoon and the rest of the week was your own, although some players did engage in a little extra work off their own bat. Once I came close to being run down by a car in a heavy snowstorm near Haughhead on the main Hawick to Denholm road. It was a Sunday evening. I decided to go out for a run in the snow and had done about two miles at the edge of the road. Because of the snow I didn't hear the car coming behind me. It whisked past the edge of my shorts, happily without injury. But I had that goose-pimply feeling of shock at what might have been.

Players and officials in those days still took the game, and their preparation for it, quite seriously. Certainly at Mansfield Park the aim of the Hawick side always was to win, and nobody in a green jersey every liked losing. But no one regarded it as a disaster of mammoth proportions if we lost, well, not unless against Gala! In those days, forwards had one priority – to get the ball for their backs to run and score tries. To some extent, ignorance was bliss in that players operated 'off the top of their

146

heads' in the main, and although there was a certain amount of planning in order to thwart the opposition it dealt, in the main, with having an idea about who the most dangerous opponents would be and how to be on guard to deal with them. Training was usually led by the captain, but there frequently was an 'elder statesman' who would give some guidance. For instance, I can remember the Hawick forwards of my day spending a lengthy spell dribbling in unison up and down the terracing touchline under the command of Tom Wright. He had played as a forward for Hawick in the post-war years and was the club groundsman but doubled as a kind of coach. He was a wise and friendly man, quiet and encouraging with his advice, and he imbued us with a due sense of responsibility to the club. He got across to us the honour of wearing the green jersey and how important it was that it should not be sullied in any way. Tom was the father of three boys all of whom played for Hawick – Tommy, capped against Australia in 1948 and Jock and Eddie, and I hold him in very fond memory. Rugby clubs have owed so much over the years to people like Tom and Pat McDonald, another most likeable enthusiast, who have given so much of their time towards serving the club and the game. One can only hope that they will continue to do so as the game becomes more professionalised, with players getting their 'slice of the cake', team managers being appointed at huge salaries and incentives being held out by clubs to entice top players into membership.

The game was played in a more sporting spirit than it is today. Players didn't cheat the way they do nowadays. Nor did they try to intimidate referees; they wouldn't have dared to do so. There was a kind of unwritten code by which most players operated. You just didn't do certain things. And no one ever thought about what they might make out of the game. The lines separating what you could and could not do were clearly drawn and, what is more, officials ensured that there was no deviation. No one every thought of stamping on opponents or kicking heads or taking-out players who did not have the ball. I was inclined occasionally towards tackling an opponent smaller than myself by banging my hands down on his shoulders, grabbing his jersey and throwing him down so as to stay on my own feet. One day, I was walking along Hawick High Street when I heard the tap on the window of the National Bank. A finger beckoned me into the bank. There I was ushered into the inner sanctum of the manager, R.L. Scott, president of the SRU. I was quaking, having walked the gauntlet of all the tellers' eyes. Mr Scott closed the door. He referred grimly to that method of putting opponents on the floor. 'Billy,' he said, 'you must stop that. It doesn't look right.' I hadn't seen anything wrong in it but that was that. I almost crept out of the bank. I even felt ashamed. When I compare that incident with what goes on today in the form of unorthodox tackling, apart altogether from the modern tactic of taking-out players well away from the ball, I realise how times have changed and how my method, which was used only sparingly, would be accepted today as quite harmless. My attitude then was that of any player weaned on the Hawick method that called for un-compromising vigour and hard but clean play, although different inter-pretations might be possible; my father always enjoyed telling of the occasion when he was seated beside a very large Kelso farmer at one Kelso v Hawick game and this vociferous son of the soil referred to 'that big, dirty, black-headed bugger, McLaren.' My father thought it wise not to let on that the large one was referring to his son.

The fact is that in those days anyone who went over the score, not only had to face a strict referee but also, almost certainly, would be scorched by an aged member of the club committee, who was concerned that the club's reputation should be upheld. Nowadays in many cases ex-cuses are found for players guilty of unacceptable conduct. Surely there could hardly be a bigger indictment of the modern game than that the legislators have had to allocate powers to the touch-judges in top matches so that they can assist the referee in dealing with players who in-fringe the foul-play provisions. They didn't have any need of such arrangements in the immediate post-war seasons. I only wish more touch-judges would use such powers more frequently so as to drive home to the hard men that there really are three pairs of eyes on the look-out for evil doing. There was more fun and genuine enjoyment in earlier times too. There was not, however, the unsmiling strain, the gaunt faces, the fearsome exhortations associated with the modern game. It has all become so deadly serious, the need to win so paramount that players are hyped up to a pitch of endeavour, their minds solely attuned to the business of winning, so that nothing is permitted to intrude into their thoughts and minds. One wonders how some of the great jokers and leg pullers of the past would be greeted nowadays, especially by coaches thumping their fists into their palms as they call for the ultimate in effort. It all nowadays speaks for a high spate of professionalism in preparation and endeavour never experienced by previous generations, or so it would seem; I once heard a club side chanting in unison in their dressing room as they thumped their studs on the floor. When they were shunted back some twenty metres at the first scrummage, I remember thinking what a fat lot of good all that motivation had been!

That great Scottish forward of the immediate post-war years, Douglas Elliot, was telling me not so long ago that prior to one Scottish game against Wales at Murrayfield he had attended a brief Scottish team get-together on the Friday afternoon but, as his father was not well, Douglas drove back home to the family farm some way out of Edinburgh and the car ran out of petrol four miles from home. He ran all the way home for petrol and back to the car, did some shearing and other farmwork before dark, was up with the lark because a field drain had to be repaired which took two hours, then took off for Murrayfield to join the Scottish team just in time for kick-off. What is more, Scotland won! Compare that with the demands of the international game today – squad sessions on Sundays, some lasting over three hours, special Wednesday-night sessions for the forwards, full squad sessions on Thursdays, a short run-about on the Friday morning, mainly for the benefit of the media, video-watching sessions at the squad hotel, final squad briefing on the Saturday, then the game. It was at one post-international press conference that Scotland's captain Finlay Calder said jocularly that the squad next would be attending the official dinner for both teams, 'that is unless Jim Telfer decides to have a rucking session on the way up The Bridges'.

Rugby Union for the top players has become almost a seven-days-a-week affair, when one considers their preparation work with club, district and national squads, not to mention their own additional running or strengthening work they feel necessary to keep them in the top flight. Once, Craig Chalmers, the Melrose and Scotland stand-off was eligible for three national sides at different levels, all at the same time. You can imagine the demands that made on his spare time although he is such an enthusiast that all the training is as meat and drink to him. Once, I interviewed Stuart Reid, the promising young Boroughmuir, Edinburgh and Scotland 'B' number 8, who reckoned that he had barely had a Sunday free all season because of squad work at various levels. But, as he said, you just had to work hard if you wanted to reach the top rung and, when it was in the national cause, it was worthwhile. All the same, for those players who live a distance away from squad training grounds, travel can be sapping and irksome. I was quite fascinated by an article written by Stewart Jardine, the Scotland 'B' scrum-half, during his research into players' attitudes to scientifically designed training regimes as part of his sports degree in Cardiff. Apart altogether from the demands of squad sessions, he claimed that travelling also was taking its toll and that some players had wondered if they would continue much longer in international rugby because they did not know if they could cope with the stress of another season. He reckoned that sessions should be shorter and more intensive, that in American football they had discovered that when daily five-hour sessions had been shortened to no more than ninety minutes, with a rest day between each one, there was a noticeable improvement in their fitness and overall standard of play.

It concerns me, too, that because winning has become so important, there is much wider inclination to play to a strategy that is aimed at error elimination with little obligation to provide spectacle and entertainment value. Prior to the crucial Grand Slam decider between England and France in March 1991, the former England captain, Steve Smith, said in TV interview that he would be perfectly happy if England won by a penalty goal to nil. I am sure that Steve's view would be shared by many players of international standing, but I have to admit that I would want more than that from any victory. I would want at least to try and put on a bit of style, to really reach out for something closer to the genuine fifteen-man game, what Jim Greenwood, the former Scottish captain, has referred to as 'total rugby', with an amalgam of rousing forward play and, when it was on, wide spread play. But too many sides nowadays hold to a cautious format of seldom letting the ball past the stand-off, of frequently turning it back to their forwards so that the game is played, in the main, around the pivot five with centres and wings being used mainly in a tackle-and-chase role, the chase usually under a hail of garryowens. The Scottish division one club campaign in 1990-91 was extremely disappointing in that too many players sought to play the game on the floor and very few sides really were prepared to sweep the ball to their wings even when overlaps beckoned. The boot, with those few exceptions, was dominant alongside the constant crump and thump of forwards clattering into each other in close-quarter combat.

Nor did the players in the lower echelons receive in 1991 much of an inspiring example from the hot-shots, if one excludes the French and the Irish. To see England, mainly through Rob Andrew, punting for touch at the corner from Scotland's '22', almost made you feel like weeping when you consider the quality of the players Andrew had outside him. Of course, the lad punted with pin-point precision and within the tactical format that aimed to give the Scots no error opportunities upon which to thrive. And it worked. England won well and did the same against France with the same kind of careful strategy. They can point to their first Grand Slam since 1980. Nor should others point the finger. Scotland, after all, won their 1984 Grand Slam with the policy built around the accurate punting of John Rutherford and the sniping work of Roy Laidlaw in conjunction with a superb loose-forward trio. The Scots didn't really let their hair down in that series until the Triple Crown was assured and an unassailable lead had been created against Ireland.

Perhaps it is something of an indictment of the Rugby Union game that those safety-first tactics, based on punting, fringe thrusts and use of the narrow side, have proved so successful. It seems far easier to prevent tries than to create them. And yet the game still has a great deal to offer in the way of inspiring spectacle if one is to judge from those recent games that stay in the memory. Scotland versus Ireland at Murrayfield in 1989 was a marvellous match of ebb and flow in which eight lovely tries were scored and virtually everybody went away happy. And when England outplayed Wales and France in 1990, they did so with two of the finest demonstrations of the total game you could ever wish to see – magnificent ball-winning and surges by the forwards, swift ball transference and power running by their backs with the two sometimes being blended into a marvellous amalgam of spectacular action. That was England at their very best. England playing in that vein and winning the 'Grand Slam' would have given a huge uplift to the game. Instead, in the 1991 Five Nations Championship, it was the French, with a quite dazzling display, especially against Wales in Paris, and the Irish, with thrilling back play that should have brought them a deserved win at Murrayfield but didn't, who really lit the fires.

I get pretty fed up with managers, coaches and captains who claim to be advocates of the fifteen-man game and whose teams then go on to the field and play to a cautious pattern in which there is plenty of hoof and far too little pass. I have found the England manager, Geoff Cooke, to be very co-operative and helpful, and the trouble he took to provide me with a BBC interview at very short notice in Cardiff was much appreciated, not least because he was such an ideal interviewee. But it was a bit ironic that he was reported as having included in his 1991 report to the RFU an expression of disappointment that England had not won the Grand Slam with the free, open style that they had hoped for. England had the personnel, the ball and the chances. But they played it safe, scored only five tries and did not make folk sit up and take notice as they had the potential to do.

Having said all that one has to admit that the modern game is immensely popular if one is to judge by the numbers wishing to attend the big occasions. Even the modern stadia in which internationals are played just aren't big enough to accommodate all those who would like to attend. Unfortunately, it is more often than not the faithful club supporter, who braves all kinds of weather to encourage his or her local heroes, who misses out when there aren't enough tickets to go round. Those new modern stands that have been, and are being, erected in international grounds certainly provide a seat in the dry and accord with the act covering safety at sporting occasions. But the effect has been to reduce capacity drastically. Murrayfield housed 104,000 for Scotland v Wales in 1975. Since the East stand was erected in 1983 the capacity has dropped to just 54,000. The great sea of faces on the old East terracing at Murrayfield was one of the distinctive features of the big occasion there, but the new stand holds far fewer at just under 11,000. Because big matches are now all-ticket and soon to be all-seated, crowds don't turn up as early as they used to do. Folk would arrive at Murrayfield just after midday in order to get a good vantage point on the terracing and there was any amount of good natured banter and singing. But no longer. Nowadays the international grounds don't fill up until just before kick-off and much of the early atmosphere has been lost. Even the singing at Cardiff Arms Park isn't what it used to be, although there remains something very special about the way the Welsh sing 'Land of my Fathers' just before kick-off. And nothing in my memory has come near to equalling that volume of song as over 50,000 Scots joined their team in giving forth with 'Flower of Scotland' prior to the 1990 Murrayfield game against England.

In Chapter 12 I was critical of the International Board, claiming that they were not doing too good a job of standardising the interpretation of the game's laws. The same charge must be levelled, with even more conviction, when it comes to the matter of the amateur code. Sometimes one gets the impression that they would rather just not know, not face up to the existence of wide-spread contradictions and anomalies. This undoubtedly has been at the core of the controversy over whether players should receive material reward for off-field, non-rugby-related activities. I remember being quite taken aback when I was in New Zealand for the World Cup to see Andy Dalton, the All Blacks captain, as the central figure in quite a lengthy TV advertisement for a farm tractor. Now, I don't purport to know whether Dalton made any personal financial gain for doing the advertisement, which must have taken quite a lot of shooting time to complete. I presume that he didn't do it for nothing. What was certain was that no player in the United Kingdom would have been permitted to make such a television advertisement. The next day, after attending a Scottish squad session, I had a chat with Alan Tomes, the Hawick, Scottish and Lions lock, who naturally questioned why Dalton could do such an advertisement while players at home couldn't. Clive Rowlands, manager of the Welsh squad, obviously realised what might follow: 'You know what's going to happen, don't you? All our boys are going to go home and they are all going to want to drive bloody tractors.' What an accurate prophecy, because it was their experience at the World Cup in which they noted that players in different countries were not being treated alike, that first set in motion the desire of players in the United Kingdom to gain some financial benefit on similar lines to that enjoyed in the southern hemisphere. No one should blame them. Will Carling, Brian Moore, Rob Andrew and others just wanted to have similar opportunities to those enjoyed by players in the southern hemisphere.

Sir Ewart Bell, chairman of the International Board, did point out that law changes had been made because players in certain countries were concerned that their situation was managed in a different way. At the World Cup he said they came across the New Zealand commercial dimension and started asking questions. You may well ask why the International Board didn't put its foot down at the first sign of players gaining material reward in contravention of their own law book, which stipulates that the 'game is an amateur game.' Wayne Shelford, the former All Blacks captain, admitted in a television interview that in New Zealand players can be offered a good job, a flat, and/or a car if they undertake to play for a certain club. If that isn't 'material reward', what is? For years, there have been stories about French clubs attracting players by financial means, and a surprising number of players from the southern hemisphere become virtually full-time players by joining a European club during our season and then going home for their own domestic season.

You might think that there is nothing very wrong about a club looking after a star player in this way and assuredly it is now fairly common practice. The danger is that the well-off clubs can corner the market in the best players and the less fashionable clubs, who more often than not, have reared those players from an early age, lose them. In former times, players played for their clubs out of loyalty to their home town or to their old school, but there is a danger nowadays that loyalty will take second place to financial gain. It has been said, indeed, that some players don't go to Rugby League because they just can't afford to do so!

Where the International Board have fallen down is in not ensuring that the laws relating to the amateur concept in the game have been strictly applied in exactly the same way in all the countries under the Board's jurisdiction. The International Board certainly has provision in the laws for dealing with transgressions but, of course, the argument often is that it is very difficult to find hard evidence of malpractice.

More recently the International Board clearly decided to adjust its laws to accord with practice rather than the other way round, so that reward is now permissible to players for non-rugby-related activities. What a non-rugby-related activity is, when players are only going to be invited to speak at functions, give special interviews, open shops or whatever, simply because of their fame as rugby players, I'm not too sure. But now that the way has been opened up, it is hardly surprising that players will leap at the opportunity of making a bit of extra income as due reward, in their eyes, for all the hard work they put into the business of reaching the top echelon in the game. As Will Carling has said, players do give a lot of enjoyment to thousands of people. Of course they've done that for over a hundred years. The big difference nowadays is the amount of spare time players have to give towards preparing for playing the game, and the number of intrusions into their private lives by the media thirsting for interesting copy that they have to tolerate.

I think the demands on players' spare time have gone beyond the acceptable. Here again, the International Board has not taken action to limit the amount of preparation time for international squads to accord with their own laws. So that not only have the number of representative commitments multiplied in virtually every grade, but players are required to attend a shower of squad sessions as each country seeks to stay upsides with the others. It is surely an indictment of the modern game that Will Carling suggested that he might give up the game in his mid-twenties because of the demands and the pressures. Once I rang Roy Laidlaw on a Monday evening but Joy, his wife, told me he was out running. I was surprised because Roy already had squad sessions commitment at club, district and national level; but, as Joy explained, Roy reckoned it was essential to do that extra work in order to stay at the top. It's hardly surprising that players who put so much in, should want to get something out; nor do I believe that the average supporter would object to that. All the same, players never were meant to 'get a slice of the cake.' The cake was meant to go towards the general betterment of the game, for helping clubs, for the upkeep of grounds and facilities and for aiding injured players.

Rugby Union players are the luckiest sportsmen in the world where employers are concerned. The amount of leave of absence from work required by players for representative match preparation and play and for the now annual national tour at the end of the season, not to mention the World Cup, must be close to the limit that some employers are prepared to grant. It certainly was a significant development when Save and Prosper allocated £30,000 towards providing a temporary replacement at work for Geoff Cooke, the England manager during his absence with the England squad on tour in Australia and Fiji and at the World Cup. In the past, managers and coaches have carried out their functions without such assistance.

I hold to the view that players should be helped financially if that is required, so that they can represent their country. No one should be debarred from representing his country or the Lions because his firm cannot afford to pay him his wages when he is away. Nor should he be out of pocket in relation to fair expenses when he is on international duty. Wives and sweethearts also should derive due recognition for the supportive role they play. But I would have stopped short of allowing players to make money through their fame in the game. Some scoff at the value of the amateur concept in Rugby Union and with some justification when you consider the in-roads made into what at one time was genuinely amateur. The game has flourished through many decades and is now more popular than ever, partly because of the moral and spiritual values associated with its amateurism. I may be wrong but I find it hard to believe that the game will benefit from the changes now in force. Human frailty being what it is there is a danger, as the Nottingham coach, Alan Davies, suggested in the splendid BBC television programme 'Public Eye', that some players might now think more of improving their income than of improving their rugby.

Already there have been unfortunate side effects. Look what happened after England's long awaited Cardiff win over Wales in 1991. The England squad decided against giving any interviews after the game. According to their manager, Geoff Cooke, the reason was that they were all mentally and physically exhausted after such a historic effort. Others reckoned it was because the demand for £5000 for giving interviews was turned down. Whatever the reason, it was a sad business that reflected badly on the game.

Legislators, I believe, should beware of 'player power'. I'm all for players expressing their views about how the game should be played and administered and it stands to reason that they will want to benefit themselves in every possible way. But I am not so sure that they are the best people to decide what should be allowed and what should not. The game and image it presents are far more important than players, even allowing for the vast amount of time and effort they give towards producing their best on the field. Incidentally, it isn't only the top boys upon whom heavy demands are made in relation to match preparation. What with squad sessions, individual fitness, player improvement, and the extra sessions for special games, the average club player and coach now have to give a lot of extra time. Shouldn't they get a slice of the cake as well?

For someone of my vintage it was a shock to read that the Queensland squad threatened to strike if Michael Lynagh was suspended by their provincial union for what appears to have been a breach of their rules. Lynagh is one of the most gifted players I have ever seen and one can understand him seeking financial reward through advertising. But the laws have to be applied equally to everybody and that includes the greatest in the land and whether the law might be a bit of an ass or not. It would be some shambles if everybody adhered to the laws they liked and ignored the others. And the thought of a squad of Rugby Union players threatening not to play unless an elected union backs down provides a sad commentary on the current situation. Player power indeed! And to think that, at one time, players were delighted to turn out just for the honour of wearing the jersey of the club, district or country, and for the love of the game. That was the only reward they sought. Happily that Queensland situation seems to have been resolved at least to the extent that Lynagh will be available for the World Cup. Australia without Lynagh is hard to imagine.

However, the International Board has opened the door for players and others embracing certain commercial opportunities, although it escapes me just how it can claim, through its much respected chairman, Sir Ewart Bell, that in 'bringing the regulations up to date the principal of amateurism should remain paramount'. To my way of thinking, Rugby Union is no longer a purely amateur game. Indeed it hasn't been that for quite a while. Now Rugby Union certainly has moved officially into the commercial world and the hope must be that the game itself will not suffer as a consequence. Certainly I can just imagine what reply a group of players would have received from, say, Alf Wilson or Herbert Waddell, had they threatened to go on strike. Changed days indeed. I thought Dudley Wood of the RFU made an important point, too, when he said that thousands of volunteers slaved away and gave long service in various ways through their love of the game. How many of them might now say that, if this is the way the game is going, it is no longer for me?

15

Seven Is A Magic Number

Seven-a-side rugby has been very much part of my rugby experience since the earliest days and it's easy to create a kind of love-hate relationship with the game, not only as a former player but as a commentator. Of all the radio and television commentary assignments I have undertaken in Rugby Union, by far the most demanding and worrying has been coverage of sevens.

I stipulate Rugby Union because I have undertaken one or two commentary commitments in other fields with no great appetite or desire for repetition. Once I was persuaded, much against my better judgement, to do television commentary on the Royal Family's visit to Holyrood House in Edinburgh. Probably the less said about that the better! On two consecutive years I also covered the Edinburgh Military Tattoo and was much indebted to producer Alan Rees who guided me through that minefield with such care and understanding that I was actually praised for my contribution. Alan deserved most of the praise, and my own feelings about not being too conversant with the history and tradition of the event persuaded me that twice was enough! It took three telephone requests from the BBC in Glasgow before I reluctantly agreed to provide television commentary on a Scotland v England tennis international at Largs and then an open tennis tournament at Montrose. I struggled through them both, but with no great relish to repeat the process!

I have always felt a commentator should really specialise in the one sport. I know there have been exceptions, broadcasters who could turn their hand to covering more than one sport, and successfully too, but in my own case I felt that one sport was enough to be going on with. Thus, in the sixties, I turned down a request by BBC Scotland to take up football commentary. That would have been highly rewarding in financial terms because it would have involved a weekly commentary commitment with the occasional break to cover the big rugby occasions, but I just couldn't see myself operating at Ibrox or Tannadice when things of great moment were going on at Goldenacre and Netherdale, not to mention Mansfield Park! Rugby Union was my game and I meant to stick to it.

But, getting back to sevens, well, that can be something of a nightmare, both from the point of view of identification and that of the preparation process. At one time or another I have provided commentary on virtually every senior Border sevens tournament on the famous Middlesex sevens at Twickenham since the late fifties, on the prestigious Hong Kong sevens which are something else and, in May 1991, with a return to cover the Ulster sevens at Ravenhill in Belfast which I had previously done in 1975. It shows what an impression I made at the Ulster tournament that it was sixteen years before I was invited back!

I like to have a couple of sentences of background about every player and replacement in the tournament as well as details of the sixteen clubs concerned. You can never be sure of which clubs will make it past the first round so you really have to be prepared to do commentary on matches involving any and every one of the sixteen competitors. This entails circularising each club with an information sheet about their selected players and a request that they fill in the details and send it back as soon as possible. Clubs generally are very helpful and I've been very grateful to them over the years, but not all officials and players appreciate the value of commentators having accurate information. Once the information arrives I transfer all the details to my own sixteen team sheets so that by the Friday evening, I hope to be fully prepared.

The big concern is over identification. At the Middlesex event there will be a 112 players taking part and, in addition, close on fifty replacements. Of 112 original choices I probably can identify at a glance only some twenty or thirty, leaving some eighty-or-so strangers running about the paddock at one time or another. You have to depend on identifying players by their numbers, in which regard you hope fervently that the numbers given are accurate and that each player has put on the right jersey. Equally important is that the thousands of supporters who have paid a pound for a programme should be entitled to accuracy of information.

Once you are up in the commentary position you are dependent on the relay of information to the commentary box. It's made all the harder by the fact that sevens is such a quick-fire game, the ball often being transferred from player to player as if it was a bit of red-hot charcoal. Sometimes not all of the first-round ties will be covered, thus affording the commentator the opportunity of furthering the identification process. When I first did commentary work at the Middlesex event in the late sixties, virtually every first round-tie was covered. How I managed to survive that I just don't know. You really fly by the seat of your pants in that kind of situation because not only is identification a problem but you have to record every score on your team sheet so that, in subsequent rounds, you can up-date viewers in what has gone before. Trying to keep those score details and, at the end of each tie, adjusting your sheet so that next time round they come up in the right order is quite a problem especially as, at Middlesex, there is very little time between the end of one tie and the start of the next, and at Border tournaments one tie follows another without a break.

Nowadays it is even harder because quite a proportion of the Middlesex tournament goes out live on the BBC's 'Grandstand', with the semi-finals and final live on BBC2. This was the case in 1991 when identification was even harder because a record number of the less fashionable clubs had qualified for the final day. There are those who would change the format of the Middlesex event to include once again star-studded, composite sides such as Public School Wanderers, Barbarians, Scottish Saltires, Crawshay's, Penguins, Co-optimists, Irish Wolfhounds and French Barbarians to pep it up just a bit. They claim that the big audience aren't all that enamoured of seeing two sides from the same club in opposition as, for instance, happened in 1991 when Harlequins 1 met Harlequins 2 and Rosslyn Park 1 met Rosslyn Park 2 in the quarter-finals. There was some disappointment, too, that the likes of Wasps, London Welsh and London Irish were not represented and that no fewer than six of the so-called 'junior' clubs, Askeans, Basingstoke, Millfield Old Boys, Old Beccehamians, High Wycombe, Guildford and Godalming, had made it to Finals Day. No one can deny that crowds love to see star players in action. At the 1991 Ulster international club sevens at Ravenhill, almost all the Irish clubs were eliminated in the opening round and the quarter-finals featured Swansea, French Barbarians, Scottish Saltires and Irish Wolfhounds. Even when the final produced a French v Scottish clash, barely anyone in the crowd left the stadium. Just to see the huge French forwards such as Abdel Benazzi and Philippe Benetton and the sizzling pace of international backs Stephane Weller, Bernard Lacombe and Aubin Heuber was a treat in itself. But it was following a protest at the Public School Wanderers' success in reaching consecutive Middlesex finals in 1972 and 1973 by calling on such seven artists as J. J. Williams, Keith Fielding, Ian Robertson, Nigel Starmer-Smith, Andy Irvine, Bob Wilkinson and Norman Barker, that the organisers introduced a new rule effectively eliminating such classy outfits. One of the pleasures of the Middlesex tournament is to see the delight of players in the less fashionable sides at having the opportunity, probably for the only time in their lives, of competing against such heavyweights as Harlequins, Richmond, London Scottish, Wasps and the like on the famous Twickenham turf and in front of a crowd of some fifty thousand. That has to be the experience of a lifetime for those players and it would be sad indeed if that delightful aspect of the event was to be eliminated.

The aspect of sevens play at Twickenham that impressed me most was the electrifying pace of the fast men of whom there seemed to be a considerable number. Having been born and bred in the home of the abbreviated game in the Borders of Scotland, I was accustomed to a quick player being on the wing in each seven but, in some of the Middlesex tournaments, teams seemed to have two or even three genuine speed merchants. Over the years one has marvelled at the speed and strength of such as John Ranson (Rosslyn Park), Colin Gibbons (London Welsh), Mike Bulpitt (Blackheath), Keith Fielding (Loughborough Colleges), Bob Lloyd (Harlequins) and, of more recent vintage, the dramatic running of Martin Offiah (Rosslyn Park), Andrew Harriman, Will Carling and Everton Davis (Harlequins). It has been a joy to see such effortless acceleration, superb body balance, and ability to change pace. When Orrell competed on the Border circuit in the seventies they had a blonde bullet called Barrie Fishwick who needed just a sniff of space and he was gone. Fielding has to be one of the greatest sevens wings I have ever seen. If my memory serves me right he once scored just under a dozen tries at one Middlesex event and I remember his contribution to that marvellous England seven who won the first World Sevens tournament to mark the Scottish Rugby Union centenary celebrations at Murrayfield in 1973. That was some seven: Keith Fielding, Peter Preece, Peter Rossborough, Steve Smith, Fran Cotton (captain), John Gray and Andy Ripley. In a memorable final, they beat Ireland with the inimitable Mike Gibson as captain and scrum-half, and Vinny Becker, Paul Dennison, Wallace McMaster, Terry Moore, Donal Caniffe (a scrum-half playing as hooker), Fergus Slattery in support, 22-18.

One would rate Gerald Davies along with Fielding as a class sevens wing. I rather prided myself in having picked him out as a future international wing when I first saw him play for the Loughborough Colleges seven at Twickenham and on the Border circuit in the sixties. He was so quick and jinky and, being Welsh, he wasn't short of 'bottle'. He was just a laddie then but became one of the world's greats.

There have been some quite stunning sevens successes over the years. London Scottish set a record of appearing in six consecutive Middlesex finals that lasted from 1965 to 1991 when Harlequins equalled it. The London Scots had pace and power everywhere – Ronnie Thomson, a flying runner-in, Jim Shackleton, a work-horse at centre, Iain Laughland, the maestro tactician and himself very quick off his mark, and Tremayne Rodd, a burly tackling scrum-half who could break tackles. London Welsh fielded some cracking sevens at Twickenham with the likes of Billy Raybould, John Dawes, Tony Gray, John Taylor, Geoff Evans and a little chap who never got a cap but who was a star turn in the short game, Gareth James, who had studied at St Luke's in Exeter. Those class sides of the sixties and seventies, London Scottish, London Welsh and Loughborough Colleges, were the first I had seen who commanded such pace and ball-handling surety as to be able to play sevens rugby on retreat as they slowed the pace of play with intuitive running off-the-ball until a gap appeared. Then one of the quickies was gone before the gap could close. Borders didn't approve. I remember Loughborough once being roundly booed at Melrose as they handled and shuffled backwards almost to their own line before erupting. The Border style was one of 'up-and-at-'em', of giving the opposition as little time on the ball as possible, of taking the game to the opposition and harassing them into error by making first tackles count. And although there have been successes in Scotland by invading sides, more often than not they have been seen off. The mighty Barbarians have played in Border tournaments some half-a-dozen times but have yet to take away a trophy. Gala folk were thrilled when their champion side of the late sixties and seventies beat Loughborough Colleges by 38-5 in the 1969 Netherdale final. Duncan Paterson, now convener of Scotland's selectors, scored five tries at three points apiece in that final. He was a mighty talent as a sevens scrum-half, and there also were three Browns, Arthur, Peter and Johnny, in a Gala seven that dominated the period 1969 to 1972. Hawick had a similar spell, winning ten senior tournaments in a row during 1966 and 1967 with special craft and skill at half-back from Harry Whitaker and Colin Telfer. More recently, the men of Poynder Park, Kelso, have been the dominant force with such outstanding sevens specialists as Andrew Ker, Roger Baird, Bob Hogarth, John Jeffrey, Gary Callander, Ewan Common, Jim Hewit and Clive Millar. They have seen off some really heavy artillery – Sale, Metropolitan Police, Public School Wanderers, Swansea, Rosslyn Park, the Racing Club de France, Glamorgan Wanderers, and the Scottish Saltires.

Curiously, very few Scottish sides have made an impression at the Middlesex event, tending to be invited either before or after they come to a boil. Since the war some twelve home Scottish clubs have been guests at the Middlesex event and only two have proved winners: Heriots F.P. in 1949 and Stewarts Melville F.P. in 1982. But that isn't such a bad record when set alongside the fact that out of 66 Middlesex tournaments, guest sides have won on only six occasions.

As a family – and Scottish at that – we have had some enjoyable experiences at the Middlesex sevens. All four of us, Bette, Linda, Janie and I, were in the enclosure seats in 1963 when Hawick reached the final and lost narrowly (11-15) to a great London Scottish seven of that time. We were there too when our son-in-law, Alan Lawson, played for the London Scottish seven who got to the 1979 final and when Alan led Heriots F.P. to the final five years later. I was lucky enough, too, to be providing commentary when London Scottish created a shattering upset in 1991 with a dramatic last-seconds winning try over the hottest of favourites, Harlequins. As a Scot I was thrilled by that win even though the exiles had proved me so wrong. A bit earlier in the tournament I had described the Harlequins as one of the strongest sevens I ever had seen. They had the sizzling pace of Harriman, Davis and Carling and splendid ball-winners in Peter Winterbottom and Chris Sheasby. But after taking an early 12-14 lead, perhaps they became a little over-confident and that proved fatal against the London Scottish seven with not a capped player in it who, throughout the tournament, had responded to adversity by stepping up the pace with pride and perseverance. There was such a dramatic end to that final, with Kevin Troupe scoring the vital try with the last move of the game, that we all got so excited, including the transmission director, Johnny Watherston, whose brother, Rory, played in the last London Scottish seven to win at Twickenham in 1965, that we almost forgot about the conversion by Mark Appleson. No one seemed to mind. The Twickenham audience, who always give unashamed support

to the underdog, were on their feet to salute an unexpected and remarkable triumph by a team whose superb fitness owed so much to
Olympic 100-metres champion, Alan Wells, and his wife, Margo.

Yet for a supreme example of players being thrown together with virtually no preparation, and succeeding in putting it all together in winning
style, the French and Irish take the biscuit. When Melrose held their centenary sevens in 1983 the French Barbarians played a wing as prop, a
scrum-half as hooker, a full-back as general utility and walked off with
the trophy. At the same venue in 1991, the Irish Wolfhounds met for the
first time on the Friday night. Dennis McBride, the captain, had never
before come across his two wings, Brendan Hanavan (Fylde) and David
Beggy (Currie). The squad of nine had a brief practice session on the
Saturday morning as much as to be able to recognise each other from a
distance as for the gelling of minds! But class will out. Those Wolfhounds kept things simple, let their skills and their judgement speak for
themselves and waltzed off with the spoils.

The tournament that really stands out, however, is the Cathay Pacific
and Hong Kong Bank sevens in Hong Kong, which has been going now
for sixteen years and which, in every sense, is a world sevens competition. I've been lucky enough to have gone out there for the BBC in
the last three years. I'd heard a great deal about it beforehand from
players, officials and supporters. I had been invited by Willie Purves,
chairman of the Hong Kong Bank and a great rugby man from Kelso, to
go out there some three or four seasons previously, but had declined on
the grounds that I would have required more leave of absence from
school duty and the Education Committee already had been most gener-
ous and understanding. I didn't want to go to the well too often. However, once I had retired from teaching I succumbed to the blandishments
of Willie and of Ian Robertson, former Watsonians and Scotland stand-
off and BBC TV and radio commentator, who occasionally creates an
impression of almost running the Hong-Kong sevens all by himself! Ian
is a remarkable personality for whom I have developed a deep respect
and admiration. Nothing seems to bother him. He is a fund of information, unfailingly cheeky and funny in a very acceptable way and he
takes my breath away by the manner in which he will take on the most
difficult commentary assignments. Ian will cope with Singapore v
Malaysia, all the players so alike, without turning a hair! He just goes
down to their dressing-room before their tie and bosses them into lining
up for an identification parade. That's Ian!

There are some aspects of the Hong Kong event that I don't like. I find over a dozen hours on an aeroplane, even one as comfortable and as delightfully organised as a Cathay Pacific jet, really tiresome. Folk used to think that my reluctance to travel on Lions tours and to Hong Kong was owing to a fear of flying. Not so. I am totally fatalistic about air travel and feel no apprehension at all at the prospect of flying. How I might feel if something went wrong during the flight I'm not so sure, but it is that interminable journey that I find irksome. Nor do I enjoy the close, dampish heat of Hong Kong. I revel more in a crisp coolness, even a sharp breeze. Nevertheless Hong Kong is quite amazing and the folk there very friendly and hospitable. We stay in the Hong Kong Hilton. The manager is a strict yet genial Scot from Fife, James Smith. He and his lovely wife, Julia, are kindness itself. The hotel is a model which reflects the organisational ability and the discipline of the manager himself. Willie Purves bosses everybody but nothing is too much trouble for him, he gets things done and his Thursday evening dinner receptions for the Scottish Border club squad in 1990 and the Scottish national squad in 1991 were thoroughly enjoyable functions and an indication of the desire on the part of Scots in Hong Kong to ensure an enjoyable stay for their fellow country men and women.

The visit in 1991 was a memorable one, because Bette and I were accompanied by our daughters, Linda and Janie, both keen rugby followers, who joined us in marking our fortieth wedding anniversary on the Friday, the eve of the sevens tournament. At the Willie Purves reception, Bette and I received lovely gifts and on the Friday we were very touched by an arrangement made between James Smith and the Scotland captain, John Jeffrey, for a reception attended by the entire Scottish sevens squad and at which a huge anniversary cake was wheeled in by the chef. John made a delightful speech and it was a lovely gesture that the family appreciated very much indeed.

Covering Hong Kong sevens has to be the most testing undertaking of all. There are all kinds of pitfalls in-so-far as identification is concerned because, to a European, so many of the players look alike. The Japanese, Koreans, Thailanders, Sri Lankans and Malaysians have very little in the way of blonde or ginger hair, bald heads or beards as a means of identification! The Fijians and Western Samoans also are quite hard to distinguish. There is another little problem. The lads from the Arabian Gulf don't have numbers on their jerseys but Arabic symbols! Fortunately, I have never had to commentate on any of their games but Ian Robertson has. I should mention here that I. Robertson Esquire, who once scored a try and a drop-goal for Scotland in the first half against Wales at Cardiff Arms Park, took the Arabic script in his stride!

Other than that, the tournament is just fabulous and the dissemination of information to all members of the media is quite excellent. I remember a big south sea islander saying that, in his view, the Hong Kong sevens were really the Olympic games of Rugby Union. Certainly, the Hong Kong event encapsulates all the really good things that the game has to offer – splendid organisation, wonderful sporting spirit, universal camaraderie, admirable field behaviour, the most enjoyable crowd participation, the chance for emergent nations with no great rugby union tradition to lock horns with the mighty men of New Zealand, Australia, Fiji, Wales, Scotland and the Barbarians. There is, too, scintillating running and handling which is what the game is supposed to be all about. I was delighted when the Scots followed the Welsh lead of 1990 and sent a fully representative national squad to Hong Kong in 1991. They didn't do as well as the Welsh, who shook everybody by eliminating the fancied Australians in the 1990 quarter-final with three battling tries from Arthur Emyr, before succumbing to the Fijians who went on to beat New Zealand in the final. Scotland were outrun, hustled and bustled into shock quarter-final defeat by the Canadians. But the point is that they went as Scotland and I hope that England and Ireland will follow suit. If a world international sevens tournament is to be established on a regular basis after the one planned for Scotland at Murrayfield in 1993, it should be staged in Hong Kong where so many countries have found a vehicle for the expression of their love of the short game and, what is more, their skill and aptitude for it. Hong Kong could do with a bigger stadium but the colony is the very heart of the international sevens.

During my three visits there I have seen some quite staggering sights. In the 1989 final Australia played an all international seven. Just have a glance at this line up: David Campese (42 caps), Acura Niuqila (5), Michael Lynagh (30), Brad Burke (1), Jeff Miller (16), Simon Poidevin (50) and Steve Tuynman (28). Campese, who scored six gorgeous tries, and Lynagh, with 56 points, provided one magical moment after another. Yet they lost 10-22 in the final to a New Zealand side that contained several uncapped players I hadn't even heard of – Dallas Seymour, Scott Pierce, Kevin Putt and Eric Rush. The little Waikato scrum-half, putt-putt-putted his way home for two tries in that final and it was the first time I have marvelled at the silky-smooth acceleratory powers of

Eric Rush, an Auckland flanker who proved a tournament personality. The point about those young New Zealanders is that when you added in John Schuster, Terry Wright, John Gallagher, Zinzan Brooke and Pat Lam you had nine guys, each of whom could score from long-range and whose running off the ball was simply mesmeric. There was one little episode that underlined the incredible skills of those New Zealanders. They were 6-10 down to Fiji in the semi-final with time running out and were forced to touch down. Their captain, the 6ft 2in and 16-stone Zinzan Brooke, hinted at kicking the 22-metres drop-out to the left but, a glance to the right showed him that Dallas Seymour was positioned, bird alone, on the right touch-line. Whereupon Zinzan placed the drop-out with his weaker left foot on a sixpence behind the Fiji wing and Seymour, all anticipation, raced on to the bounce, scored between the posts and a John Gallagher conversion took the New Zealanders through by 12-10.

One other aspect of New Zealand sevens play that impressed me was the physical ferocity of much of their tackle engagement. No standing-off and letting the other guys play but 'up-and-at-'em' with a series of shuddering, bruising tackles that were fair but intimidatory. Ironically, it was this very same virtue which allowed the Fijians to turn the tables on the New Zealanders in both the 1990 and 1991 finals. The Fijians sailed into their tackles like men possessed, upsetting New Zealand confidence and rhythm. Nor could I believe what I was seeing in the 1990 final when, in one astonishing move, Waisale Serevi, the young Fijian stand-off magician, manufactured a blind, split-second pass over his head to Noa Nadruku, who promptly passed it between his legs to Tomasi Cama who stayed just in front of John Gallagher for the winning try. It was typically audacious handling play by the Fijians who tend to make it up as they go along. Serevi, with his running hitch-kick to deceive opponents, was a little genius. In 1991 Nadruku ran in 11 tries with an amazing demonstration of power running, and who could ever forget the thundering try-scoring feats of the massive Mesake Rasari. That was some sight. I'd only seen him once in fifteens before but had witnessed him eat a huge breakfast in the Hilton Hotel and that could have been listed as a tourist attraction! Mesake enjoyed his breakfasts.

It is small wonder that players, officials and referees all regard the Hong Kong sevens as a unique and rich experience, and that the tournament has been described variously as 'a mardi-gras cocktail of fun' and 'a blend of sport, culture and bier-fest'. The running of the tournament reflects immense credit on the chairmen of the sevens committee, Dermot Agnew and Don Watson, and their committee men and helpers.

I used to enjoy playing sevens although you have to be something of a masochist to take that view. Sevens is a form of physical torture that has to be experienced to be believed. Seven minutes each way may seem a bit of a dawdle, but on a full-sized pitch of a hundred and ten yards by seventy-five (100 metres by 69 metres) it can leave you absolutely 'puggled', your throat raw and dry, your legs heavy and pooped. Scrummages, with only three against three, can be surprisingly taxing and there are hardly any opportunities for taking a breather except in the case of injury. Nor is your will to go on more severely tested than when you are faced with a long retreat run to cover an opposition punt downfield and when you find yourself with the ball in your hands near your own line and the open prairie in front of you with nothing else for it but to take off and run till you drop. In such circumstances the length of that pitch can appear to be about five miles! At the same time if you really are fit it can be a joy, providing so many opportunities for running with the ball in your hands, for showing your skill in transference, in support running and in general decision-making. When the short game was first launched at Melrose in 1883 as the brain-child of Adam 'Ned' Haig, it did provide an attractive form of relief from the moving melée-orientated type of game played then in the fuller version. To some extent the same applies today. The fifteen-a-side game is so highly competitive that much of the playing is of the percentage variety. In sevens you have long-range tries and ball-transference from one side of the field to the other and back, then there are the dramatic sudden-death, extra-time provisions and the pleasant social and even carnival atmosphere, which makes for wonderfully attractive, fluent play.

There is something very special about winning a sevens tournament. That winners' medal, given at all the Scottish Border tournaments, represents a goodly portion of blood, sweat and tears, and it was particularly enjoyable when Hawick won their own tournament in 1947 because just the week previously we had been knocked out in the first round at Melrose by a penalty-goal kicked by Archie Lockie for Kelso. So we restored our prestige a bit at Hawick and I had the pleasure of scoring the opening try against Stewarts College F.P. in the final, although I didn't have far to run and Jimmy Chalmers, our stand-off, reckoned that he was the one who pushed me over the line! We had big Wattie Scott, a wing, playing as a prop and what a success he was. I was the other prop and the hooker was Cecil Froud, a rare personality, a little bundle of energy, tough as nails. In that final he had a slight difference of opinion with Rolf Koren, a giant of 18-stones. There was a bit of head bumping and 'yahoo' in each scrummage between the little and large of sevens hookers, but it was indicative of the spirit of the times that, at the local Palais de Danse that evening, Cecil and Rolf danced the tango together, none the worse for wear.

A week later we met Stewarts F.P. in the Jed-Forest final and this time they took the spoils. I remember once playing at Langholm after a dry, hot spring and following one tackle, I was coughing and spluttering with dust from the hard ground. You needed a thick coating of vaseline on your knees for that kind of ground condition. Recently, I went to Langholm to report their sevens for the *Glasgow Herald* after a dry spell that had rendered most grounds very hard. But Langholm had taken precautions. I think it was Walter Hislop, their former hooker, who told me that the Langholm club had pumped 35,000 gallons of water in order to soften the pitch on the Thursday, only to find that it rained most of Friday! Just Langholm's luck! They are a great club on the Western fringes of the Scottish Border rugby area, a bit isolated from the other senior clubs and more often than not struggling to maintain their status because of limited playing resources. But they keep going, with town pride and tradition to spur them on, and it is always a pleasure to go there – not least on their sevens day, which draws the Scottish season to a close. One of their most loyal supporters is Sir Hector Monro, former Minister for Sport, and a splendid forward stalwart in the post-war years when Langholm were a genuine force in the land, with the likes of Jim Telford alongside Hector in the front row of both fifteen-a-side and sevens. Hector has always been one of the great defenders of the sevens tournaments and I side with him in the belief that it provides a very special type of rugby football that we should always treasure.

In 1981, BBC Scotland decided to provide TV coverage of the Langholm versus Gala game at Milntown which would decide the division one championship. So I drove up to Langholm on the Thursday night to attend their training session and so identify players I hadn't seen before. In a chat with their committee I gathered that their main concern was that their outstanding forward, Hector Barnfather, should not be ordered off. Hector was every inch a competitor, totally committed to the Langholm cause, a typically uncompromising Border forward good enough to have played for the South on a number of occasions and notably against the 1975 Wallabies. Hector also had a bit of a short fuse. The committee's concern was that he might be goaded, in the heat of the battle, in a fiercely ferocious Border rivals game, into action that he might later regret, with consequent damage to Langholm's hopes of a famous victory. They were spot on! The match was still in its first quarter when Hector was given his marching orders. Gala won with a bit to spare. But Hector, ever the enthusiast, is now helping with the preparation of Langholm sides with the principle aim of seeing the club climb back into division one in Scotland's National Leagues.

One final point about sevens. Ever since the turn of the century, rugby folk in the Scottish Border country have allocated all of April and part of August-September to the playing of sevens at some eight senior tournaments. The 'blue riband' of that circuit is the Melrose event at Greenyards where the first-ever sevens tournament took place. In 1991 an estimated 14,000 attended the Melrose event and each of the other tournaments attracts a good crowd, and this is true of the Selkirk and Kelso events which are staged at the beginning of each season. The sevens mean a lot to each of the Border clubs who stage them, not only from a financial point of view but also as a social event in which the entire family can participate. There is a threat, however, to the Border sevens circuit from those who would use April for a Scottish Rugby Union knock-out cup competition. I would be all in favour of such a cup competition because, as has been shown in Wales and England, cup play generates massive interest, with crowds of 50,000 plus attending the finals, and the sudden-death element lends such games a special flavour. But not at the expense of the Border sevens. So long as the Border clubs want to continue in their sevens tournaments they should be allowed to do so and any cup competition should be fitted around them, so that teams are not shorn of their class men. So far the Border clubs have not been tempted by the financial blandishments held out by the prospect of cup play. Perhaps one day but so far the general Border attitude has been; *not at the expense of the short game.*

16

The People You Meet!

Rugby Union over the years, has spawned some rare characters of all shapes and sizes, some of whom have enlivened the scene by their distinctive reactions to certain situations or by their special brand of humour, others having created an impact by standing on a few toes in creating controversy, argument and annoyance.

Two real characters to whom I will always feel indebted are Cliff Morgan and Alan Mouncer. The strongest influence on my broadcasting career has come from them. I will be forever grateful for the encouragement given to me in the earliest days by Peter Thomson, who had charge of BBC Scotland's sport output, and whose faith in me was an important factor in my progress, and Archie Henry and producer Bill Stevenson also guided me along the way. You can imagine what a lift I got when Peter sent me the following letter in March 1968:

A few weeks ago I received the following minutes of the sports department meeting in London which is chaired by Mr Bryan Cowgill, head of sports programmes, television.
Rugby: Head of sports programmes, television, congratulated Mr Alan Mouncer and Mr Dewi Griffiths on their magnificent presentation of the All Blacks rugby tour, adding that the commentator, Mr Bill McLaren, had emerged as **THE** commentator of the season.

Peter then added 'great stuff' before signing his name.

The happiest and most rewarding experiences, however, were in the company of Cliff and Alan. Cliff named us 'the three M's' – Mouncer, Morgan and McLaren and we were responsible for most of the early transmissions of 'Rugby Special', Alan as producer, Cliff as presenter, commentator and interviewer and myself as commentator. It was a privilege for me to work with them. Alan was a producer of exceptional gifts, full of sound advice which he proffered in a quiet, easy-going manner. He had so much to do with moulding my style, especially when I came in for a bit of flak in earlier times for yapping too much. One letter from a chap in Myddelton Passage, London, referred to my 'monotonous monologues . . . like a sullen, aching tooth,' and informed me 'your voice is always there, one cannot concentrate on the play. Would it not now be courteous for you to give some consideration to wishes of viewers who, indirectly, are the persons who pay your fee?' In my reply I stressed that a lot of the 'Grandstand' viewers were not rugby specialists and rather enjoyed receiving background information about players and explanations of refereeing decisions. Two months later I received the following letter from the same critic:

Honour where honour is due. I must congratulate you on your commentary of the Scotland versus Wales match on Saturday. Gone were the irrelevant details, gone was the aching tooth, for you gave pauses in which we could appreciate the atmosphere of a rugby international. My wife and I passed a pleasant afternoon watching a good match and listening to a good commentary. Don't forget that I would like to buy you a drink sometime. You deserve it. Perhaps it could be when you come here for the England versus France match on 22 February.

Actually I had tried to cut my cackle a bit to accord with Alan Mouncer's sage advice 'just be conscious of your pacing'. Like Bill Taylor after him, Alan always wrote a letter of thanks at the end of the season and I got quite a kick from one I received from him in April 1969. It said:

I couldn't let the season end without expressing my admiration and gratitude for your excellent commentaries and for all your other contributions to 'Grandstand'. It really was a marvellous season, from the rugby point of view and for you personally. Out of the many compliments I have heard paid to you, the most memorable one comes from Joe Mercer. Five days after one of the internationals I met him for lunch and he spent at least ten minutes talking about your scene set interview with David Coleman. He was really impressed with your knowledge of the game – as indeed we all are.

Cliff always has been great company and a fine host, with a fund of cheery stories. He was always the true professional; he would amaze me by turning up without a note of any kind, and yet would stand in front of that camera and introduce a 'Rugby Special' programme as to the manner born. Once, I conducted an interview with Cliff after a Scotland v Wales game at Murrayfield and before he answered the first question he doffed his trilby to the viewers. It took a big trick. I heard more about that little courtesy from folk at home than about anything in our interview. That is Cliff. Some character. Once for an international at Lansdowne Road, Cliff and I had to be at the ground at 10.45 on the Saturday morning in order to do a scene set for 'Grandstand', after which we usually would return to Jury's Hotel, there to be guests of Telefis Eirean at lunch, always a delightful experience, with commentator Fred Cogley and producer John O'Brien, two of the nicest guys I have ever come across, as our hosts. On this day, however, Cliff suggested we have a burnt sausage and coffee in a wee hut behind the East stand at the ground. There, he was greeted like a long-lost son by an aged female, brown as a berry, with lived-in features, and a boisterous personality, who served us burnt sausages and sweet, milky coffee. I'll never forget those burnt sausages. I like my food birstled like that. It wasn't quite in the class of the gorgeous lunch at Jury's but very enjoyable all the same. And the 'crack' was good too.

No one had greater influence on Scottish rugby than Herbert Waddell, a strong, somewhat autocratic personality, who had been an outstanding stand-off for Glasgow Academicals and Scotland and had earned undying fame through his drop-goal, then worth four points, that won the Grand Slam for Scotland in the 14-11 defeat of England at Murrayfield in 1925. Herbert lived and breathed Rugby Union. He had a clear imprint in his mind as to how the Scottish game should be played and he influenced the thinking of many rugby men all over the world. Towards the end of 1968 I received a series of letters from Herbert, all written staccato style in short sentences, all wonderfully informative. Once he wrote me two full pages about Scotland's stand-off Colin Telfer:

I am very pleased with Telfer, frankly. He is quick off his feet. His reactions are quick. He has perfect hands. He must choose his breaks. Better from a heel against the head. The scrum wheels the right way. He can go left. The opposing wing forward is put two yards further away. Four breaks in a game is the maximum. *They must all be*

TRIES. His forte is passing and then backing up. The New Zealand stand-off once came in *outside* his outside-centre. Perhaps Telfer could try that. It means very fast running . . .

In another letter Herbert accompanied his text with drawings to show how best a stand-off could create space and time for himself in a drop-goal attempt from a scrummage. He was an extraordinary citizen. He was responsible in large part for the publication, *Raise The Standard* in 1956, a 32-page booklet based on lectures given at the Scottish Rugby Union's early coaching conferences. Its purpose, as outlined in the fore-word by W. Maxwell Simmers, president of the Scottish Rugby Union and another of Scotland's greats, was to focus attention on some funda-mentals of Rugby Union 'which seem to have been lost sight of in modern rugby'. It certainly did that. Of course it laid stress on the value of the 3-2-3 scrummage as an attacking set-piece, compared with the 3-4-1 because in those days the Scottish hierarchy still held faith in the scrummage wheel and dribble which had been the lynch pin of Scottish attack strategy during some halycon earlier times. Few modern forwards have ever heard of the 3-2-3 scrummage. But, in many respects, that Scottish Rugby Union booklet underlined requirements that are still very much part and parcel of the modern game and one can almost feel the Waddell influence behind one of several bald statements: 'Unneces-sary touch-kicking should be stopped. Players do not train hard just to see other players continually kicking the ball out of play on Saturday afternoons. Many touch-kicks do not merit applause – the reverse.' If only modern players would take more heed of that advice. Certainly Herbert took immense satisfaction from seeing his beloved Barbarians, for whom he was the fifth of that famous nomadic club's six presidents, eschew safety-first play by running and handling whenever possible – and sometimes when it wasn't – thus giving huge pleasure to thousands and thousands of supporters and players. I can't help feeling that Her-bert and many of his cronies, who gave so much to the game, would be saddened by some trends in modern times. Once I accompanied a local golfing companion, Raymond 'Jock' Oliver, to Muirfield, there to join Herbert for a round of golf and lunch. Herbert said I would be provided with a caddy. I said I would rather deal with my own clubs. Being Her-bert, he insisted. So I had a caddy who succeeded in clubbing me wrong almost throughout! I was Herbert's partner. He was a competitor. He liked to win. So did I. But we didn't! I thought my caddy was to blame.

Herbert was not amused. But he treated us to a magnificent lunch. Muir-field can be a beast of a course for the uninitiated and, indeed, for the in-itiated, but the lunches are something else, and in this case it com-pensated for that caddy!

The Irish have more than their fair share of personalities. Once, at the World Cup, I introduced my wife to one of the greatest Irish players and administrators at virtually every level of the game, Syd Millar. He took one look at me, one at Bette and then said, 'Ah, Jaisus, Bette, you could have done a hell of a sight better!' One of the favourite quips of the former Ireland stand-off, Mick Quinn, whenever a young lady is in-troduced to him is: 'Ah, hello again. How are yee? Oi didn't recognise you wit' yer clothes on!' Over the years, the story has been told of Tom Reid, the great garryowen' and Irish lock of the fifties, describing that moment of terror when someone passed to him in an international at Twickenham: 'Jaisus, der wos oi, in the middle of Twickenham wit 60,000 looking on, and wit dis ting in me hands.' That was a plaintive reference to those days when forwards were there to get the ball for their backs and not for any fancy handling such as they do nowadays!

Two of the most remarkable personalities I have come across were both, like myself, born and bred in Hawick – Hugh McLeod and George Stevenson. When I was starting out as a radio commentator and writer, Hugh and 'Stevie' were just establishing themselves in the Scottish side and I found them most agreeable and helpful companions, especially at Scotland's away matches. I was very proud of both of them because they were outstanding players who brought great credit to our home town of Hawick, Hugh gaining 40 caps and two Lions tours as a prop, George playing 24 times for Scotland as centre or wing. They were, and still are, great buddies and yet totally different in approach; Hugh, serious, dedi-cated, totally committed; George, a happy-go-lucky extrovert, always poking fun and performing quite outrageous deeds on the field of play. Their contrasting attitude was underlined when Stevie gained his first cap against England at Murrayfield in 1956. After some ten minutes of play and during an injury break, Stevie sidled over and said to Hugh, 'Hey, the girls aren't in their seats yet!' – this in reference to their young ladies, Myra and Jessie. Hugh simply exploded: 'Do you mean to tell me you've been watching their seats in the stand to see if they have arrived yet? Listen, pal, it's England yee're playin' th' day, no Greenock Wanderers.' Hugh is one of the straightest men I've every come across, absolutely forthright, a wee bit dogmatic at times, but one who doesn't shy away from an argument and who says exactly what is on his mind.

Stevie is just good fun. Once he was driving Bette, Barrie Laidlaw, the international referee, and myself to Edinburgh Airport for the flight to Dublin and on the straight along the top of Soutra Hill, he gave a waggle on the wheel that frightened the living daylights out of all of us. When next he came up to go out to dinner with us, I was sitting in our lounge, blindfold, with The Holy Bible in my hands, and insisted on being led out to the car. Stevie was driving!

Once I had to play a blind shot from down the hill on our fifth hole on Hawick golf course and was delighted to find that I had holed a six-iron for an eagle two. Then I detected a ruse in which my wife was a fellow conspirator. Stevie had run a hundred yards to pick up my ball which had gone wide of the green, popped it into the hole then had sprinted back before I got up the hill. That's Stevie!

It might surprise his Lions contemporaries to hear that Hugh has become something of a specialist in dog-shows, mainly through his acquisition of a quite magnificent bulldog, which he and Myra named 'Spike'. What a character he was, and with such a pedigree that Hugh became thoroughly interested in showing Spike, who became something of a star turn and competition winner. Being Hugh, of course, he studied the process of dog preparation in all its detail. Spike sadly succumbed to respiratory failure but I have a feeling that Hugh and another Spike soon will be gathering in the 'best of breed' and 'best in show' awards before very long.

I've already mentioned Andrew 'Jock' Wemyss, the one-eyed doyen of Scottish rugby correspondents in Chapter 6. He was the Barbarians historian. He hardly missed one of their matches. He was also one of the co-founders of the Scottish Co-Optimists, along with George St. Clair Murray. What an enthusiast Jock was and what a deep love he had for the game. He reacted very strongly to anything that besmirched the game and he didn't stand for any nonsense. Once at a Scottish trial at Murrayfield two young thugs came along towards the press box, clanking seats as they approached. As they were about to pass us, Jock suddenly reached over, grabbed each one by his shirt collar and bodily lifted them over the Press seat rail, growling into their faces a grim warning about what would happen if they continued to risk damaging the Murrayfield stand seats, before promptly depositing them on the other side. They didn't hang around. Jock always said to me that my rugby education would not be complete until I had attended the final of the French club championship. I haven't done that yet but hope to do so, accompanied by Bette, before 'I hand in my dinner pail'.

I count among my friends John Reason. That bald statement might make me a few enemies, because if ever a Rugby Union journalist has laid about him with rare gusto and without much concern about who he offends, John Reason is the one. He is the bravest rugby writer I know and I admire him very much for having the courage to write what he believes. He must have a lot of friends as well as enemies, if one is to judge by the amount of information, classified and otherwise, that he elicits from various sources to provide background for the most compulsive rugby reading of all: 'Norling Omission blows Whistle on World Cup chaos'; 'Chaos reigns as Board fail to do their Duty'; 'Railroaded R.F.U. steaming headlong into the buffers'. Those are just some of the recent headlines to John's stories in the *Sunday Telegraph*. I know that the journalist doesn't write the headlines but, in John's case, they fairly reflect the meat and tone of his text. He is not infallible and I have told him frankly that he can be very hard on Scotland. Even when Scotland won the Grand Slam in such spirited fashion against England in 1990, John hinted that England had given it away rather than that Scotland had risen to the challenge brilliantly on the day. He was wrong about how Bill Beaumont would turn out as a player and captain although eventually he did concede that B.B. had developed into one of the greats of his day. But, make no mistake, J. Reason's contribution to the literary aspect of the game and the way he encourages his readers to give careful thought to what is happening in the game, by keeping them informed in a way that no one else has managed to do, have been quite remarkable, and although there are those who will put out the flags when he lays down his pen, there are many others who will miss very much his pungent comments and his barbed wit. Nor can one imagine a more fascinating dinner companion. Many are the eve-of-international meals I have enjoyed in the Reason company although, once in a classy Edinburgh hotel, the bill was like something resembling the national debt. As it was 'the Reason's' turn to pay, his remark was very much to the point. He took one look at the bill, smiled wanly, then delivered at the pit head: 'This, Pollock, has been rather a bruising evening'.

One BBC producer who has had quite an influence on my career has been Dewi Griffiths of BBC Wales, another remarkable chap, talented, outgoing, full of fun, but very much the professional TV technician – imaginative and innovative, and insistent upon the highest standard from everybody concerned. Dewi is another who has led me by the hand along the paths of Rugby Union commentary. He has a way of boosting your confidence because, apart from anything else, you know that he is on top of his job and that you can depend on his help and encouragement at any time. Mind you, he sometimes became so enthusiastic as to feed you bits of information that weren't quite accurate. 'And here is Barry Llewellyn with seven caps,' Dewi would chatter into the commentary ear phones, when I knew perfectly well that it was only Barry's fifth! That apart, Dewi has been a great guy to work with and one of the reasons why I always enjoyed covering a match at Cardiff Arms Park, although there was one occasion when Dewi had to work with an unfamiliar camera crew. They weren't on top of the job and Dewi told them so in no uncertain terms. There was I already in full commentary flow and all the while, in my earphones, was Dewi's voice telling the camera men to 'get your bloody fingers out!' They did! Dewi was a man of many parts.

Prior to the World Cup Final in Auckland, Dewi arranged a dinner party attended by the World Cup Final producer and his wife, Nigel Starmer-Smith, Bette and myself. Scotland's representative on the International Board and the 1991-92 SRU president, Gordon Masson was having a meal in the same restaurant and it was a kind gesture on his part to send us a gift of wine for the evening meal. After which, Dewi demonstrated another of his talents by rattling the keyboard to brilliant effect as we sang and danced the evening away.

Charlie Drummond of Melrose and the Scottish Rugby Union was a good friend for, although I have never been a great one for the social scene in which Charlie revelled, we always somehow kept in touch, usually through Charlie's chronic inability to get to sleep before two or three in the morning. He had the unusual habit of ringing you in the early hours 'just for a wee blether' and many is the time that I've stood shivering by the telephone as Charlie, and occasionally his great pal, Alf Wilson, as well as Kathleen, Charlie's charming wife, chattered away about the game and current affairs. And yet you could never take umbrage. Charlie used to be an outstanding threequarter and a bruising tackler. Once at Selkirk sevens I was clear away for a try when a building fell down on me, or that's how it seemed. Charlie hit me with the force of a tornado. You got the feeling that his shoulders were constructed out of brickwork, and he was so quick that his tackle-impact was shattering. Charlie always had a word for everyone and was another of those cheery, larger-than-life characters who helped to enhance Scottish Rugby's standing in the world game. Once after a very rough Wales v Scotland game at Cardiff I was told that Herbert Waddell and Charlie had unofficially told Welsh committee men that if they didn't discipline two of their players Scotland wouldn't play Wales the following season. As it turned out, they did. Bette can also testify to Charlie's dancing ability although the kilted Charlie knew only one step, the polka. So it was a polka whether for quick-step, tango or fox-trot! But no one ever minded. Charlie was a fellow you just couldn't help liking.

Another of the larger-than-life characters I have come across in my rugby travels has been Ian McLauchlan, capped as a loose-head prop out of Jordanhill College 43 times and who still holds the record of having captained Scotland in 19 major internationals. His international career lasted from 1969 to 1979 and in that time he created a reputation as one of the most feared scrummagers in the game, in which regard he had a sage and uncompromising guide in the Jordanhill and Scottish coach, Bill Dickinson. McLauchlan wasn't taken seriously when he first hit the big time. For one thing he had a roly-poly build and weighed in at just over 13 stones. I have to admit that when I first came across him I thought he was just too small for the international game that, at the time, had props such as Ken Gray, Alastair Hopkinson and Brian Muller of New Zealand, John O'Shea of Wales, Syd Millar of Ireland, Mof Myburgh and Hannes Marais of South Africa. They were all big men and I doubted that a player of McLauchlan's physique could hold his own with such giants. Hold his own? He gave them all a hell of a time! He posed all kinds of different problems for them because of his shape but also because of his strength which, along with his weight, was being boosted by special training supervised by the crafty Dickinson. Indeed at that time Jordanhill's two props, McLauchlan and Struan McCallum, had an aggregate weight of barely 26 stones but they gave rivals of all shapes and sizes a very hard time indeed.

There was one famous picture of McLauchlan, on tour with the Lions, lifting one huge South African prop clean off the ground in a scrummage. McLauchlan could scrummage comfortably at heights that caused such discomfort to bigger men and once he had got them down there he had the technique and strength to embarrass them. When Scotland played England on consecutive Saturdays in 1971 at Twickenham and then a week later at Murrayfield in the centenary international there was a story that after the first match, one Englishman had complained at the front row tactics of McLauchlan and had made a comment on the lines that 'we just do not play like that down here'. Whereupon McLauchlan, with that forthright Tarbolton (Ayrshire) way of his, snorted: 'Well, pal, you have exactly one week to find how to do it.' A week later it was much the same story. Scotland won 26-6. He was a hard, tough, unafraid little man with a ruthless streak that brooked no half measures and his teamtalks as Scottish captain were models in their pride in wearing the thistle and in creating the right mood.

I had the pleasure of having Ian as summariser during television commentary of the Scotland v Ireland game at Murrayfield in 1989. That was a rich experience. One of his comments made my hair curl. It was when the Irish lock Neil Francis had a lick at someone but missed. Ian told several million viewers that Francis must beware of gaining the reputation of a softie because 'there isn't much point in having a go at somebody unless you make sure that you connect'. Of course commentators have to be careful not to incite young viewers into reprehensible acts by glorifying them on the field, but that was Ian. Straight from the shoulder. It still is. I enjoyed working with him. And make no mistake, virtually all of his contemporaries would agree with the feeling that if you were in a situation where the shrapnel was flying Ian McLauchlan would be one guy you would want by your side.

Another BBC producer to whom I owe a great deal is Brian Rogers, whom I first met when I shared the 1987 World Cup commentary coverage with Nigel Starmer-Smith. I covered the earlier stages of the competition in New Zealand whilst Nigel took on the Australian section. Brian was my producer but he proved to be much more than that. He smoothed my path throughout the series as map reader, chauffeur, guide, philosopher and friend. He had an uncanny knack of finding his way to wherever we wanted to go and he made sure that when it came time for commentary everything was in order and ready. Once, when we headed for Wellington by car to see one of the early ties, I was navigator which explains why we became unsure of our route! So we stopped and asked a huge farmer, with a face like a burnt walnut, which way we should take for Wellington. Like most things in New Zealand his answer was succinct and informative: 'First left and follow yer bloody nose.' We did and made it in time. You always did with Brian.

Bill Dickinson of Jordanhill College was another of rugby's unusual characters for whom I have very high respect. He once claimed to have scored a try for Hillhead High School F.P. against Hawick in a match that I played in. I treated his boast with a pinch of salt. I mean, had any Hillhead F.P. ever scored a try against the 'crème de la crème'? But I checked the record and he was justified in his claim! That earned him my admiration for a start, which was increased when he became Scotland's first officially appointed coach in the seventies. It was no secret that some of the SRU committee were not in favour of a national coach. Indeed the word 'coach' was never mentioned. Bill was termed the 'advisor to the captain' as the Union wanted to ensure that the captain's role in leading the side along the tactical minefield would be maintained. So Bill had to operate in somewhat difficult circumstances. But he got on with it and earned the players respect by his craft, wide tactical knowledge, unfettered enthusiasm and far-sightedness. Scotland gained a new respect under his guidance. Indeed, his tactical astuteness helped engineer one of the most successful periods in Scottish rugby history, 1971-1977 in which Scotland lost only one of fourteen games at Murrayfield; among their victories were four over England, including margins of 26-6 and 23-6, two over the mighty Wales of the seventies and two over France, 20-9 and 19-6. Bill was a genuine hard man who certainly put fire into Scottish bellies. He created one of the most formidable Scottish packs of all time comprising Ian McLauchlan, Quintin Dunlop or Bobby Clark, Sandy Carmichael, Alastair McHarg, Gordon Brown, Nairn MacEwan, Peter Brown and Rodger Arneil. He was a scrummaging expert who brought a new meaning to that phase of play and influenced the thinking in other countries.

Once, Bill had made some aggressive comments about a forthcoming match against England that brought from the England coach, John Burgess, who, like Dickinson, was forthright and unceremonious, the comment: 'I've seen this Scottish pack rucking. If it's blood on the boots they want, that's what they'll get.' The opening few minutes of the match at Twickenham were the fiercest I have seen, a bit akin to the Australian v England fracas which ended in Mike Burton being sent off in 1975. At Twickenham Nairn MacEwan was carted with a split head after only two minutes and replaced by Ian Barnes but it soon settled down into more civilised action. Dickinson had made his point. So had Burgess. In any event Dickinson deserves praise for overcoming early difficulties and prejudices and setting guidelines by which people could operate. Dickinson also succeeded in making the role of advisor or coach respectable. No one could have given more to the task and it was regrettable that, although, Scotland came close in 1973 and 1975, Dickinson didn't have a

Triple Crown to show for his valuable role in leading the way.

My job has brought exciting perks. For instance, I did appreciate the compliment in 1978 when Bette and I were invited to 10 Downing Street when the then Prime Minister, James Callaghan, held a reception to mark the feats of the Welsh rugby team in winning another Grand Slam during their second 'golden era'. That was an enjoyable experience, during which the Prime Minister showed us around the cabinet room. Fellow commentator Nigel Starmer-Smith and his wife, Ros, were there too and I thought it was a delightful gesture to have invited the two of us who, as commentators, had the pleasure of covering the brilliant rugby football played by those splendid Welsh sides of the seventies.

Bette and I have also been lucky enough to be invited twice to Royal Garden Parties at the Palace of Holyrood House in Edinburgh. On the first occasion we were accompanied by our older daughter, Linda, and I remember feeling a bit uncomfortable on entering the spacious lawns to find that I was one of comparative few who had opted for the permitted dark lounge suit instead of morning dress. When we came across a group of Scottish Rugby Union dignitaries I found that, in their toppers and tails, most of them were as uncomfortable as I was! On the second occasion I did opt for topper and tails. Daughter Janie was with us that time and we were very excited at being presented to Her Majesty the Queen. I remember Her Majesty making the point that Rugby Union seemed to have a place for every type, whether large or small, heavy or light. Janie, who had been at Ascot the previous week, congratulated the Queen on having had two winners there. In no time at all the Queen and Janie were engaged in an animated chat about horse racing with me a rather miffed bystander! That occasion, though, was a real thrill and as Her Majesty approached, I could feel the same stomach butterflies of nervousness as before the start of every commentary. I was quite astonished by, and filled with admiration for, the charming manner in which Her Majesty made people feel at ease and how she was so au fait with every subject, although clearly her preference was for horse racing.

It was in December 1979 that I received an MBE for services to Rugby Union. I felt quite undeserving when considering the thousands of volunteers in the game – gate-men, car-park attendants, tea ladies, groundsmen, club officials, coaches – who willingly give so much of their spare time simply through their love of the game and of their own club. I have been fortunate enough in my role as teacher of physical education to have organised primary school rugby in Hawick over a number

LEFT Bill Beaumont (Fylde and England) on high with a little help from Phil Blakeway

Famous personalities in Dublin, 1956. Left to right: Alf Wilson, self, Charlie Drummond, Bette and Sammy Walker

ABOVE Syd Millar (Ballymena and Ireland): 'Ah, Jaisus, Bette, you could have done a hell of a sight better!'

ABOVE RIGHT Willie Duggan (Blackrock College and Ireland): 'The quickest way to take the edge off your form is by training'!

Cameron Michael Henderson Gibson (NIFC and Ireland) – the most capped Irishman with 69 and simply the greatest back of them all

ABOVE LEFT Two sides to Michael Lynagh (Queensland and Australia) – here the pin-point punt . . .

ABOVE . . . there handling ignition

David Campese (ACT, NSW and Australia) moves the ball out of the tackle. This time they caught him. Often they didn't

ABOVE Colin Meads (King Country and New Zealand), known as 'Pine Tree' (second from right), is first on the scene with, in behind him, two great Springboks, Frik du Preez and Hannes Marais. Some trio!

Hugh McLeod and Spike

ABOVE LEFT The greatest Frenchman –
Serge Blanco (Biarritz and France) –
more caps, more tries than any of his
countrymen; more caps than anyone in
the history of the game

ABOVE RIGHT Jacques Fouroux (La
Voulte and France) – 'Le Patron' –
Grand Slam scrum-half and captain in
1977; Grand Slam coach in 1981 and
1987

With Douglas Elliot on the day they
named the Elliot Country Lounge at
the Carfraemill Hotel after the
famous Edinburgh Academical, a
mighty force for Scotland in the
postwar years

RIGHT The most dangerous wing I ever saw – Gerald Davies (Cardiff and Wales) – scoring a try against Scotland that I thought should have been disallowed. But as Gerald said afterwards: 'Oh, actually that wasn't my impression'!

Delme Thomas (Llanelli and Wales) rises like a spring salmon to make another spot-on lineout deflection, this for England–Wales against Scotland–Ireland at Twickenham in October 1970

ABOVE LEFT They seek him here – Barry John (Cardiff and Wales), the Red Phantom! . . .

ABOVE RIGHT . . . and another try for his Cardiff and Wales side-kick, Gareth Edwards

The inimitable J.P.R. Williams (London Welsh, Bridgend and Wales) – nose bleed and all, but still full of aggressive intent in taking them on. A linchpin in the second Welsh 'golden era'

TOP LEFT John Reason: 'This, Pollock, has been a very bruising evening'

TOP RIGHT Cliff Morgan (Cardiff and Wales): great player, great colleague, great friend

ABOVE RIGHT Clem Thomas (Swansea and Wales) – cheeky comments about my food intake, and great company

ABOVE LEFT McLaren and Edwards prior to a big match broadcast from Cardiff Arms Park of years and that had been a particularly pleasurable part of my teaching obligation and I have been doubly fortunate in having been able, through television commentary, to cover for a big viewing audience some of the most memorable events in the game. But I was thrilled, and the family had a wonderful time in London on the day of the investiture, especially as we had delightful company in Audrey and Andy Irvine. Scotland's most capped full-back was having his services to the game similarly marked and I followed Andy in the order of presentation. Her Majesty said, 'Do you know that young man who has just gone through?' I replied, 'Ma'am, everybody in Scotland knows that young man as one of the most exciting rugby players in the world.' Afterwards we all adjourned to the BBC at the typically thoughtful invitation of Cliff Morgan, who had so much to do with the success of BBC outside broadcast coverage in those days, and who had organised a lovely party to mark the occasion.

As I write in our lounge at home I can look upwards at the beautiful painting of Hawick's Wilton Lodge Park, by Adam Robson, Scotland's 1984 Grand Slam president and 1991 World Cup representative and former head of art at Dollar Academy, where our three Lawson grandchildren, Gregor, Rory and Lindsay, are pupils. The painting was a gift from all the rugby clubs in Hawick to mark my retirement from teaching and, especially, from coaching rugby among Hawick's youngest players, and is one of my most treasured possessions. It is the work of one of the most respected rugby men to come out of Hawick and whenever I gaze up at the painting it revives memories of some of the most enjoyable experiences of my teaching career, for it depicts the beautiful park and rugby pitches where I did most of my coaching.

It has embarrassed me to have been presented with treasured mementoes for what was, to me, pure enjoyment. I have received two tankards from the *Rugby World and Post* for services to the sport. The first was received on my behalf by one of my favourite Scots, the late Bill Taylor, the BBC producer, as I couldn't attend because of teaching commitments. For the second I got myself togged up in my blue Hong Kong suit and thoroughly enjoyed the presentation function sponsored by Whitbreads. It was especially pleasing that the presentation to me was made by Cliff Morgan.

It was in late 1972 that Hawick Rugby Club asked me to produce a book entitled 'One Hundred Years of Hawick Rugby' to mark the club's centenary. It was a considerable task made easier by the contributions from many local personalities who had given much to the game in Hawick, and from three guest writers, 'Jock' Wemyss, Norman Mair and John Methven, the last-named a school-master at Hawick High School and, later, a devoted stalwart of the Kirkcaldy club. I researched and wrote much of my contribution in Hawick Cottage Hospital as I was having a hernia put right, where I was looked after by another of my favourite townsfolk, Mrs Eileen Bonnerman, a wonderful Red Cross stalwart, and where, at the same time, Andrew Bowie, who gave a lifetime of service to the game, was a patient in the same ward. I did so enjoy hearing many of Andrew's stories of past Hawick rugby teams and players and that enabled me to feel the real flavour of the club from its early days. After the centenary book was published, Andrew, the club president, Willie MacTaggart, a flying Hawick threequarter in the twenties and thirties, and Wattie Scott, who had been desperately unlucky to miss out on a cap, arrived at our home to present me with a beautifully inscribed wine decanter and glasses for my work in collating and editing the club history. Here again I was being rewarded for performing a most interesting and agreeable function. Compiling that history was akin to much of my commentary preparation – hard and time-consuming, but very much a labour of love.

Once upon a time I was much concerned that people might think that I had insulted Sebastian Coe. The great middle-distance runner had been conducting a fitness course at Gleneagles Hotel and our daughter, Janie, and husband Derek had decided to attend. There was to be a farewell dinner and discussion with film of some great athletics feats with Sebastian in the key role. Daughter Linda and husband Alan as well as Bette and myself were invited to attend on that evening. I was simply thrilled to meet Sebastian Coe whom I regarded as the greatest middle-distance runner Great Britain has ever produced. We are so lucky to have such an athletics tradition and such dedicated men and women athletes as to be able to produce at the same time two such dominant middle-distance men as Coe and Steve Ovett, not to mention the Linford Christies, Tom McKeans and Peter Elliots of modern times.

Like so many of the truly great sportsmen and women Sebastian came over as a modest and friendly young man, so that what was to follow proved embarrassing to me and to our family. Things got a little behind time as they are wont to do on such occasions when folk mingle over a pre-dinner cocktail. By the time Sebastian started his talk and film show we were anxiously scanning our watches because it was absolutely essential that we were back at Linda and Alan's home in Limekilns, some forty minutes away, to relieve their baby-sitter, whose timings had to be spot on. Very reluctantly, and in the semi-darkness, we had to bid Janie and Derek au revoir before we crept out, like thieves in the night, to make our way home. That would have been fair enough as Janie and Derek had undertaken to explain our predicament to Sebastian. Unfortunately, at one point during his talk Sebastian said how pleased he was to have in his audience the BBC television rugby commentator, Bill McLaren, whereupon with the lights up, the audience all turned to have a look and found no McLaren. Of course, Janie and Derek made our apologies but you can imagine how I felt on hearing of that episode. It was a fascinating talk that Sebastian was giving and I felt really badly about having embarrassed him, but he understood that some things have higher priority and keeping to your word to your baby-sitter is one of them.

17
Not Tempted

Quite a number of folk found it hard to understand why I turned down the opportunity of joining the ITV commentary team for the televising of the World Cup. I suppose the plain answer is that I always have been a BBC man and was hopeful of continuing to be so for as long as they wanted me to do the job. It had come as quite a shock to all at the BBC when the contract for televising the World Cup was awarded to ITV. There were probably a number of reasons for this but I was of the view that BBC Scotland had played a part in that their coverage of the Scottish scene had not been extensive enough. Indeed, I wrote to the Head of Sport in Glasgow some years before the World Cup contract was decided, suggesting that more Scottish games should be covered. As one example, there were Edinburgh v South matches deciding the inter-district championships of 1986, 1987 and 1988, which, apart from their intrinsic importance, featured a veritable host of international players. The cameras should have been there, but they weren't. Sure enough BBC Scotland eventually did put its best foot forward with much fuller coverage of Scottish rugby and with their own 'Rugby Special' programme on Sundays. But it was a bit like shutting the stable door after the horse had bolted. The World Cup was lost and with it several rivetting confrontations, such as the Scottish and English tours to New Zealand and Argentina and Wales and England in Australia in 1991. Soccer is Scotland's national game and commands massive support, and it is right and fair that it should have the major role in TV and radio coverage. But I felt at the time that Rugby Union wasn't getting a fair whack and this view was reflected in comments I heard from folk in the game, including SRU representatives. The Friday evening half-hour preview is interesting and very well done but there is just too much football coverage, although happily season 1991-92 has started well with John Beattie as interviewer in several well directed rugby slots. In any event, I was approached by Bob Burroughs and David Scott on behalf of ITV in February 1990. They wanted me to join their commentary team for the World Cup. I think they would have had me sign a contract there and then. I found them pleasant and persuasive, and perhaps, they were surprised that I didn't accept their invitation. They seemed to be of the view that I could just pop over to their side for the World Cup and pop back to the BBC for the Five Nations Championship and the rest of the domestic contract. Of course I would have enjoyed covering the World Cup on television. I had been one of the BBC commentary team at the inaugural World Cup in Australia and New Zealand, and although the thought of fifteen hours on an aeroplane had bored me stiff, and the thought of being away from our home for any length of time was a mite unpleasant, I had revelled in the experience, even though it was darned hard work and set a new series of challenges. On the other hand, I had been a BBC commentator since 1953. The BBC had been good to me throughout all those years. I had had the pleasure of working with gifted professionals, knowing that, like me, they had a real feel for the game and wanted to show it at its best. I just couldn't turn my back on them. I felt that they were entitled to my loyalty. They asked me to join their group for their presentation to the Four Home Unions committee for the domestic contract and I agreed. If the BBC won the domestic contract for three years the chances were that I would be part of their commentary team. I also really did believe that the BBC, with all its experience and expertise and because of what they had learned from losing the World Cup contract, and because of their vast library of recorded material, were the better equipped to present Rugby Union into the 1990s. If the BBC had not obtained the domestic contract, my days as a commentator with them surely would have been numbered, for their own coverage of Rugby Union would have been drastically curtailed. It was clear to me also that by the time the domestic contract decision was made, ITV probably would have completed their commentary teams for the World Cup.

Virtually all of my friends had recommended that I accept the ITV offer, take the money and let the future look after itself but the BBC had first given me the rare opportunity of a career as a rugby commentator and my association with them over all the thirty-eight years had been friendly and agreeable. I can't say anything about the BBC presentation of its case except that it was quite brilliantly done, a credit to Jonathan Martin and his aides, and although I am no great judge of such things I couldn't see how the Home Unions committee could turn them down, except on the cash factor. That the BBC gained the contract was wonderful news, and although I will not be providing TV commentary on the World Cup I'm delighted that the BBC have asked me to share their radio commentary so that I will be working again with old friends such as Charles Runcie, Ian Robertson, Nigel Starmer-Smith, David Parry Jones and Jim Neilly. It has been twenty years since I did any match commentary on radio so that will be something of a challenge, although some of my critics have maintained that, on television, I have always virtually done a radio commentary anyway! The prospect is fascinating. One of the irritations inherent in all the talk of whether I would sign on for ITV was the number of telephone calls I received from newspaper men keen to be up-to-date with the situation. As I had worked on a newspaper myself for nine years and have written a weekly column and match report on rugby for the *Glasgow Herald* for over twenty years, I had much sympathy with the reporters, most of whom, happily, were rugby men themselves. But I got a bit testy with one whose first paragraph stated that I was on the point of signing up with ITV. That just was not true. It surprised me, too, when ITV called a press conference to explain what they hoped to do in relation to matches covered, whether live or recorded, and when, after they had said that they would like to have me on their commentary team, another of their top table got up and referred to BBC's coverage as 'tired' and then said that ITV did not want to have their viewers being 'lectured to by a retired school-master'. I hope he wasn't being personal! It was a difficult and anxious time for all of us, those of us who were friends from the TV commentary box including Chris Rea, Bill Beaumont, Eddie Butler, and all the lads in BBC Wales, and there was a feeling of relief all round that the BBC would continue to cover the Five Nations Championship and other top games for the next three years.

18

That Little White Ball!

As the only golfer in captivity who has played the first five holes in Hawick Golf Club's summer competition in 3,18,4,4,3, I have come to the conclusion, after some sixty years' experience of the agonies and the ecstasies that temperamentally I am totally unsuited to playing the game of golf!

It is true – and this will surprise some of my former pupils not to mention some of my own generation – that I once was down to a handicap of 6 and have gone round our course, called the Vertish Hill, in 68 – yes, all putts holed, and with witnesses to prove it in the persons of Alan Potts, Jim Purdie and if memory serves me right, Drew Deans. That was in the good old days. I also have managed to socket a drive to near 12 o'clock when I was aiming for 9 o'clock, and recently I had the salutary lesson of being out-driven fully forty metres by two former pupils, each standing about 4 feet 10 inches and weighing no more than eight stones!

The Vertish Hill, as the name suggests, is a hilly course. You have to be a bit of a mountain goat to cope and when the wind blows and the ground is bone hard, some parts of it can be almost unplayable. In mitigation of that 18 at the second hole I should explain that Hawick Golf Club boasts just about the most fiendish start to any course in the country, in that the two opening holes are played alongside a busy road with the greens absolutely flush with the road fence. I have long claimed that a ball out of bounds should be penalised by only one and not two shots. It isn't as if the tees at those two holes provide any safe angle of shot. They are flush with the road side as well. On the occasion of that unusual start I was playing in the summer competition, which also doubled as the Club Championship qualifying rounds, with Tom Scott

189

as my partner. Tom was known as 'Lefty', a left-hander with a beautifully rhythmic swing. He was a most agreeable golfing companion and a
darn good player as well. On this morning we had been given special dispensation to go out at the head of the field because Tom had a church
meeting about midday. Having played the first in par 3s, we found that a
lad, playing on his own, was about to drive off the second tee, whereupon Tom asked him if he would mind letting us through as he had to be
finished by a certain time. 'By all means,' said the fellow, 'I'm a rabbit at
the game anyway.' Tom then sent his drive whizzing down the centre of
the fairway. I followed by sending my first drive, well enough hit, over
the road into the field. My second drive followed exactly the same trajec-
tory. So did the third and the fourth. The four balls were lying within
fifteen yards of each other all out of bounds. I had played nine and
wasn't yet off the tee! Not only that, but an acquaintance of mine, Drew
Ford, had been coming down the road after having been searching for
mushrooms. In watching each of my drives going over his head, Drew
had tweaked his neck, and he now continued his walk with his head to
one side and, so far as I could gather, making several uncomplimentary
remarks about my golf swing. So it took me eighteen to complete the
hole and I felt a right twit, especially as the lad who had let us through
had described himself as a rabbit! So I started that round par, fourteen
over par, par, par, birdie. The story of my golfing life is encapsulated in
that start – going along nicely, thank you, and just waiting for the next
disaster to turn up. It never fails to do so!

That lovely man of golf, Henry Longhurst, referred to 'the humps and
hollows of golfing fortunes' and, like every man who ever swung a golf
club, I have felt those ups and downs in rapid profusion. Once, I drove
off the first at Gullane number one course. That is 315 yards and is a
good belt. I made the green. Admittedly the ground was hard and there
was a following breeze. But it was a pretty good lick just the same. On
the other hand there is engraved in my memory that occasion at Gullane,
where I am a country member, when Bette and I were waiting to play off
with some twenty or so assorted Queen's Counsels, Privy Counsellors,
retired Lieutenant-Generals, Inspectors of Education, Rear-Admirals
and the like. Jim Scotland, the starter, an uncle of the famous Scottish
full-back, Ken Scotland, and a friend of ours, rang the bell and
announced in a loud voice, 'Mr and Mrs Bill McLaren on the tee.' Bette
took one look at the assembled multitude and said that, under no circumstances, was she going to play off under such pressure. She would

start at the second. I gently reminded my beloved that I had just paid £6 for her to play and would she kindly get on with it. 'No,' she said. 'Oh yes,' I replied. After further encouragement, including the threat to stop her house-keeping allowance, Bette teed up and smacked a beauty some 180 yards down the middle of the fairway. My turn. I hit from the top and duck-hooked my drive just twenty yards into heavy rough on the left of the fairway. That was bad enough, but the final humiliation was when all of our distinguished watchers had to totter over to help me find my ball! One of them was heard to mutter, 'I hope this chap is a better commentator than he is a golfer.'

It was off Gullane's first tee that I once hit a huge slice right over the wall of a handsome house overlooking the fairway, whereupon I heard four Japanese golfers, waiting to play off behind us, chuckling and chortling at my embarrassment. When eventually I got to the green and looked back, there were the four of them, miles apart, three in knee-high rough and the fourth on another fairway miles off-line. I thought, 'What a blinking cheek they had poking fun at my shot!'

Once, I was playing with my friend Alex Waldie and when we hit off the fifteenth tee at Hawick I sliced, he pulled and we reckoned that we played our second shots at least half a mile apart! It was on the last tee at Hawick that Alex coined the phrase 'Hitler youth' to describe our grandchildren. The name stuck, although our daughters and their husbands, were not amused at such a description being given to their off-spring.

I have been lucky enough to play golf since I was seven. My father was devoted to the game and he lit the fire to my own enthusiasm by taking me to play in company with his factory friends, Joe Hunter, George Watters, Walter Weir, Archie Davidson, Tom Kyle and Tom Cairns, and by showing me the ropes in our regular games when we went on holiday to Silloth. Silloth always seemed to be over-run with heather and there was one bunker on the inward half that seemed about 200-feet deep. Once, I lost the rag at hitting a bad shot and chucked my clubs into the depths of the bunker, which resulted in a rocket from my father and a traipse all the way down and back up again with my clubs. My father was a steady golfer who played off about 12. He was the only person I ever came across who could hit a drive with a cigarette in his mouth, and about one and a half inches of ash on the end of it. When he'd completed his drive the ash was still in place!

Gullane has three courses and is situated near North Berwick in East Lothian's golfing country. It is a joy to play. Bette and I feel beautifully relaxed and happy as we walk along the first fairway there with summer dew on the grass and the sun beginning to spread its warmth. The Lord is very much in his heaven in those conditions – especially if, as occasionally happens, He lets me hit a straight drive out of the meat and not get out-driven! I think the most beautiful hole I have ever played is the seventh on Gullane number one course. The elevated tee has a magnificent view across Gullane Bay to Muirfield, the Open Championship course, on the right side, and the stunning beauty of the Forth estuary straight ahead, with the hills of Fife in the background. Bette once stood on the tee and gave an eloquent description of that beautiful view only to find that she was talking to herself. I had hit a good drive and already was fifty yards down the fairway.

I've tried desperately hard ever since I took up the game to keep my head still throughout every shot but with unfailing regularity I have succeeded in lifting it with disastrous results. It's all very well suggesting that I should watch the ball with my left eye, or fix my gaze on the make of the ball, or wear a cap with the brim tilted down or any other cleverdick ideas but the effect I fancy would still be the same. Out of the blue and for no reason at all my head will move and I'll make a real botch of the shot. I've become philosophical about the whole matter. After all, when you have hit a 3-wood into the breeze right over the last green in Hawick's first open tournament, bounced it on the road and forced half-a-dozen watching spectators to move their cars further up for safety, then topped the second and heard the Waldie fog horn remark: 'Aye, that's a bit more like it,' there are not further depths to plumb! Just the other day playing with Bette on our own golf course here in Hawick I started out with 3,5,4,5,3,8,7. Lord, will it never end?

One of my most pleasant golfing experiences was taking part with Peter Alliss in his 'A Round with Alliss' TV series in which you play a few holes with Peter taking occasional stoppages for a wee chat about your views and experiences. My already high respect for Peter as a golf commentator rose even more because he was so pleasant and helpful, and like every good commentator he had done his homework. We played over the Rosemount course at Blairgowrie in Perthshire, a beautiful stretch of country, but with quite a bit of wood growing in strategic places. Bette and I went up the day before to reconnoitre the course. I was keen to discover where I should play an old ball! Our recce was completed in solid water, rain lashing down throughout, then we were guests of the BBC at dinner with Peter and the BBC production staff.

Peter was like a host at the meal. He had as many stories as 'Jock' Wemyss, but told them in a different accent. The following day I stood on the first tee, apparently calm and composed, inwardly petrified. It is one thing to play ham-and-egg golf in company with a loving and under-standing wife. Quite another to expose your frailties to the world of TV watchers. Peter had noticed, as I had a brief practice swing, that I had a form of loop at the top of the back swing. It was some loop. Only the Lord knows how I ever got the club back to the ball. Peter took one look at it and told me: 'I can do nothing for you, William.'

It was an exciting experience. The audience at the start was just a hand-ful of local golfers but, as we played, more and more appeared through the trees like little prairie dogs. Happily, I didn't play badly and Peter was a most sympathetic companion. At a hole that required a fairly good lick with a drive over water Peter's shot hit a branch and his second, a full 2-wood, was blocked out by the trees. He explained his intention to bend it round the trees to the edge of the green. I didn't think it was on but he played it exactly as described. Pure magic! I have no hesitation in nominating Peter Alliss and Peter O'Sullevan as the two most outstand-ing commentators I have ever heard. Alliss is so knowledgeable, simply lives his sport, and introduces those delightful touches of humour that provide light and shade; O'Sullevan simply amazes me with his uncanny identification and his instant assessments of prospects and positioning. Has he ever placed a horse wrong in his entire career?

One other likeable aspect of the Alliss-O'Sullevan delivery is that they are so easy to listen to with dulcet tones which never grate. I also have admiration for the presenters. Folk such as David Coleman, Frank Bough, Bob Wilson, Dougie Donnelly, Steve Ryder and Desmond Lynam are true professionals, because it takes a special kind of person-ality to sit in the 'Grandstand' studio for five hours, introducing a variety of sporting situations and, toughest of all, keeping it going when things don't go according to plan. I had just the one experience of that kind of presentation. Once, I was asked to go to the BBC studio on the Sunday following the Scotland v Ireland game to introduce fifty minutes' worth of clips of the game. That meant producing something like five introduc-tory bits lasting from forty-five seconds to a minute and a half to in-troduce each bit of action. I'd prepared my links but the fellow who was providing the action clips had over-run his mark and it took him some time to get back to the right place so that he could show the bit of action required. In the studio, of course, I'd already made my link and the bit of film should have come up with the action on it. Unfortunately it didn't. Now when that happens, you just have to keep talking. I don't know how many times I repeated myself but I was in a cold sweat by the time I eventually got the green light to tell me that the bit of action was ready and I could lead to it. I will never forget that: it certainly raised greatly my appreciation of those presenters who have to do the job through a whole five hours. They are remarkably gifted people. Not only that but in those days at that time on a Sunday, the regular programme featured an American detective. I think he was called Hiram Holliday and he was very popular with youngsters. As soon as Scotland v Ireland started, with McLaren's face on the screen, the BBC got something like a hundred-and-fifty telephone calls from irate parents claiming that their children were sitting waiting for Hiram Holliday and wanting to know why were they having to watch Scotland v Ireland when it had been played and shown the previous day?

It was against my better judgement that I accepted an invitation to compete (subsequent events suggested that 'compete' was hardly the right word) in the Terry Wogan Golf Classic at Limerick Golf Club on Saturday 15 June 1991. I say 'against my better judgement' because I nowadays play only fun golf ('fun', now there's an inappropriate adjective if ever there was one) and am totally unaccustomed to playing in Pro-Am or Cel-Am tournaments and also because my golf of late had been so patchy and, at times, pitiful. Having been asked twice before, however, and having turned down the invitations, and having a keen admiration for Terry Wogan and the contribution he makes to television and to good causes, as well as the general sense of fun he imparts, I decided to gird up my whatever it is Scotsmen gird and have a go. What a marvellous weekend that was. The whole affair was organised by a big, bluff Irishman from Portmarnock, Michael Lynch, and his wife Elizabeth, and they did a superb job. The only blemish was that the local weather-forecasters had predicted a sunny afternoon for the tournament whereas it came down in sheets, and with hailstones, for good measure, that caused flooding of greens in no time. A galaxy of talent had been gathered together: Frankie Vaughan, Henry Cooper, Geoff Hurst, Jasper Carrott, Eddie Large, Hale and Pace (both very knowledgeable Rugby Union fans), and a host of others, including a strong representation from Rugby Union, among them: Kevin Flynn, Philip Matthews, Paul Dean, Michael Bradley, David Irwin, Colm Tucker, Rob Andrew, Paul Ackford, Gary Rees and Jeremy Guscott. For Bette and myself it was a special treat to meet Frankie Vaughan and Henry Cooper. We found Frankie a charming man and it wasn't difficult to appreciate why Henry is so much respected and held in such affection. I was fascinated when we had a long chat about boxing, which always has been one of my favourite sports, and to hear Henry talking about the likes of Len Harvey, Jack Doyle and Joe Louis, who were heroes of mine when I was a youngster. There was, too, one of the my best friends in broadcasting, Fred Cogley, who does the Rugby Union commentaries for RTE in Dublin. We've known each other for many years and have shared the joys and sorrows of commentary, and Fred has that ability to enliven the proceedings with his cheery personality and unfailing modesty. Before one Scotland v Ireland match at Murrayfield Fred asked me to join him in a three-minute interview for Radio Eirean on the eve of the match. Fred got the chat started and things were going along fine but I had a suspicion that we were going on for longer than expected. Eventually Fred brought the proceedings to a close, whereupon I asked how long the interview had lasted. 'Oh, it was near on 20 minutes,' said Fred, 'but they were quite enjoying it so they just let it go on.' There are none to compare with the Irish when it comes to producing the unexpected!

Can you imagine a magnificent banquet at Bunratty Castle at which Jasper Carrott and Eddie Large had the gathering rolling in the aisles, and there was delightful entertainment from the Bunratty Entertainers against a rich medieval tapestry, and a choir of lovely lasses gave us a rendering of 'Danny Boy' that brought the house down? Good, because the less said about the golf, the better!

I was lucky enough to be representing Aughinish Alumina Ltd whose managing director is a Scot, Frank McGravie, who, like me, set no heather on fire in shot-making but was the kindest of hosts. Our other partners were the Canadian Ambassador, Michael Wadsworth, a big powerful man who had played grid-iron football, and another very pleasant personality, Pat Lynch. I don't know if you have ever had the experience of standing on the first tee of a celebrity-amateur tournament when you are the alleged celebrity and there are some two hundred folk all wondering if you are going to make a botch of your first drive. Let me tell you, it is one of the most nerve-racking experiences I have ever known! As you address the ball you are saying, *sotto voce*, 'Please, Lord, just help me to keep my fat head still, and please don't let me snatch, and please keep my ball out of those thick trees on the right of the fairway.'

Of course he listened to only half of my plea. I didn't snatch but my head moved so that I hit it not too badly but with a touch of unintentional fade. A bad bounce and I was in the trees. I found that I could play a shot, a simple 9-iron to the green. But this time my head moved earlier, I duffed it and finished with a 6 which should have been an easy 4. I won't bore you, dear reader, with the painful details of the rest of my performance but sufficient to say that my comment to Frank on the Friday night, that, where celebrities were concerned, he had drawn the short straw, was proved absolutely spot-on. Happily we all got soaken wet, and the process was brought to an end at the tenth. That evening there was a banquet in the Limerick Inn Hotel. What a feast and what a cabaret! Roger de Courcey, Jasper Carrott, Eddie Large, the Batchelors joined with other Irish stage people to provide a marvellous programme of entertainment, with Bill Cole and his traditional jazz band taking a particular trick with me because I just love the music of New Orleans and the Blues. It was three o'clock in the morning before we heard the final word of thanks from Terry Wogan who had been such a wonderful host throughout, although he did express the opinion to an assembled multitude that, being a Scot, Bill McLaren was unlikely to throw his ball to the crowd at the end of the round! Terry had a word for everyone and made at least three speeches during the two days, each one full of fun and cheek. It was the first really big tournament of its kind that I had attended. On the pure basis of my golf I will never be invited again. But even just that once it was a real treat, not least because of the kindness of the golf and rugby folk of Limerick and the friendliness of the famous folk of stage and screen who give so much of their time to such worthwhile causes.

Incidentally, isn't pressure a strange phenomenon? Before a big crowd at Limerick I played like a prune. I would have had difficulty hitting our town clock. Yet on the Monday, Tuesday and Wednesday on our return I scored 79, 78 and 79 over our own course. That may not seem very impressive but to me it was hot stuff.

Pity I hadn't been able to do that at Limerick!

19

Looking Back – Mainly With Pleasure

It stands to reason that out of some thirty-nine years of commentary, certain incidents will stand out in the memory as being extra special. For instance in one of the very first inter-city matches between Glasgow and Edinburgh that I covered for BBC radio there were five Camerons playing. You can imagine the problem there of always having to give the Christian name of each Cameron so that listeners would know which one of the clan was involved. The trouble was that, as is the case sometimes with Fijians such as Lutumailagi, Koraduadua, Tikoisuva and Naucabalavu, by the time you got the names out they had scored the try and kicked the goal!

One great day was when our son-in-law Alan Lawson scored two tries in the 22-12 defeat of England at Murrayfield in 1976. Alan James McGregor Lawson is one of the really good guys and a dashed good scrum-half who loved to run at opponents, had little time for the punt-and-hope attitude, and who at one time drew from that famous man of the Barbarians, Mickey Steele-Bodger, the comment: 'What England need just now is a really good scrum-half, but unfortunately the best scrum-half in England is Alan Lawson.' That was when Alan was playing for London Scottish. His first try against England was out of the very top drawer because it started inside Scotland's '22', when David Shedden of West of Scotland ran the ball out and Mike Biggar (London Scottish), Sandy Carmichael (West of Scotland) and Alan Tomes (Hawick) provided handsome linkage for Alan to sprint the last twenty-two metres for a try that brought the house down. I can still see Mike Biggar motioning to Sandy Carmichael to veer left! Alan's second was from loose ball and his exploitation of a gap like a barn door. I have to admit to being quite

197

excited especially at the first score because long-range tries are the stuff of exciting commentary, or certainly should be, and to score such a try against England gave Scots immense pleasure. The same can be said about Jim Calder's try against Wales at Cardiff in 1982. It was another magnificent effort, also from long-range, and also involving both sections of the side. Remember how Gareth Davies (Cardiff) chipped ahead and Roger Baird (Kelso), covering back, took the ball on the run? Most players would have just hoofed to touch to stabilise the situation but Roger took off up the left touch-line and from his own '22'. Iain Paxton (Selkirk) and Alan Tomes took it on (it's surprising how often the 17-stone Tomes got into the long-range try-scoring act) and as he was sunk by Clive Rees (London Welsh), his pass found Jim Calder who plunged over. Not many score a try from so far out against Wales. It was a try also that set Scotland on the way to their best win ever at Cardiff – 34-18, five tries to one. Considering the indignities that had been showered on Scots on that great Cardiff Arms Park pitch, there was a sweet revenge in such a memorable win.

*

Rugby Union and the BBC have been good to me. In addition to being a teacher of physical education in my home town, with the pleasure of seeing three whole generations of Hawick families growing up, I have been able to cover in commentary, at a rough estimate, some three hundred international matches as well as umpteen other games at club, district and county level. I was asked to cover two Varsity matches at Twickenham, and recall being so appreciative of the efforts of two Watsonians, Ian Robertson and David Bell, both Scottish internationals, in helping me to overcome identification problems. Once 'Robbo' held a Sabbath day practice at Grange Road, Cambridge, which I was allowed to attend in order to sort out the players; and when I wasn't able to get to an Oxford University practice for the same purpose, David Bell, the Oxford captain, went to the trouble of lining up his players before they had lunch on match-day and introducing each one to me. I felt like royalty doing an inspection of a guard of honour and it was a wee bit embarrassing. Nor was it ideal. There is no substitute for seeing players running about and for quietly (in case folk think you have a screw loose!) doing a private commentary to yourself as they do so. But, just seeing the Oxford boys was a help and I was grateful to David for taking the trouble to interrupt his team's set routine in order to help me in my task.

That was in 1972 and whilst I got through the commentary without mishap, it stiffened my resolve to go out of my way always to attend practice sessions prior to each game.

Once I was called down late to provide commentary on the Midlands v Fiji game at Leicester in 1971. Cliff Morgan was scheduled to do the commentary but suffered a heart-rending family bereavement. I arrived in the Fijian team's hotel at 10.30 on the Friday night. Only the Fijian manager and a friend were available. I explained my predicament. I had not seen any of the Fijians on the tour and the manager agreed to let me attend a special squad meeting in a hotel room at 9.00 on the Saturday morning. That was good of him but all the lads were coloured and it really was just impossible in that short time to identify each one. I remember noting that George Barley wasn't quite as dusky as his colleagues, so George got quite a few mentions during the commentary! I just had to do the early part of the commentary by numbers until I familiarised myself with differing characteristics. The Fijians scored two tries in the first ten minutes and luckily, on each occasion, it was the same try-scorer and he had his back to our commentary box so I saw his number quite clearly. The name has stuck to this day – Sovau, a big lump of a lad. What a relief! Had he been running towards me I don't believe I could have recognised him so early in the game. Luck was on my side. It was in that game that an eighteen-year-old was introduced to the Midlands team. The name was William Henry Hare, then of Nottingham. He was called in as centre. Little did I realise then that this youngster was to become one of the most kenspeckle players in the English game, 'Dusty' Hare who, as full-back, played twenty times for England and held the English record of forty two points in a Five Nations Championship until that was beaten by Simon Hodgkinson of Nottingham in the 1991 Championship. What a coincidence that two Nottingham full-backs should attain such fame, and that Hodgkinson should beat the Hare record with almost a replica of the relaxed, smooth, stroking, goal-kicking style of his predecessor.

*

On the trip to Bucharest in 1984, when I was not permitted to attend the home team's training session, I had one of those experiences that you can well do without. I came in from school on the day I was to leave for Bucharest to find my wife packing several tins of food into my case. Bette explained that the *Evening News* of Edinburgh had telephoned to our house to tell her that their rugby correspondent, Bill Lothian, had told them that the Scottish team were not getting enough to eat and could I bring out some food with me. Bette was packing some tins of sausages and beans, powdered milk, Mars bars and corned beef. I wasn't too happy about the whole affair as I had no idea how their customs people would react at Bucharest airport to a Scot bringing in a horde of foodstuffs. After all it was behind the Iron Curtain in those days and I had visions of being interrogated by men in grey suits under a bright light. But Bette insisted that Scotland couldn't hope to win without some sausage and beans inside them so off I went, although not, I hasten to say, with unbridled enthusiasm. On my arrival at Bucharest airport, imagine my horror when I was asked to stand aside whilst the security man with the big, black moustache and the deadpan expression sought assistance from another security man with a big, black moustache and a deadpan expression, in dealing with my case. I was beginning to fear the worst. I could hear the clang of the cell door closing. Happily, the trouble was not the food but the fact that my passport described me as a teacher of physical education, whereas the document we had to fill in during the flight showed me as being in Bucharest as a television commentator. It took ages to get that sorted out, whilst an assortment of security men with big, black moustaches and deadpan expressions came along to see what was going on and pushed off again. It was a nerve-racking period and I was so relieved to be sent on my way, sausage and beans and Mars and all. At the team hotel I asked Jim Renwick if he would share out the food to the players. When I saw him the next day and asked how he had got on he replied: 'Oh it was grand. They ate the tins as weel.'

*

Jim Renwick was one of the game's brightest characters with quick wit and an impish sense of humour, as well as being a player of immensely high skill-level, sharp awareness and possessed of every gift of deception. As a pupil of mine at Drumlanrig-St Cuthbert's primary school in Hawick, he was quiet and modest and, even at eleven years of age, was a 'natural' and destined for high achievement. I recall him once telling the whole Scottish team, whilst showing them his right palm, that he had got that from Bill McLaren when he was at school! In actual fact I do not remember Jim being in any trouble at school. He was a very good pupil, this perhaps attributable in part to the fact that his parents and other members of his family had been devoted to the cause of the Salvation Army. Jim also was involved in one of the proudest moments of my life. The painting I was given to mark my retirement from teaching in 1988 which is mentioned in Chapter 16, was presented by Jim Renwick. Whenever I look up at it I think of all the enjoyment and fun I had during all those years. And at the presentation function I was thrilled when the Hawick Club president, Gerald Adams, introduced Jim Renwick to make the presentation. He never could resist poking fun and part of his speech referred to my coaching. 'Do you think,' he had been asked in a BBC interview, 'that you would have gained 52 caps if you had not been coached by Bill McLaren?' He had thought for a moment then delivered at the pithead the answer: 'I think I would have got 70 caps if I hadn't been coached by Bill McLaren.' It brought the house down. Jim has a gift for doing just that.

I was delighted, too, that alongside the famous guests at that gathering were the folk who had given me such invaluable assistance in organising the rugby for Hawick's primary school pupils. Fellow teachers, volunteers and those who gave up time to help the youngsters in the rugby clubs. I owe a lot to all of them for their unfailing enthusiasm and interest – especially George Scott, Mrs May Sinclair, Bill Bothwick, Duncan McKenzie, and Alan McCredie.

A less fond memory is of that doleful occasion back in the early sixties when I was asked to provide radio commentary on a race at the Edinburgh Highland Games at Murrayfield. I turned it down on the grounds that I was not really an athletics specialist. The BBC in Glasgow rang back and said that I would cover only one event, that it would be a 440 yards race in which there would be just six competitors and that Jack Crump, the AAA secretary, would be at my side as a race reader if required. I allowed myself to be persuaded. Came the day, Jack Crump wasn't there. My studio manager took ill and I was left, bird alone, up at the back of the Murrayfield stand. When I had to go 'live' in radio commentary the race in progress was a three-mile team race in which there were 85 runners who were stretched round the entire track! The only two I recognised were Len Eyre of England and Ian Binnie of Scotland. Happily they led throughout but it was when they lapped the other runners that my difficulties multiplied. What an ordeal! It will not come as a surprise that I have not covered athletics on radio or television since, although some years ago the BBC in London did offer me the chance of going down to live in London to cover athletics in the summer and rugby in the winter. I took one look at the London traffic and compared it with the lifestyle that I had in Hawick, our home on the hill with its beautiful views of Wilton Lodge Park and Sunnyhill, our golf course just half-a-mile up the road, the enjoyment I had as a teacher in my own home town and the peace and restfulness of the Border hills not far from our front door and I realised how lucky I was. So I said 'No' to that attractive BBC offer.

*

Ever since my earliest days I have had a sweet tooth! As a young schoolboy one of the delights I used to look forward to was that of scraping out the huge pan in which the Irvine sisters used to make the tablet they sold in their shop. The Misses Irvine, Margaret and Netta, had a beautifully stocked general grocer shop in Weensland Road, some 200 yards from our home, and it was a favourite haunt of mine. They took a keen interest in my welfare and I was a frequent visitor to their shop either for some messages for my mother or for sweets or just to say 'hello'. I had a great affection for the two of them. Whenever I had to go to their shop for a message I always used to time myself with a view to setting a new record for the trip. Or, on the way, I would sidestep every lamp post and used to frighten the life out of people by running at them and then swerving or sidestepping past them. Cleaning out the tablet pan was a very special perk. I just scraped it with a spoon and had a wonderful meal in the process! Whenever I was at a Hawick rugby match I always had to call in at the Irvine shop in order to tell the sisters how Hawick had fared. They used to tell folk that, even as a lad of 9, 10 and 11, I could give them a detailed account of exactly how the game had gone and who had scored. So even in those early days that desire to do sports reporting manifested itself again as in the long, detailed reports of rugby matches, Olympic Games, golf tournaments etc., that I wrote down in my big ledger. I have fond memory of Margaret and Netta, two gentle and kindly ladies of an old school.

Maybe it was all due to scraping that tablet pan, but I have enjoyed a sweet ever since. I used to always take a tin of Hawick Balls with me on commentary assignments. They are pleasant mint sweets contained in a colourful tartan tin and manufactured, initially by the Hill family in Hawick, and now by Billy Smith of the local bakery firm. Gareth Edwards developed a taste for them and always used to ask me in the Angel Hotel if I had any to spare. It cost me a fortune keeping the Welsh team supplied on Gareth's insistence! Bill Beaumont and Fran Cotton also enjoyed a 'sook' at a Hawick Ball. Once I offered one to Paul Rendall, the Wasps and England prop, and told him that it would put a yard on his pace. Paul, a very pleasant man who never seemed to get uptight about anything, and who never was liable to break the sound barrier, simply replied in that Slough accent of his: 'Well, in that case, you'd better give me the whole bleeding tin!' Prior to the North and Midlands versus New Zealand game at Aberdeen in December 1978 I was out on the pitch checking the conditions when the home players appeared and Scotland's international scrum-half, Ian McCrae, shouted to me: 'Hey, Bill, have you any of those Hawick balls?' I had a tin in my briefcase and in no time they had disappeared as the North and Midlands lads made their way to their dressing room crunching away like hail stones on a tin roof. The North and Midlands were inspired in the first half, at the end of which they were only 3-4 behind. At full-time the score was 3-31 and I think it was Ian who voiced the view after the game: 'It's a hell of a pity that we didn't have another tin for half-time.' Nowadays it is the Scottish squad who like to satisfy their taste for Hawick Balls, especially John Jeffrey. Of course the Scottish squad had already acquired the taste because Colin Deans had taken several tins to the World Cup and they didn't last long.

*

Despite everything Twickenham remains one of my favourite grounds. The 'everything' I refer to is the number of painful results for Scots at that renowned graveyard, virtually most of which I have had to report on radio or television since 1953.

It was at Twickenham on the morning of an England v Scotland game that I arrived early one day, and, as usual, went on to the pitch to check ground and weather conditions. I was quite alone and proceeded to give a rendering of the opening verse of 'Flower of Scotland'. I didn't think it sounded all that bad. Anyway there was I on a totally deserted Twickenham pitch singing my full-hearted rendition of what was to become a rugby anthem, when I heard a voice from the Heavens saying, 'It's a good thing, McLaren, that you are a slightly better commentator than you are a singer.' I looked up and there, in the commentary position checking all the equipment, was my producer, Bill Taylor, a Scot to his boot soles and clearly unappreciative of my singing capabilities. I had a real soft spot for Bill Taylor. There was no fuss or frill about Bill, he was as straight as a dye, spoke his mind and was quietly very helpful. He understood the commentator's problems and loved his Rugby Union. When the Ireland v England game was postponed owing to snow in 1984 Bill, fighting a courageous but losing battle against cancer, and I had a most enjoyable lunch with the former Gloucester and England prop forward, Mike Burton, after which Bill looked after our luggage whilst I went to check if there was a plane going out to Glasgow. Bill had heard an announcement that a Glasgow plane was due to leave very soon and there he was, ashen-faced, struggling down the stairway to bring my luggage to me. I could have cried. When Bill died I knew I'd lost a very good friend for whom I had the deepest respect and admiration.

20

Scotland Rejoices

Of all the great names and occasions I have been lucky enough to cover, undoubtedly the most emotional event was Scotland's Grand Slam success over England at Murrayfield on 17 March 1990. there are lots of reasons for that. It undoubtedly was one of the most widely publicised Rugby Union internationals of all time. It was, after all, the first time in the hundred-and-nineteen years history of international Rugby Union that two home countries had met with everything at stake for each of them; 'Grand Slam', Championship, Triple Crown and, as it was between the 'auld enemies', the Calcutta Cup as well. During the entire week leading up to the match the media had given huge coverage to the 'game of games'. Everywhere you went folk spoke of the coming confrontation. The stakes were very high. Scotland had won the 'Grand Slam' only six years previously, but that had only been their second. England had promised so much but, flattering to deceive, had failed to achieve their potential and so had no Championship, Triple Crown or 'Slam' to show since Bill Beaumont had led that great England side to their 'Grand Slam' in 1980. The Scots remembered with some trepidation that that had been climaxed with a 30 points to 18 win at Murrayfield. Not only that, but another 'Grand Slam' for England would put them one ahead of Wales in the total number of 'Slams' won. Most Scots who know a bit about their rugby acknowledged that England were a superbly equipped side with barely a weakness – massive forwards who could scrummage till the cows came home and who had those twin control towers, Wade Dooley and Paul Ackford, to guarantee ball at the lineouts. Scrum-half Richard Hill had the quickest hands in the business, his partner Rob Andrew had developed his game significantly in terms of vision, option choice and technical skill and, in Rory Underwood, Will Carling, Jeremy Guscott and Simon Halliday, they had pace and power aplenty. To all that had to be added the points-gathering of Simon Hodgkinson (74 in his five previous internationals). During their championship campaign, England had outplayed France in Paris (26-7) and crushed Wales at Twickenham (34-6). In those two matches they had touched a peak of total rugby at high pace which was marvellous to behold. Scotland had entered the championship a fortnight after the others, were caught cold by the Irish in Dublin and were fortunate to squeeze through by 13-10, thanks mainly to the try-scoring capability of Derek White. Scotland led France at Murrayfield by only 3-0 when Alain Carminati was ordered off by England's Fred Howard for allegedly trying to re-arrange, with his boot, the features of John Jeffrey. Scotland then stretched away to two fascinating tries. The first was eventually credited to Finlay Calder although initially I gave it in commentary to Sean Lineen and, what is more, having seen it on video, I still believe that Sean Lineen got his arm on top of the ball for the try before Finlay arrived. But referee Howard indicated that Finlay had scored and that is how it will remain in the record books. The other try was typically Iwan Tukalo. He is a dogged little campaigner, very elusive and stays well on his feet. This time he stumbled, got up and away from Pierre Hontas, pushed-off another tackler and just made it to the line at full-stretch. At Cardiff Arms Park the Scots faced a Welsh side being coached by Ron Waldron for the first time and containing seven of his Neath side. Clearly Ron hoped that that heavy leavening of Neath players would result in Wales playing like them and with their confidence as well. After all, Neath were the kings of Welsh club rugby. The trouble was that at international level you just have to carry physique and ballast in the frontal exchanges and this is what Wales lacked. Brian Williams at 14 stone 2 pounds and Kevin Phillips at 13 stone 7 pounds were tremendous forwards in broken play and lacked nothing in 'bottle' and effort but they were giving away too much beef. Scotland had much the better of the scrummages. Indeed when the Scots found that they could cope comfortably with the Welsh scrummage they were able to withdraw John Jeffrey from scrummages near Scotland's line in anticipation of pick-up moves and drives up Scotland's left flank by Mark Jones. Wales did just that and Jeffrey, aided by Derek White, simply stifled the moves at birth. What Wales should have done then was instruct Mark Jones to feed Robert Jones, the scrum-half, on the Scottish right flank. That would have been more of a problem to the Scots although Finlay Calder and Gary Armstrong would have been primed. But the Welsh never did make the change and the Scots survived, although Wales scored what many rated the try of the championship. Paul Thorburn turned the ignition switch with a sizzling intrusion. Robert Jones and Mike Hall added their bit, Jones made a delicious reverse pass, and Ritchie Collins showed excellent vision with a long miss-pass that enabled Alan Bateman to send Arthur Emyr pounding home. But a third penalty goal by Craig Chalmers kept Scottish noses in front for a 13-9 victory margin.

So to the big day – well, not quite. Bette and I attended the final England practice session at Peebles on the Friday morning. I just wanted to check that all the players were fit, that there were no doubts (it is so helpful to know if a player may not come to the starting gate so that one can look up background details of any new player who might be added to the squad, just in case of emergency) and just to assess the atmosphere in the England camp. We saw virtually a perfect session. For just over half an hour the English players ran through their repertoire at high speed. It was like clock-work. Not a single pass was dropped. The continuity, even allowing for the lack of physical opposition, was very impressive. Afterwards Geoff Cooke, the England manager, who has always been very approachable and helpful, and Brian Moore, expressed their satisfaction at how things had gone. I have to admit that I found it hard to envisage a Scottish win against such an accomplished side as England. How glad I was to be proved wrong.

Incidentally all the suggestions that the English players were arrogant and thought all they had to do was turn up to win were off the mark. Bette and I found the squad primed for a very hard battle indeed. None of them under-estimated the task in hand or the quality of the Scottish squad. I thought it was the media, or certain elements among them, that did all the boasting, not the English players.

On the morning of the big day, Bette and I drove out to Edinburgh Airport to greet our daughter, Janie, up from Buckinghamshire for the game, festooned in tartan and convinced that Scotland would win. Janie obviously is a better judge than her father! The airport was absolutely heaving with folk from England pouring in to see the game. I could sense that this was going to be different and very special. As usual I was at the Murrayfield ground by 11 o'clock and had had a word with Derek Brown of Melrose, the Scottish Rugby Union's ground committee convener, and with Bill Ellwood, the ground manager, about the conditions and state of the pitch. There is just another aspect of union committee work that critics tend to forget. Derek had been at Murrayfield since seven o'clock that morning. And, of course, Bill tends his pitches with loving care and may the Lord help anyone who damages them! It was in lovely order. I always like to be available just in case BBC's 'Grandstand' programme runs into early problems and needs someone to do a 'fill-in' chat with Desmond Lynam. Even the stewards at Murrayfield were in a specially animated mood, including their chief steward, George Reid, who has done that job for 25 years. After a plate of soup, Scotch Broth – what else? – I took up station at the entrance to the dressing rooms so I would be able to confirm that there were no late changes. Sometimes I like to pop in and wish the referee and touch judges an enjoyable game. I was delighted at the 1991 Scotland v Ireland match when Australian referee, Kerry Fitzgerald, whose style of adjudicating helps the game to flow, presented me with an Australian Referees' Association tie.

On my way up to our commentary gantry I suddenly was aware of the privilege of doing commentary on such a vital match and, indeed, of a certain amount of additional pressure on me in the guise of an over-whelming desire to do a really acceptable job. After a brief word with BBC's Ian Robertson, I settled into the commentary position alongside Bill Beaumont who simply exudes an aura of good sense and friendliness. I have worked with quite a number of fellow commentators or, as they used to be called, 'summarisers', from one whose almost sole comment was 'this is a jolly good game of rugger' to Eddie Butler, the former Welsh captain, who is very observant and sharp on tactical influences. Providing 'inter-round summaries' at a televised rugby international is a testing business and having gained a number of caps as a player, whilst clearly a considerable aid, still does not guarantee total success. The summariser has to avoid just repeating what the commentator has said and, instead, should be seeking to make points that will stimulate viewer interest. Nor is it easy for recently retired players to avoid concentrating on their own countrymen and being so engrossed in what is happening on the field that they forget the need to sit back and be scrupulously fair and objective.

I enjoyed working alongside Gareth Edwards. I had admired him so much as a player and always identified him and his fellow Welsh stars with a very pleasurable period of commentary for me during Wales's second 'golden era'. It was a joy to be in the commentary box during much of that exhilarating rugby played by Wales between 1969 and 1979 and to which Gareth made such a significant contribution. I had an arrangement with Gareth that whenever he wanted to make a contribution he was to tap my shoulder and I would stop talking. So I did feel a bit 'miffed' when, on a 'Sportsview Personality' programme, Gareth replied to a question about how he was getting on as a summariser with the comment: 'Fine, that is when Bill McLaren let's me get a word in edgeways'. Admittedly I do go on a bit but I was genuinely very keen to see Gareth establish himself in that function and he certainly could have contributed more often had he wanted to do so. Nor do some summarisers appreciate how much preparation they should do prior to the match, especially in the realms of identification and simple detail. Once ten minutes before kick-off Gareth leaned across and said: 'Hey Bill, could you give me a note of the Christian names?' But it didn't take him long to appreciate that there was a bit more to it than met the eye and I thought he brought out some interesting points, although I felt that there was far more of the lore to come that he had stored away during his illustrious tenure of the Welsh and Lions scrum-half positions.

To some, the summarising requirement can come easily and naturally. Once in Dublin no summariser had been contacted and I was called from the commentary box not long before the start of our transmission to try and persuade Ciaran Fitzgerald, the former Ireland and Lions captain, to do the job for us. He was a mite reluctant because it had just been put to him. When I explained that he could pick his own moments to do his bit he eventually agreed. As it turned out you would have thought he had been doing the job for ages. He was splendid. I have always had the feeling that the summariser should embellish the commentary and, indeed, in explaining why that happened or didn't happen, he should make his commentator say to himself: 'Fascinating. I never thought of that.' Ciaran had that gift and made a big impression on me.

Fergus Slattery is another who is analytically very sharp and has sound television discipline and, on the only occasion that I have worked with Jamie Salmon at the 1989 France v Scotland game, I thought that he too read the trend cleverly and was a natural communicator.

I have always felt very comfortable working with Bill Beaumont, whom I've known since his great days in the England jersey. We used to exchange pleasantries at English practices and it used to amuse me when Bill would leave the practice to ask if I had any of my regular mint sweets, the Hawick Balls, then saunter back with one for himself and one for Fran Cotton. Bill and I have an arrangement that whenever he wants to contribute, he just taps my shoulder, I shut up and he does his bit. But if ever I have had to put a point to him he always has responded naturally so that we have established a kind of conversational partnership that seems to go down quite well. (Bill returns the sweety compliment by occasionally presenting me with a tin of Uncle Tom's Mint balls made in Wigan. They certainly make you suck in your breath, not quite on a par with Hawick balls, but distinctive and highly edible.) A brief word with French TV commentator Pierre Salviac, then it is time to check microphones, to check communication with the director, Mike Abbott, to ensure that I will be able to hear Desmond Lynam, and his handover to me in the 'Grandstand' studio, and then it is a question of feeling that inevitable nervousness as I await the cue from Mike 'Cue Bill' – and off we go. The atmosphere was almost over-powering as England's warriors took the field. When the Scots followed the noise was deafening and such was the sense of occasion that I have to admit I did not notice that David Sole had marched his team on to the field, instead of running, in the grimly determined gesture that became front-page news the following day. I have never known such a lengthy greeting for a Scottish side in all my experience of international attendance. I remember feeling a sense of satisfaction that 'God Save the Queen' was given a comparatively unhindered and vociferous rendering and then came the moment that Scots will never forget – the sight of Scotland's fifteen joining with the fifty-three thousand-strong crowd in the most inspiring rendering of 'Flower of Scotland' that one ever could imagine. It was quite overwhelming. As a commentator I always have sought to be objective and fair but as a Scot, and proud to be a Scot, I have to admit to a feeling of high emotion and intense national pride at that wonderful rendering. It seemed as if the whole of Scotland was united in anthem behind the national side. I don't know what it did for the English players but it certainly stirred the blood of every Scot. Rob Andrew said that even on four visits to Cardiff Arms Park he had never felt quite the same challenging atmosphere as that at Murrayfield on that 'Grand Slam' occasion. In all my experience of rugby grounds I have never come across anything in terms of atmosphere and national passion to match the singing of 'Land of My Fathers' at Cardiff Arms Park. Even as a Scot I always felt the goose pimples and the hair bristling on the back of my neck whenever the Welsh sang their hearts out at that anthem. But on 17 March 1990 my countrymen and women reached the same heights of inspiration and challenge. And, believe it or not, whenever I play the record of the Scottish team singing 'Flower of Scotland' or watch the start of the video of that historic match, I feel quite emotional with a lump in my throat.

It certainly was a great day to be a Scot. The match, supported by the Royal Bank of Scotland, lived up to the occasion, if not in continuity of spectacle, certainly in total commitment and in the ebb and flow of rival fortunes. When Jeremy Guscott dummied through for a try created by a scrummage pick-up by Mike Teague, a beautifully weighted pass from Richard Hill that rendered Scott Hastings fractionally off-line in his tackle engagement, so that Will Carling was able to demonstrate his flaring acceleration, there were many Scots who feared the worst. But one of the key factors was the inability of England's lineout giants to dominate that phase as they had done against their other rivals, because Ian McGeechan, Jim Telfer, Derrick Grant and Douglas Morgan had evolved the masterly strategy at the lineouts that upset England's well-laid plans. The Scots opted out of conventional lineout positioning and, instead, moved their jumpers around so that virtually no line was the same as the one before it. This set the English forwards an examination they hadn't faced before, and when coupled with unceremonious Scottish engagement on England's throw, it proved vital in the battle for possession. There was, too, a repeat of Scotland's dedication to making tackles count that had marked their entire championship approach. From Gavin Hastings to David Sole, number fifteen to number one, every man tackled as if his life depended on it. And it was copy-book tackling by the legs so that the ball-carrier virtually every time was grounded and so momentarily put out of the game. The tackle contribution from Scotland's tight five forwards was a crucial element. One recalls Craig Chalmers's tap tackle at full stretch on Pierre Hontas. If the Frenchman had escaped, a try was certain and the entire trend of that match could have changed. Then, against England, there was the perfect example to youngsters watching of how to cut down a player from the side and behind. Rory Underwood was virtually certain to score when Scott Hastings launched himself and brought him down. It is true that Gavin Hastings was covering behind his brother but Underwood is such an elusive runner with instant take-off and change of pace that I believe he would have scored. Finally, there was that moment when Will Carling was in full-cry with ten metres to go, when he must have got the impression of having hit a tidal wave of blue as the entire Scottish pack supported Craig Chalmers's tackle and simply swept England's captain backwards at a rate of knots. Of course, there was the point that if England had taken penalty-goal changes in the first half they could have created a handy cushion, but the fact is that they didn't. As for Tony Stanger's try it was a special thrill to me to be providing the TV commentary because he is from my home town and is a former pupil who started his rugby as a ten-year-old at Wilton Primary School in Hawick where one of the women teachers, Mrs May Sinclair, had a lot to do with his initial development and enthusiasm in the game. That move will be engraved on the minds of all Scottish rugby folk for a long time – John Jeffrey's pick up and feed, Gary Armstrong's cleverly judged pass, the Gavin Hastings punt that was placed on a sixpence and Tony's reach and dive. I wonder if that try would have been scored if Tony had been only five feet nine instead of six feet two? His height and reach made all the difference. It was an Englishman who expressed the opinion that Tony hadn't touched down properly. Tell that to the fifty-three thousand Scots who were there! A wee country like Scotland has long periods of hunger and of failure and short bursts of wonderful success. This had to be the greatest day in Scottish rugby history. It was a day Scots never will forget. And whilst I hope that my commentary was unbiased it was some day for me as well.

21
Cancer Scare

It was on 6 January 1991 that I was told I might have cancer. You can imagine the shock that caused for Bette, myself and our family. I had arranged a meeting with surgeon, David Bremner, just to check if there was any point in doing anything more in the way of surgery that might ease my varicose problem. It had created another symptom, a lump in my left groin. It was during examination that David, a keen rugby man, drew attention to a small dark spot on my left ankle. I couldn't remember having seen it before. I noticed an immediate change in his demeanour and he clearly was a bit more concerned at this discovery. That set my alarm bells ringing and it was with that goose-pimply feeling that spells genuine fear that I came straight out with: 'Are you telling me that I might have cancer?' The answer in the affirmative brought me out in a cold sweat. David made it quite clear that he could be wrong but that he wanted further tests done. By the time I had probed him about the possibilities, I realised that, if David's diagnosis proved accurate I had real trouble that could hold out dire prospects. I was in a kind of half-daze as I decided to tell Bette exactly what had happened. Bette had been by my side throughout my tuberculosis episode. I knew that if I didn't say anything she would know that something was amiss. We always had trusted each other implicitly. When I told her the news Bette just couldn't believe it. I had no illness complaints and was in reasonably good nick. There started eight days of misery and fear for us. It's hard to explain the effect of such a prospect when it comes out of the blue. I suppose there was some semblance of the confused feelings I had experienced at the South v Edinburgh game. It is so difficult to concentrate on what you are doing, because your mind is constantly returning to all the aspects of the

213

new situation and just what the future might hold. I had awful visions of having to make preparations for what might become inevitable. Bette and I walked for miles during those eight days. The effect could be gauged on the fact that, whereas we usually play a round of golf each day, we didn't once go near the golf course. That represented the bleakest period of our forty years together. I'll never forget a comment by Bette during one of my most depressed spells: 'I just cannot believe that anybody would take a big, handsome fellow like you away from me!' It was arranged for me to have a biopsy, which entailed taking a tumour out of my left ankle. I'll never forget that journey to the Borders General Hospital for the operation. Jack Swanston, as friendly a neighbour as anyone could wish to have, drove Bette and I there at 8.30 in the morning. I was released at 6 o'clock in the evening to be collected by Bette and another very good friend, Roy Burton. I had a bit of a haemorrhage from the operation wound that evening and had to call in a young doctor to help to staunch the flow. The following day I drove to Edinburgh for a complete scan at the Royal Infirmary, that process of entering a chamber for a series of X-rays, a somewhat claustrophobic experience but one conducted with gentle understanding by all of the staff concerned. After the tests were completed I asked if I could have a chat with the professor who had been studying the finds. He was a nice man who said that there was nothing in the evidence gained that raised any cause for concern. I was clear. It is hard to describe how I felt at that moment, but I have to admit that when I dressed and left the unit and saw Bette and Linda coming down the corridor, anxiety written all over their faccs, I couldn't hold back the tears of relief. Actually Bette and Linda feared the worst until I blurted out: 'No, it's good news, it's good news.' Of course there was still the pathologist's report to come but that evening David Bremner phoned and his first words were: 'Bill, have I got good news for you?' I was so grateful to David for that call. Of course we telephoned Linda and Janie, who was just about to fly North to be with us. Janie didn't have to make that journey. There were quite a few tears shed that day.

We were all so relieved. It was wonderful just to feel normal again. I always have been a religious soul, not through church attendance in which I fail miserably but in personal prayer several times a day. On this occasion my prayers had been answered. Hopefully, we will never have to go through such an experience again.

22
Nostalgia Can Be Beautiful

One of the disappointments I experienced was over a proposed series of television programmes under the heading 'McLaren's Men'. The idea came from Nevin McGhee, a sports producer with BBC Television in Scotland and a former rugby correspondent of the *Belfast Telegraph*. It consisted of me selecting a World XV from all the players I had seen from the commentary box over some three decades. Then I would travel to interview each player in his own home environment about his memories, the players he played against, the great matches he had played in, all of this 'painted' with action and other archive material. There were to be 16 programmes of about 25 minutes each and they were to be transmitted on the BBC2 network during 1984-85. The thought of filming Colin Meads on his own farm, for example, was exciting and although I have never been any great shakes as an interviewer and am not very socially inclined, the idea seemed to be a good one and hopefully would have made interesting viewing. Just to compare, for instance, the relative merits as full-backs of Bob Scott, Don Clarke, Pierre Villepreux, J.P.R. Williams, Andy Irvine and Tom Kiernan would have created some controversy for a start. But the idea didn't get off the ground. For what reason, I know not.

As for 'McLaren's Men', now it is hard enough picking the best Scottish team from the last 40 years, not only because of the number of candidates for each position but because the game has changed so much in fitness levels, attitude, preparation method and time allocation. I believe, for instance, that Douglas Elliot (Edinburgh Academicals), acknowledged as one of Scotland's greatest players and a giant in the post-war years, would still have made massive impact in the modern game although it might have irked him not a little that he would be required to give far more of his time from his farming to attend so many squad sessions. Trying to pick the best from all the players in the world, however, is another kettle of fish altogether. Who would be the best pair of centres from this galaxy – Jeff Butterfield, Malcolm Phillips, Clive Woodward, Jeremy Guscott, Will Carling, Jim Renwick, Ian McGeechan, Ian Laughland, David Johnston, Mike Gibson, Brendan Mullin, Steve Fenwick, Jack Matthews, Bleddyn Williams, Roland Bertranne, Jo Maso, Philippe Sella, André Boniface, Jacques Bouquet, Claude Dourthe, Didier Codorniou, Franck Mesnel, John Gainsford, Danie Gerber, Bruce Robertson, Joe Stanley, Craig Innes, Andrew Slack, Michael Lynagh, Michael Hawker? And that is just a list of centres from the original eight International Board countries. However, off the top of my head and without going over the lists and lists of players for each position, here is one World XV that sure would take a lot of beating: Andy Irvine, Gerald Davies, Danie Gerber, Mike Gibson and David Campese; Cliff Morgan and Gareth Edwards; Fran Cotton, Colin Deans, Piet du Toit, Steve Cutler, Frik du Preez, Ian Kirkpatrick, Benoit Dauga and Fergus Slattery. Just one Englishman, one All Black and one Frenchman? All the same those fifteen, at the time of writing, have amassed an aggregate of 658 caps so they had a bit of experience and ball-winning capacity in all departments and they would want to put on the style. And if you wanted a side to give them a run how about: J.P.R. Williams; Rory Underwood, Philippe Sella, Jim Renwick and David Duckham; Michael Lynagh and Nick Farr-Jones, Ken Gray, Tom Lawton, Sandy Carmichael, Colin Meads and Delme Thomas, John Jeffrey, Dean Richards and Kel Tremain.

It's a daft game, really, trying to pick all-star sides from different eras, but what it does show is the mass of talent that has passed our way in the past forty years or so and how lucky the ageing generation are that they have been privileged to see so many wonderful players in action and have been able to compare them with those of a different decade. There are players who might never be selected or, indeed, considered for one of those mythical World XV's, but who have been giants in their own way and much respected by team-mates and opponents alike – players such as Elie Cester, the French lock, Geoff Wheel, the great Welsh mauling lock, Jan Ellis, a splendid South African flanker who once brought Twickenham to its feet with a magical run up the West stand touchline for a great try, David Morris, Wales's Mr Perpetual Motion as a flanker, and those numerous denizens of the front row who slog away in the darkened recesses and in their own little world where no others dare to tread; men of considerable girth such as England's 'Stack' Stevens and Paul Rendall, Scotland's Ian McLauchlan and Hugh McLeod, Ireland's Phil Orr, Wales's Denzil Williams and such as Robert Paparemborde and Amadee Domenech of France. There are so many more and the mention of each name conjures up wonderful memories. Nostalgia can be beautiful!

23

Grand Stand Finale

From a purely personal point of view the 1991 Rugby World Cup was something of a challenge in that I was returning, in a sense, to my roots so far as broadcasting was concerned. Having turned down the opportunity of joining the ITV commentary team, a decision about which I have never had the slightest regret, the invitation to take part in the Radio 5 coverage for the BBC meant that I had to go back to where I had started in 1952 – to radio commentary. I was nervous about that, firstly because I hadn't done any radio commentary for 30 years although there have been those folk who reckon that even on television my commentary is closer to a radio style! Secondly, my suspicion that it would be darned hard work proved to be absolutely spot on. No-one had warned me that not only would commentary for Radio 5 be involved but so would an interview here for Radio 1, an update there for Radio 2, a contribution to a chat show on Radio something else and, of course, previews and interviews for various news and sports programmes. It shook me a bit when I found that on the day of the opening match between England and New Zealand at Twickenham, I had to be at the ground by 7.20 am and had completed two separate broadcasts by 8 o'clock! I was up and down those Twickenham steps to and from the commentary gantry four times. I nicknamed those steps 'coronary hill' and I was pretty nearly a hospital case by the time that lot was over! I once found myself standing on the concourse behind Twickenham's West Stand doing an interview for a children's programme! That's radio for you – they were slave drivers! But I really did enjoy the entire experience for a number of reasons. I was fortunate enough to have a very acceptable programme of matches. I felt very privileged to share the opening commentary at the England v

New Zealand game at Twickenham with Ian Robertson and Mike Burton. Thereafter I was part of the coverage of all of Scotland's games, which reduced the amount of travelling time and kept me in familiar surroundings. It was a delight for me to be invited to cover the Ireland v Australia match in Dublin on the day after the Scotland v Western Samoa match, even though the prospect of doing two games in two days was quite daunting. The Dublin match turned out to be a thrilling affair in which the Irish reached such heights of endeavour and inspiration that their whitewash demise in the following Five Nations Championship seems incomprehensible. The Scotland v England semi-final had all the atmosphere and trappings of a great sporting occasion without, unfortunately, the spread and flow that would have given infinite pleasure to all. It was a special thrill to be involved in the final – a riveting affair in which, curiously, the roles were almost reversed from those expected – England moving the ball about the paddock, and Australia, on shorter rations, using more of the boot than usual.

Before the start of the World Cup the BBC decided, very sensibly, to give me a trial run just to get me into the swing and discipline of radio work again. The vehicle chosen was Romania v Scotland in Bucharest on 31 August. Rugby journalists tend to go pale when told that they have been assigned to a match in Bucharest because the food leaves a lot to be desired and communications can be a bit dodgy. Dodgy, on this occasion, was hardly the word. I was to liaise with Ion Ghitulescu of Romanian Radio and he would ensure that all my needs would be attended to. On arrival in Bucharest, I immediately 'phoned Ion's number only to be told that he was on holiday! At this point I became indebted to a Romanian friend, George Raetchi, who had been the official rugby correspondent on Romanian visits to Scotland. George was a gem. He smoothed my path all the way. For one thing he gained me entrance to the Romanian squad's training session. You may remember me mentioning a previous occasion in Bucharest when no-one was permitted to do this. This time it was even more important to see the Romanians training because it was very much a new-look squad and I knew that the commentary position at the National stadium was fairly distant from the pitch. George was a personal friend of the new Romanian coach, Petre Ianusievich, and could explain that all I was interested in was being able to identify the players. Petre was a delightful young man, bright and enthusiastic, and he couldn't have been more helpful. Not only that, but I noted right away that he was incorporating into his training regime the quick-fire, criss-cross skills work with which the All Blacks and, in particular, their fitness guru, Scots born Jim Blair, had startled the rugby world at the inaugural World Cup in 1987. The Romanians didn't achieve quite the same pace and error-free levels that so marked the work of the New Zealanders but they clearly found this new style of training very enjoyable and entertaining. As I watched them going through their drills it did strike me that they might be more of a handful for the Scots than some suspected. That was borne out by the score – a Romanian victory by 18-12 and two tries to one. That was quite a shock to the Scots, who were virtually at full strength with the exception of Gavin Hastings, Chris Gray and John Jeffrey. It pointed a clear warning to Scotland that the World Cup would be no cushy number, even against some of the emerging countries. Disappointingly for the Romanians their deserved win over the Scots was not an overture to a powerful World Cup challenge. Although they beat Fiji with three splendid tries to none, one a spectacular effort by their captain, Harilambi (Harry) Dumitras, they were already out of the World Cup, having lost to France (3-30) and Canada (11-19).

In Bucharest Scotland played Finlay Calder in his 29th international at the age of 34 and he proved his fitness and stamina for the World Cup campaign after having been out of the international scene for a full season. Ian McGeechan, Scotland's coach, had always been keen to have Calder in his World Cup squad. As well as his rich vein of experience from captaining the British Lions to their splendid Test series success in Australia in 1989, he was an inspirational figure both on and off the pitch. It must have been irritating for Calder and his host of friends and admirers that he should be involved in two unsavoury incidents during the World Cup. Irish people were incensed, believing that Calder punched fullback Jim Staples into a dazed state when following up a garryowen punt. My own view is that Calder, in charging in, aimed to knock the ball from Staples's grasp. What angered the Irish was that a dazed Staples mishandled the next garryowen at crucial cost to Ireland. What came over Calder in the play-off with New Zealand when he headbutted Sean Fitzpatrick, one cannot say. The contest, of course, being for clear third place in the World Cup and with the Scots still very much in contention, was bound to be tense, but people who know Calder were quite aghast. Certainly, as one who has seen him play for some years and long before he was capped, I can testify to his fairness on the field. I have never seen him guilty of such a violent reaction.

That Romanian trip stays etched on the memory. As I was to provide a weather update and preview of the game from the commentary position about a half an hour before the kick off, I was down in plenty of time only to find that the commentary box was deserted – not only of personnel but of equipment as well! On the previous day George had managed to persuade a friend to provide his own TV set so that I could see re-runs of scores during the game. That hadn't arrived, and neither had a microphone or earphones. I began to get a wee bit edgy as the time came closer to the preview. George popped off to try to unearth an engineer of some description. Meanwhile, on spotting a telephone in the press area below the commentary box I tottered down the steps (I seemed always to be going down or climbing up miles of ruddy steps in the interest of Radio 5) and tried to get through to the Radio 5 studio in London. I thought it was a forlorn hope so you can imagine my delight and surprise on hearing: 'Hello there, Radio 5 here'. The wonders of modern telecommunications. Should I do the preview over the 'phone as the commentary box is deserted? I asked. 'Not at all, old chap, just pop into the commentary box and we should be linked up fairly soon.' I didn't share his confidence but, lo and behold, on climbing back up to the commentary box who should I find but George and, a sight for sore eyes, a young geezer who couldn't speak a word of England but who, in a magical sequence that took the breath away, produced a microphone and earphones. With just three minutes before our scheduled preview to London, contact was made and the broadcast completed. Not only that but a large, unshaven soul, sweating profusely, carted a TV set into the box, stuck in a plug, fiddled for a moment or two then pointed proudly to the black and white picture on the screen. Things might not happen immediately in Romania but eventually they fall into place! The Lord be praised for George Raetchi! I am also indebted to Radio 5 producer Pat Thornton who directed the programme from London. Pat is brusque, organised and efficient, and even though I had difficulty hearing her against a rival commentary in my earphones from, I think, Aston Villa, her words of encouragement saw me through the match. It was Pat who drew to my attention the occasional pauses in my delivery and reminded me that, whilst that is the TV commentary method, on radio you have to keep going all the time. She seemed right on top of the job.

It was slightly irritating for me that I only had to provide patches of commentary during the first half because Radio 5 switched periodically to the first division soccer grounds and to the cricket grounds to get an update on proceedings there. Having to pick up commentary cold, several times, was a new experience for me but, with Pat's direction, it seemed to go quite well and during the second half I did continuous commentary which was more enjoyable. I had been told that BBC Scotland would contact me for two post-match reports but I doubted whether they would be able to get through. Yet, dead on time, I heard the voice of Dougie Werham, the radio sports producer, as clear as a bell. What a relief. I was chuffed to have got the job done without a disaster and I had satisfied myself that, although there was some polishing to be done, I could cope with radio commentary in a testing environment.

The official dinner followed. Viorel Murariu and his Romanian rugby officials went out of their way to make things agreeable for their guests but quality food is in short supply. I had joined members of the Scottish Press, Bill McMurtrie of the *Glasgow Herald*, Bob McKenzie of the *Daily Express*, Jack Adams of the *Daily Record*, Jack Robertson of the *Evening Times* and Bill Lothian of the *Edinburgh Evening News* for lunch and dinner on the Friday. The chicken and meat courses were pretty awful as was the fish at the official dinner. A number of the Scottish squad suffered gastroenteritis and on the journey home Scott Hastings especially was really ill. I can still see him lying out on the tarmac at Timisoara Airport, white as a ghost and completely cheesed off. My own attack had a delayed action. By Monday morning all was misery and despair for 24 hours. We had to land at Timisoara, I believe for refuelling, but it was discovered that the nose cone had been damaged. Imagine trying to unearth a new nose cone on a Sunday in Timisoara! We were there for over four hours in boiling heat with nothing to do but wait. When I went for a wee walk in the shade at the side of the airport building an unsmiling soldier appeared with a machine gun and motioned to me that it might be advisable for me to retrace my steps to where the others were. Jack Adams also went for a wee promenade and got a machine gun stuck in his ribs as well. Eventually we were ready for take-off but the pilot was apparently a bit worried about the nose cone because all of the heavy members of the party were asked to make their way to the back of the plane until it took off. So there was a parade of donkeys – Chris Gray, Damian Cronin, Paul Burnell, Derek White, David Sole, Derek Turnbull, Doddie Weir, Finlay Calder and John Allan – towards the rear. Iain Milne arrived last, couldn't find a decent seat so spent his journey in the toilet! It worked. The nose went up, the tail stayed down long enough and up we went into the blue yonder to many sighs of relief. One thing about a trip to Bucharest is that notwithstanding the courtesy and kindness of the hosts and the fact that this time there were actually people who smiled, it didn't half make you glad to be home.

The high professionalism of those with whom I was associated at Radio 5 made my job an enjoyable one. I couldn't have been more impressed by the performances they gave and perhaps, most of all, by that of the senior director, Charles Runcie. I suppose some would refer to Charles, a true Scot, as a workaholic. He seems to revel in his work and nothing is too much trouble for him. He takes immense pride in getting things right. I referred to him in fun as an *Obergruppenführer* because he was the one who had to break the good news to me that I would have to do an interview with somebody or other, or that I would have to rush back to the BBC, Queen Street, and provide a bit of this or that for this or that programme. But he was tremendously helpful and I owe him a lot for his cheery guidance. I also admired the professionalism of my fellow commentators: Ian Robertson, never at a loss for a word, unfailingly happy-to-lucky but also bravely blunt when he felt strongly about something; Jim Neilly, always smiling and joking and a superb mimic; David Parry-Jones, an old and much respected friend; and David Mercer, equally at home on the tennis circuit and who really did his homework. The summarisers were also a first-class group. They avoided repeating what the commentator had said and kept the listeners interested by calling on their playing experience for specialist analysis of what had happened or, indeed, on occasions, what was going to happen – Fergus Slattery, Barry John and Andy Irvine – all were a pleasure to work with. Mike Burton was adept at providing light and shade, forthright and with a delightfully humorous edge to his pronouncements. When I once referred to the number of players who had been ordered off in internationals, forgetting that Mike was one of them, he simply chuckled in mock horror. I am also indebted to John Inverdale, the unflappable presenter of the Radio 5 sports programme, who does a remarkable job in linking all the bits and pieces together, in memorising information about a vast number of sports, in interviewing people of differing persuasions and interests and, of course, in keeping the programme going even when things do not go as planned. Unlike the TV man, the radio presenter cannot rely on the picture to tell the story. John Inverdale was out of the top drawer.

As one who had worried that the introduction of the World Cup in 1987 might mean an escalation of violence and a 'win at all costs' attitude, especially in the later stages when the heavy artillery were in opposition, I have to admit that the first World Cup rendered such fears groundless and the 1991 competition provided confirmation of that. It proved a resounding success, generating huge interest in the game, so much so that mini rugby groups all over the country gained new members, and clubs gained handsome financial benefit. On-field behaviour was of a high order and only two players were ordered off during the entire competition, and that probably wouldn't have happened if the protagonists had stopped throwing punches when the referee, Jim Fleming of the Boroughmuir club in Edinburgh, told them to do so. Of course the World Cup committee had made it plain before the competition got underway that they wanted their referees to be strict in keeping the temperature just right and there did seem to be a general desire on the part of the playing squads not to bring their country into disrepute by unacceptable behaviour.

My own feeling about the World Cup is that there should have been more expansive play. There were sides capable of producing a tremendous spectacle and attractive handling play will bring people into the game either to play it, to support it or to administer it. There were, of course, some splendid contests in which the ball was given air, such as the highest scoring pool 2 in which Scotland, Ireland, Japan and Zimbabwe battled for quarter-final places, almost every time the Australians took the field except, perhaps, in the final when they were called on for water tight defence, and from the Western Samoans. They were the surprise packet and did my heart good because they still seem to hold to old-fashioned values of accepting victory or defeat with the same good grace and because they really did get most enjoyment just from playing. And they could certainly play a bit.

Of course another value of the World Cup is that it provides the minnows of the rugby world with the opportunity of playing against some of the heavy artillery. On the same lines as the Hong Kong sevens where the likes of Sri Lanka, Singapore, Korea and Bahrain can aspire to tilting their lances against the All Blacks, Wallabies, Wales, Scotland and the Barbarians, the 1991 World Cup provided the opportunity for 29 nations to qualify for the remaining eight places in the finals. Among the 29 were the Ivory Coast, Belgium, Morocco, Poland, Taiwan, West Germany, Yugoslavia and Israel. The very first qualifying match was between Israel and Switzerland in France in April 1989 so the tournament was indeed a worldwide affair. Although some would like to increase the number of qualifiers to 24, my own view is that such a move would lengthen the tournament by several days. The demands on the spare time of top-class players are already too heavy and there are signs that employers may have reached the limit of their generosity in regard to granting leave of absence for international duty. Sixteen qualifying countries are sufficient, and prevent the likelihood of one-sided games. Not, let me hasten to add, that one-sided contests are necessarily bad for the competition. Indeed it could be argued that they are more likely to spawn the kind of sparkling interplay that shows the game in its very best light. Tense tactical battles with quite a lot of boot such as England v New Zealand in the opening match of the finals may appeal to the rugby specialist who can appreciate the whys and wherefors of the rival strategies but they are hardly enthralling for those thousands of viewers who are interested but know little or nothing about the game. Holding the ball in the back of the scrummage, inside centres taking the ball back to the forwards, punting from half back five times out of six and bodies going over the ball in a series of pile-ups, do not motivate youngsters into taking up the game. What really inspires them, I feel, is the sight of the ball rippling through the hands of players, sharp switches in direction, and the sheer audacity and adventurism that is the hallmark of class men like David Campese (Australia) and Jean-Baptiste Lafond (France). Most of that kind of flamboyant action in the World Cup was provided by the Japanese, the Western Samoans, the Zimbabweans, and, when they let their hair down, the Italians and the French.

One other myth laid to rest by the 1991 World Cup was that games not involving the home countries would be sparsely attended. Indeed, on a BBC midday programme in which I took part before the World Cup, Henry Kelly, that ebullient, cheery Irish personality, kidded that he had 500 tickets for the Japan v Zimbabwe game at Ravenhill in Belfast and hadn't a hope of selling a single one. Yet that match, the first international ever to be played in Ireland that did not involve the Irish side, not only drew a handsome crowd but produced arguably the most entertaining game of the entire tournament in which 11 tries were registered, the ball fizzed about like a fire cracker, and Japan won 52-9.

The trophy for the most sporting and most inventive country in the tournament surely should have gone to the Japanese. Of course they had to be inventive because, as always, they were desperately short of height and ballast for the frontal exchanges and so inevitably were short of quality ball. They had to use every kind of unorthodox, deceptive

measure in order to win lineout ball and had to make the best use of
every morsel of possession. Their tactic was to run everything, which
they did at such a lick and with such incredibly swift and sure handling,
that they proved a commentator's nightmare, but a joy for the spectators. Eventually of course they were worn down by the top boys and
their defenders, brave to the last, simply couldn't keep their fingers in the
dyke any longer. But they were well worth seeing and wherever they
played the audience was assured of exciting action. Their discipline was
exemplary as well, so much so that folk couldn't believe their eyes when
Masanori Takura, their tight head prop, was cautioned by English referee Ed Morrison in the Scotland game at Murrayfield. I had never seen
a Japanese player cautioned before and Takura was suitably full of re-
morse, no doubt anticipating a rocket after the game from Japan's 'Mr
Rugby', Shiggy Konno. Shiggy was a superb ambassador for the
Japanese game, ever courteous and a dedicated defender of the amateur
faith. At short notice he provided me with a radio interview after one
practice session at the Heriot Watt University campus at Riccarton that
was a delight in its vision and fairness.

The other squad who captured the imagination of all who saw them
were the Western Samoans – not only because they were something of a
surprise packet, especially with their defeat of Wales at Cardiff – but
because they married vigour and enjoyment to splendid skills and a very
positive approach. I was particularly pleased to make the acquaintance
again of their genial manager, Bryan Williams, whom I had last met
when he was a considerable force as a wing with the touring All Blacks.
He was naturally delighted at the way his players had comported themselves especially as he regarded their considerable success as a tribute to
one of their most fervent supporters, his father, who had died of cancer
not long before the World Cup began. Another likable Samoan personality was the burly wing Timo Tagaloa whom I had come across in the
New Zealand seven at Hong Kong sevens. He was such a cheery fellow
and endeared himself to the crowds with his robust approach. Some regarded him just as a battering-ram runner but he was much more than
that, for he could weave and swerve at top speed which made him, at 15
stones, even more formidable. One of the most touching episodes in the
entire World Cup was when the Western Samoans were led on a lap of
honour at Murrayfield by their hefty captain Pita Fatialofa. The crowd
simply rose to them. Pita said afterwards that they had just wanted to
thank the people of Wales and Scotland for their friendship and hospital-

ity. It was a much appreciated gesture. The spirit of those South Sea islanders was demonstrated in the volume of singing coming from their dressing room. They clearly did not regard defeat as the end of the world. Good for them.

I regarded myself as extremely fortunate to have been asked to cover Scotland's matches. They were all at Murrayfield and because I knew the Scottish squad I didn't have any particular concerns about identifying them or about background information. It was a different story with the Japanese. They are desperately hard to sort out, especially their backs who are so alike in stature and features. Also, as I've already mentioned, because they shift the ball around as if it was a bit of red hot charcoal, keeping up with them is some challenge. One area of the Japanese game that worried the Scots was their ability to steal ball through their impressive upper body strength. A feature of one Japanese training session was to set up situations in which opponents driving forward were dispossessed, and in a twinkling the ball was delivered to backs who immediately counterattacked from no matter what area of the field. It was sound thinking that such counterattack would catch the opposition momentarily in vulnerable defensive positions. So the Scots made sure that in their driving play they laid off or posted ball before they could be robbed. There wasn't much point in posing problems for the Japanese at the lineouts if you conceded ball to them at stoppage points. What pleased the Scots most was that the matches against Japan and Zimbabwe enabled them to spin the ball wide with some regularity and brought out from Scotland's backs some of the handling skills and running angles and interplay that tended to be kept under wraps in more highly pressurised matches. Thus it was a delight to see Scott Hastings and Sean Lineen indulging in clever loop and dummy scissor moves, sweet, little behind-the-back reverse passes and adjustments to their weight of pass. One had to feel some sympathy for the tiny Japanese defenders whenever the Scots produced a miss-move that brought Gavin Hastings thundering into the line. Once, towards the end, when the big full-back scored a try with two Japanese clinging to him like limpet mines, the area behind him looked like a casualty clearing station, littered with bodies that had bounced off him.

Perhaps the most disappointing match of the World Cup was that between Scotland and England in their Murrayfield semi-final. England played a tight, disciplined format that eliminated wide spread and incorporated impressive forward power and inward-looking half-backs.

Scotland had no foothold of any value at the lineouts and Jonathan Webb's two penalty goals were for collapsed scrummages. The Scots were quite unable to stitch together the flowing interplay of their pool games. Yet they had the opportunity to win. Gavin Hastings had a penalty goal from in front of the posts which he would normally have chipped over with his eyes closed but, for some unaccountable reason, this laid-back soul somehow pushed it fractionally wide of the right up-right. Had it gone over Scotland would have led 9-6 with just 18 minutes left. Not only would the psychological advantage to the Scots have been massive but England's unforced errors, of which there had been several, might have multiplied under the strain. The English, to their credit, took control of the ball-winning areas and the winning drop-goal by Rob Andrew was perfection – a manicured lineout delivery, Richard Hill's sweet pass and Andrew, from his good side, providing a languid swing of his boot.

It was sad that a match that had created such intense interest should prove so stodgy in failing to produce a single try. England had just played in similar style against France and I thought they deserved criticism, as they possessed, in my view, the fastest, most lethal backs in the competition but asked nothing of them against France and Scotland except to chase and tackle. Perhaps the French and Scots supporters should have been grateful, for if England had spun the ball wide they would probably have won more convincingly. But they sought an error-free game and the euphoria with which the supporters greeted their two victories – and they were deserving winners in each case – showed quite clearly that, to many of their supporters, victory was what counted and not the manner of it.

To their credit, however, England approached the final against Australia at Twickenham with a more expansive pattern in mind. Whether some of the criticism hit home or whether they honestly believed that their best chance of victory was through handling attack on a wide front, they really did take the game to the Wallabies and put enough pressure on them to force them into more of a punting game than in any of their previous matches. Yet Australia could have been further ahead than 9-0 at half-time, for David Campese had produced another magical sequence with a chip ahead past Jonathan Webb that seemed certain to spawn a try but an unfavourable bounce denied the great Australian wing. Another Australian personality, 'Willie' Ofahengaue, had a key role in the only try of the final that Australia won 12-6. An inch-perfect throw-in by

Philip Kearns was gobbled up by Ofahengaue who was then driven forward in a green avalanche for Tony Daly to score. What had impressed me most about those Australians was the mobility and pace of their tight five forwards. All five could run, all five were as fit as fleas. This was underlined near the end when England battered and battered against the Australian defence. Rob Andrew was clean through when from out of nowhere John Eales, the 6 foot 8 inches lock forward, launched himself in a copybook tackle that sunk England's stand-off. Those young Australians showed that effective defence is just as important as scoring, keeping the plug in as England threw everything at them. They were a superb all-round outfit and deserving world champions. Yet England had demonstrated that they too were capable of playing to different styles and had established themselves clearly as the team to beat in the forthcoming Five Nations Championship.

So the World Cup was given a fitting finale of open play, the stage having been set by Scotland and New Zealand in their play-off for third and fourth places at Cardiff. New Zealand won by 13-6 in a thrilling game full of exciting movement and magnificent defending. The margin was only 9-6 when, in virtually the last move of the game, Walter Little ran sinuously for the only try as if to rap the knuckles of the New Zealand selection system for leaving him out of the previous matches. Perhaps the most memorable act of an enjoyable game was the sight of Gavin Hastings charging, flat out, into New Zealand's unsmiling prop, Richard Loe, and knocking him backwards on to his posterior. Loe was not amused. Most others were.

One of the unusual features of World Cup media coverage was that, at some matches, radio and TV commentators were 'wired up' to the referee and so could hear him explaining his decisions. Some referees, understandably, weren't in favour. They have enough on their plates trying to ensure fairness, keep the temperature right and cope with all the cheating without also having to remember that virtually every word they utter is being heard by an unseen audience. I say *virtually* every word because it was amusing to see some referees place their hands over the microphone when they wanted to make a point that commentators were not supposed to hear. Les Peard, the Welsh referee, once made a comment in immoderate language which, unfortunately, was picked up by a nearby sound effects microphone. On a later occasion when Les, as touch judge, was about to express a view to the referee, his countryman Derek Bevan, Derek beckoned him on to the pitch before he could say anything and out of range of the touch-line microphone! I remember bumping into Les Peard at Glasgow Airport on the eve of the Ireland v Australia quarter-final. He had just been omitted from the final list of referees for the closing stages and expressed himself as 'totally gutted' at the news. I thought his omission was unfair too.

From the commentators' point of view the link-up with the referee was helpful in that you could hear why he had made each decision, although I always felt it part and parcel of a commentator's obligation to decide himself why each decision had been made. Of course it's true that in scrummaging, for example, there are any number of offences that can be committed. The same can be said of the lineout. Once, at a club match, I told viewers that a penalty had been given for barging at the lineout which, of course, I had seen myself, only to hear referee Eric Grierson's voice proclaiming: 'Number 7, you were off-side'. So undoubtedly the World Cup system did make for more accurate reporting. At the same time it was no great joy for commentators to have the referee's voice in one earpiece of his headphones and his producer's voice in the other. It just took a bit of adjustment and familiarising. What tickled me was the bluntness of those international referees in explaining their decisions. Jim Fleming, who officiated at the opening World Cup match between England and New Zealand, was like my old headmaster, Robert Burns, clipped and to the point. He really did take charge and none of the players was in any doubt as to his decisions. There was a touch of the sergeant major about his performance and it worked very well. Fred Howard of England was also full of good advice to help the players stay within the law. Once when Scotland and Ireland had drawn level at 15-15 I heard Fred warning the players at the next scrummage: 'Right now, keep it up. You don't want to lose the World Cup through a collapse penalty, do you?'

One aspect of refereeing that caused some argument was the strict interpretation of the law relating to players on the ground. The World Cup referees had been encouraged to drive home to players the need to stay on their feet whenever possible. Much of the rugby in Europe was being spoiled by players going over the ball and so preventing the quick release so conducive to flowing back play. Perhaps some referees were a touch over-zealous and New Zealanders especially claimed that they were not able to ruck. All Blacks have their own methods of dealing with offenders on the ground! All the same, the standard of refereeing was fairly high and the top men did come through to the top jobs.

The referees went out of their way to help players limit the number of offences so as to make for longer spells of continuous action. They constantly reminded players about the off-side provisions and contributed handsomely to the fluency of play. Most of them weren't too fussy about lineout tactics; they were more concerned with getting the ball out of the lineout and so allowed a certain amount of licence with shoving and leaning. I must say I agree with this because fussy referees could blow up at virtually every lineout. The important point is to check the temperature now and again to make sure that lineout specialists don't take the law into their own hands and flatten their rivals as, for instance, when Tony Copsey clocked Neil Francis in the Wales v Ireland Five Nations match three months later.

So the World Cup in general proved a great success. The final at Twickenham drew receipts of over £1 million for the first time. The message of Rugby Union was carried to the furthest corners of the world and everywhere youngsters were stimulated into taking up the game. The lesson driven home by the varying nature of team strategies was that Rugby Union is a game that has a place for everyone, no matter what build or size. The sight of the English forwards rolling and driving and commanding lineout ball surely must have encouraged all those outsize young men perhaps too big and hefty to shine in other sports. The sights of David Campese, Rory Underwood, Jeremy Guscott and Jean-Baptiste Lafond demonstrating their magical skills surely inspired all those youngsters with pace and guile to 'take up the ball and run with it' as William Webb Ellis did to such effect at Rugby School in 1823.

For Scots there was some satisfaction in that not only were Scotland the highest point scorers in the entire competition with 162 (New Zealand were next with 143) but they were the top try scorers as well with 20, one more than the All Blacks. It is true, of course, that Scotland had been in the less demanding pool 2 but they still had to do the business and they did it well enough to justify their fourth place in world ratings. After all, they had almost beaten England and they were still in contention against the mighty All Blacks until that last hammer blow of the Little try.

For myself there was a sense of relief that it was all over. My coverage ended with a Radio 5 summing up in which I took part, along with Ian Robertson, Tim Gavin, the Australian number 8 (cruelly excluded from playing in the World Cup by injury), and Russ Thomas, the chairman of the World Cup committee, with John Inverdale leading the discussion.

Gavin is a delightful personality, forthright and modest, and Russ Thomas has always been an old world gentleman although I think he felt a bit embarrassed by the fact that the committee took so long to react positively to the disgraceful attack on referee David Bishop of New Zealand by French coach Daniel Dubroca. It is understandable that feelings will run high in the pressure-cooker atmosphere of a World Cup quarter-final between two of the great playing nations, especially in Paris, but it is written into rugby law that the referee's decision is final. It is absolutely vital to the future well-being of the game at large that referees are protected from such angry outbursts; whoever transgresses and no matter what his position in the game he should be shown the door for the error of his ways. Referees are only human. They make mistakes like the rest of us. Unfortunately their mistakes are seen by thousands in the ground and by millions watching on television. The whole tradition of the rugby game has been that referees are sacrosanct. That is how it must be. Eventually, of course, Dubroca took his leave, his reputation besmirched, and Pierre Berbizier took over as French coach.

So what had been a thoroughly enjoyable experience on Radio 5 came to an end for me. It had been very hard work, not only keeping a note of results and scorers but also finding out as much personal information about overseas players as I could and attending training sessions so that identification would be spot on. The one joy of being back on TV was that I didn't have to be down at the ground by 7.20 am and take part in two broadcasts by 8 am! Radio men and women certainly earn their corn.

There never was any doubt in my mind that England should start as very hot favourites to win the Five Nations Championship of 1992 and perhaps a second Grand Slam in a row, something no-one had achieved since England in 1923 and 1924. What was more in doubt was whether England would revert to their restricted style of the France and Scotland World Cup games or take a stage further the wider spread they had thrown at Australia in the World Cup final. Some critics felt that their failure to capitalise on their handling game in the final had been attributable to the fact that they had kept the ball close to the forwards in previous games and so weren't well enough practised in the subtle arts of moving the ball by hand under pressure. This theory perhaps fails to give due credit to the organisation and commitment of the Wallabies in defence. They truly were the most dogged and copy-book markers and tacklers and my feeling was that against any other country in the competition, except perhaps New Zealand, England would have run in several tries. The question was, would they go back into their shells, or would they give it a twirl and seek not only to win the Five Nations but to do so in an attractive style? Their opening game was against Scotland at Murrayfield and they laid all their inhibitions to rest with victory by 25-7. I have to admit that Scotland's selectors and their locks proved me wrong about Scotland's lineout potential. When the team was announced I thought the selectors had missed a rare opportunity of matching England's towering lineout battalions. I would have played Damian Cronin (6 ft 6 in) as number 2 jumper – I had already seen him as a fruitful source in that berth – Andrew MacDonald, the former Cambridge University Blue, as mid-line jumper (6 ft 8 in), and Doddie Weir as number 8 (6 ft 7 in). The selectors opted for Neil Edwards of Harlequins (6 ft 4 in) and Weir as their locks – Weir still a bit stringy at under 16 stones. Those two, however, proved a splendid combination, to such an extent that they virtually cleaned out England in the first half lineouts, permitting them only one good ball from that source. Edwards is a shrewd campaigner, totally at home in the nudge-lean-hold depths of lineout play and Weir, having been played out of the lineouts by Wade Dooley in the World Cup game, came of age and had a highly profitable game. Scotland's forward play in that first half was their best of the season, new cap David McIvor acting as a rousing driving spearhead. But Scotland's backs, although contributing most of the handling spread with neat loops and feints, simply lacked penetration against an English defence that, because of the speed in the back division, allowed only minimal reaction time to Scottish attackers. There was, too, another demonstration by Michael Skinner (Harlequins) of that tackle explosiveness with which he invariably drove the ball carrier backwards.

The quality of Scotland's early forward play can be measured by the fact that they actually scored a scrummage push-over try by Derek White. Not for a moment did I ever believe that any pack would be capable of shunting England's heavyweights backwards in disarray; that the Scots did so is a tribute to their scrummaging practice under the guidance of Richie Dixon, Scotland's new forwards coach. He had been a disciple at Jordanhill College of perhaps the most astute scrummage specialist the game has ever known, Bill Dickinson, first 'adviser to the Scottish captain'. That collective power was demonstrated later when the Scots survived three close-range scrummages but, by then, England had begun to take control of much of the ball-winning and Rob Andrew once again teased the Scots with the accuracy of his attack punting. No Scot could complain about England's triumph. Scotland had had their chances in the first half but hadn't made them count, whereas England had capitalised on Scottish weaknesses with a runaway try by Rory Underwood after Gavin Hastings had the ball exploded from his grasp. I have long regarded Rory Underwood as the most lethal finisher in the game and after the 1992 Five Nations I have no hesitation in installing Will Carling as the finest all-round centre in the world. England also had an extra dimension in their back play from the combative Dewi Morris who had not only improved the speed of his pass but was prepared to take people on and, with his strength on the run, clearly posed a threat to every breakaway unit. Morris was also on hand to record a clinching try for England after a searing diagonal run by Simon Halliday, another player of admirable consistency and good footballing sense.

I had the good fortune to be asked to provide the TV commentary on the England v Ireland match at Twickenham which showed the flowering of the English game at the very height of its brilliance. They demolished brave Ireland – Ireland, remember, playing ten of the men who had held Australia to one point in the World Cup – by 38–9, six tries to one. It was an exhilarating performance in which the English backs showed their true potential in scoring all six tries. Ciaran Fitzgerald, the Irish coach, paid tribute to their ability 'to penetrate in numbers so that they always had an option'. They certainly had. But well though the English backs demonstrated their power running and noses for space they would be the first to admit that they owed a great deal to scrum-half Dewi Morris. His probing and threatening frequently tied in the Irish loose forwards so that England's backs were on a man to man situation. The match was marked by one of the fastest tries ever scored in an international when Jonathan Webb recorded the first of his two tries 23 seconds after kick off. Webb also equalled the championship record for an English player with 22 points – a mark set by Daniel Lambert against France in 1911. It was a great pleasure to commentate on England's display because I simply revel in fluent matches where the ball whistles about the paddock. Any commentary is very much influenced by the type of game being played and this one was a treat to cover as England threw off their shackles and really let their hair down.

On the day that England won the crucial match in Paris by 31 points to 13, and French rugby plumbed the depths with Gregoire Lascubé and Vincent Moscato being sent off by Irish referee Stephen Hilditch, I was in Dublin covering Scotland's 18–10 win over Ireland. It was during my commentary that a lot of folk thought that I'd had a heart attack. Because of a dispute involving the Telefís technicians, a BBC North of Ireland unit took over the TV transmission and everything was going along nicely when, all of a sudden, my commentary disappeared and viewers in Scotland were left with silent pictures. Of course all of our friends thought that I had suffered a coronary attack especially when, after some minutes of silence, the BBC Scotland radio commentary was substituted. However some wee while later my commentary was restored. Of course I had no indication in the commentary box of what had happened, so Hugo MacNeill and I were cracking on with the commentary. It was only on the following day, when I was watching a video of the two matches in our home that I said to Bette: 'Where's the commentary gone?' Happily Bette and our younger daughter Janie were with me in Dublin so they knew that all was well and daughter Linda viewed the edited version in 'Rugby Special' the following day. I never did find out why the whole commentary was heard in England but not in Scotland. One happy event during that trip which I appreciated very much was the presentation to me of a beautiful Waterford decanter by the Irish Distillers and the Irish Rugby Writers' Club through their chairman, David Guiney. Actually it was to have been a double presentation to Fred Cogley, the Telefís commentator, and myself. But because of the dispute Fred couldn't be there. That was a shame. No-one deserved such an accolade more than Fred; he has done so much for Irish sport, is a really good guy and a much respected colleague.

I rather drew the short straw for the closing two matches of the Championship – Scotland v France at Murrayfield (10-6) and Wales v Scotland at Cardiff (15-10). Both games were desperately short of sparkle and spectacle and although tense in a way, one wonders what kind of impression they made on those many TV viewers who are not genuine rugby adherents. It certainly wasn't the kind of rugby that would have persuaded them to switch on again.

Meanwhile England wrapped up another Grand Slam with their somewhat low-key 24-0 win over Wales at Twickenham. Will Carling had another super match which was specially memorable in that he equalled the record of the New Zealand captain Wilson Whineray with his 22 winning matches as captain. Carling also scored yet another try virtually from kick off when he beat Anthony Clement and Scott Gibbs to the bounce after a Rob Andrew garryowen. The game was no classic. There was so much at stake and whatever else the new Wales might lack it isn't total commitment to tackling. That match stressed what a mighty influence Jonathan Webb had been on England's success. He finished with a new England record in internationals of 246 points, beating the previous mark, 240, of Dusty Hare. Webb also set an all-time record – 67 – for points in any one Championship.

It was a great seven months for English rugby – World Cup finalists and Grand Slam winners for the second year running. Rory Underwood, Peter Winterbottom and Wade Dooley all reached the magical figure of 50 caps, and Rob Andrew became the most capped stand-off in the history of the game with 47 appearances plus one as a full back, beating the mark set by the legendary Irishman Jack Kyle. Just how changed England's side will be when the 1993 Five Nations Championship gets underway remains to be seen. But there seems no doubt whatsoever that they will start off as the prime target for everyone, the team the beat.

Index

Index